A Course in Phonetics

A Course in Phonetics

Peter Ladefoged
University of California, Los Angeles

 Harcourt Brace Jovanovich, Inc.

New York   Chicago   San Francisco   Atlanta

ISBN: 0-15-515180-0

Library of Congress Catalog Card Number: 74-9390

Printed in the United States of America

This book is for:

Lise

Katie

Thegn

And for Simba, who faithfully attended nearly all the LBFS meetings at which it was written.

Preface

This is a *course* in phonetics, not a book about phonetics. It is intended to be useful to both students of linguistics and to those who are more concerned with studying the sounds of English. How much attention is to be paid to different chapters depends on the objectives of the course for which it is used.

The first chapter presents an overview of articulatory phonetics and the technical terms required for describing speech. The second chapter is concerned with phonetic transcription and a set of symbols for transcribing English. Everyone should master the terminology and symbols in both these chapters before going further in the book.

Many of the main concepts of phonetics are introduced through a discussion of the phonetics of English in Chapters 3, 4, and 5. These chapters should be read carefully by all students, but they may contain too many exercises for some; those students who are not primarily concerned with the sound pattern of English may prefer to give only one or two examples of answers to each question.

Consonants that occur in languages other than English are discussed at length in Chapters 6 and 7. These chapters are obviously of most importance to students of foreign languages and of general linguistics. The questions at the end of each involve materials that are not essential for students of English.

Chapter 8 outlines some of the main concepts of acoustic phonetics and is a prerequisite for the discussion of vowels in Chapter 9. It is also useful to have some knowledge of acoustic phonetics before reading Chapter 10, which discusses the nature of the syllable and the use of stress, length, tone, and intonation in languages other than English. The final chapters are more concerned with general linguistic concepts.

Chapter 11 introduces the basic ideas involved in two different sets of features that have been used by linguists for specifying the sounds of languages. Chapter 12 discusses the relationship between linguistic descriptions and phonetic specifications. It gives more precise definitions of the set of prime features that can be used in phonetic (and phonological) specifications of the languages of the world. This chapter contains more material than is appropriate for students not specializing in linguistics.

Toward the end of the book, the chapters have fewer exercises—largely because varied assignments seem most rewarding at the beginning of a course. Toward the end of a course students should be able to concentrate on a single project. The kind of project that is most useful for students of general linguistics is to give a description of the major phonetic characteristics in some other language. Students of English might profitably try to describe an accent of English that is very different from their own. Each student might try to find a speaker of another language (or a speaker with a different accent) with whom to work. Then, using grammars, dictionaries, or whatever sources are available, the student could try to compile a list of words illustrating the major characteristics of that language. If possible, a tape recording of this list of words should be prepared and submitted along with written observations.

At the end of nearly every chapter there is also a set of performance exercises that involve making and hearing differences between sounds. Nobody can hope to get very far in the study of phonetics without developing this practical ability. A phonetician should be able to produce the sounds he or she describes and to reproduce sounds described by others. Some people are naturally better at doing this than others, but everyone can improve his or her ability to a considerable extent by conscientiously working through exercises of the kind suggested here.

As this is an introductory textbook, many of the ideas presented here are not new. The sources for some of the less familiar data are acknowledged in a separate section at the end of the book, but I cannot properly acknowledge all of the material I have incorporated. From a personal point of view my greatest debt is clearly to David Abercrombie of the University of Edinburgh, from whom I first learned what I took to be the commonly accepted dogma of phonetics, many of the ideas being his own contributions to the field. But, as he is always eager to point out, many are part of the general tradition of phonetics in Britain that goes back through Daniel Jones to such great nineteenth-century phoneticians as Henry Sweet. Even the details of some of the exercises that appear here (for example, the adding and subtracting of voice from an articulation) can be found in their publications.

I have also incorporated ideas from many other people, including my former teachers and colleagues at the University of Edinburgh, Elizabeth T. Uldall and Ian Catford (now at the University of Michigan), and my colleagues at the University of California, Los Angeles, Victoria Fromkin,

Breyne Arlene Moskowitz, Mona Lindau (now at the University of Iba-
dan, Nigeria), Ian Maddieson, Sandra A. Thompson, and Diana Van
Lancker. Their comments and criticisms have much improved the draft
versions of this book. Helpful comments have also been made by Kenneth
C. Hill of the University of Michigan, John Ohala of the University of
California, Berkeley, Jimmy G. Harris of the Ford Foundation, Harry
Hollien of the University of Florida, William Dyckes of Harcourt Brace
Jovanovich, and numerous students. Of course none of the above is in
any way responsible for any errors. Wherever possible I have checked the
facts with my own observations. The majority of the illustrations are based
on my own x-ray tracings or acoustic analyses.

In conclusion, I would like to acknowledge the enormous amount of
help I have had from my wife, who has judged every sentence in the book,
rewritten many of them, and in a practical sense been a coauthor. I would
also like to thank the University of California, Los Angeles, for granting
me the sabbatical leave during which most of the book was written. The
original research on which parts of the book depend was supported by the
National Institutes of Health (Grant USPHS NS 09780 and 04591) and the
National Science Foundation (Grants NSF GS 37235x and NSF GS 36045).

Contents

A Course in Phonetics

Articulatory Phonetics 1

Phonetics is concerned with describing the speech sounds that occur in the languages of the world. We want to know what these sounds are, how they fall into patterns, and how they change in different circumstances. Most importantly, we want to know what aspects of the sounds are necessary for conveying the meaning of what is being said. The first job of a phonetician is therefore trying to find out what people are doing when they are talking and when they are listening to speech.

The Vocal Organs

We will begin by describing how speech sounds are made. In nearly all speech sounds the basic source of power is the respiratory system pushing air out of the lungs. Try to talk while breathing in instead of out. You will find that you can do it, but it is much more inefficient than superimposing speech on an outgoing breath.

Air from the lungs goes up the windpipe (the trachea, to use the more technical term) and into the larynx, at which point it must pass between two small muscular folds called the vocal cords. If the vocal cords are apart, as they normally are when breathing out, the air from the lungs will have a relatively free passage into the pharynx and the mouth. But if the vocal cords are adjusted so that there is only a narrow passage between them, the pressure of the airstream will cause them to vibrate. Sounds produced when the vocal cords are vibrating are said to be **voiced**, as opposed to those in which the vocal cords are apart, which are said to be **voiceless**.

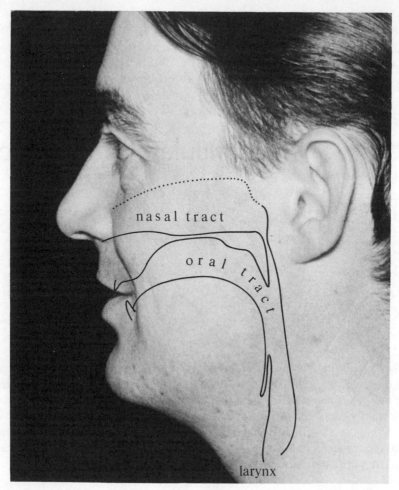

Figure 1.1 *The vocal tract.*

In order to hear the difference between a voiced and a voiceless sound, try saying a long *v* sound, which we will symbolize as [vvvvv]. Now compare this with a long *f* sound [fffff], saying each of them alternately—[fffffvvvvvfffff vvvvv]. Both of these sounds are formed in the same way in the mouth. The difference between them is that [v] is voiced but [f] is voiceless. You can feel the vocal cord vibrations in [v] if you put your fingertips against your larynx. You can also hear the buzzing of the vibrations in [v] more easily if you stop up your ears while contrasting [fffffvvvvv].

The difference between voiced and voiceless sounds is important in all known languages. In each of the pairs of words "fat, vat; thigh, thy; Sue, zoo" the consonant in the first world of each pair is voiceless, whereas that in the second word is voiced. Check this for yourself by saying just the consonants at the beginning of each of these words and trying to feel and hear the voicing as suggested above. Try to find other pairs of words that are distinguished by one having a voiced and the other having a voiceless consonant.

The air passages above the larynx are known as the **vocal tract**. Figure 1.1 shows their location within the head. The shape of the vocal tract is a very important factor in the production of speech, and we will often refer to a diagram of the kind that has been superimposed on the photograph in Figure 1.1. Learn to draw the vocal tract by tracing the diagram in this figure. Note that the air passages that make up the vocal tract may be divided into the oral tract within the mouth and the pharynx, and the nasal tract within the nose. The upper limit of the nasal tract has been marked with a dotted line since the exact boundaries of the air passages within the nose depend on soft tissues of variable size.

The parts of the oral tract that can be used to form sounds are called articulators. The articulators that form the lower surface of the oral tract often move toward those that form the upper surface. Try saying the word "capital" and note the major movements of your tongue and lips. You will find that the back of the tongue makes contact with the roof of the mouth for the first sound, and then comes down for the following vowel. The lips come together in the formation of *p* and then come apart again in the vowel. The tongue tip comes up for the *t* and again, for some people, for the final *l*.

The names for the principal parts of the upper surface of the vocal tract are given in Figure 1.2. The upper lip and the upper teeth (notably the frontal incisors) are familiar enough structures. Just behind the upper teeth there is a small protuberance that you can feel with the tip of the tongue. This is called the **alveolar ridge**. You can also feel that the front part of the roof of the mouth is formed by a bony structure. This is the **hard palate**. You will

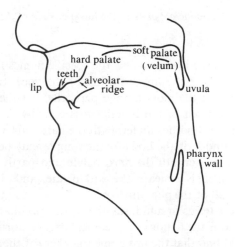

Figure 1.2 *The principal parts of the upper surface of the vocal tract.*

probably have to use a finger tip to feel further back. Most people cannot curl the tongue up far enough to touch the **soft palate**, or **velum**, at the back of the mouth. The soft palate is a muscular flap that can be raised to press against the back wall of the pharynx and shut off the nasal tract, preventing air from going out through the nose. In this case there is said to be a **velic closure**. This action separates the nasal tract from the oral tract so that the air can go out only through the mouth. At the lower end of the soft palate there is a small appendage hanging down that is known as the uvula. The part of the vocal tract between the uvula and the larynx is the pharynx. The back wall of the pharynx may be considered to be one of the articulators on the upper surface of the vocal tract.

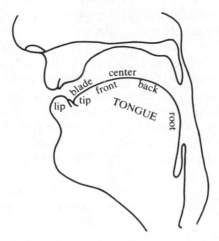

Figure 1.3 *The principal parts of the lower surface of the vocal tract.*

Figure 1.3 shows the lower lip and the specific names for different parts of the tongue which form the lower surface of the vocal tract. The tip and blade of the tongue are the most mobile parts. Behind the blade is what is technically called the front of the tongue: it is actually the forward part of the body of the tongue, and lies underneath the hard palate when the tongue is at rest. The remainder of the body of the tongue may be divided into the center, which is partly beneath the hard palate and partly beneath the soft palate, the back, which is beneath the soft palate, and the root, which is opposite the back wall of the pharynx.

Bearing all these terms in mind, say the word "peculiar" and try to give a rough description of the actions of the vocal organs during the consonant sounds. You should find that the lips come together for the first sound. Then the back and center of the tongue are raised. But is the contact on the hard palate or on the velum? (For most people it is centered between the two.)

Then note the position in the formation of the *l*. Most people make this sound with the tip of the tongue on the alveolar ridge.

Now compare the words "true" and "tea." In which word is the tongue contact further forward in the mouth? Most people make contact with the tip or blade of the tongue on the alveolar ridge when saying "tea," but slightly farther back in "true." Try to distinguish the differences in other consonant sounds such as those in "sigh" and "shy" and those in "fee" and "the."

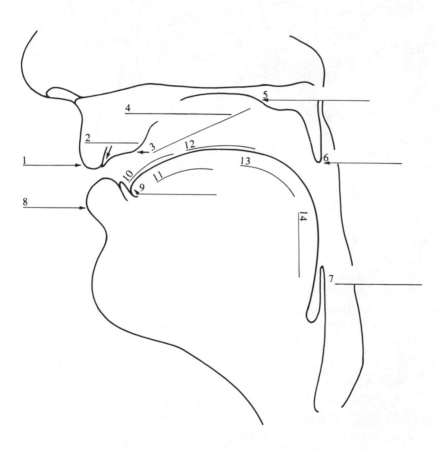

Figure 1.4 *Fill in the names of the vocal organs in the spaces provided.*

Places of Articulation

In order to form consonants, the airstream through the vocal tract must be obstructed in some way. Consonants can therefore be classified according to the place and manner of this obstruction. Some of the possible places of articulation are indicated by the arrows going from one of the lower articulators to one of the upper articulators in Figure 1.5. The principal terms for these particular types of obstruction, all of which are required in the description of English, follow.

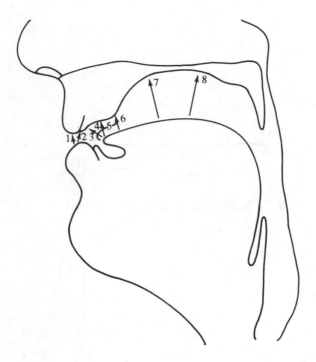

Figure 1.5 *Places of articulation :* **1** Bilabial ; **2** Labiodental ; **3** Dental ; **4** Alveolar ; **5** Retroflex ; **6** Palato-Alveolar ; **7** Palatal ; **8** Velar.

1 Bilabial
(Made with the two lips.) Say words such as "pie, buy, my" and note how the lips come together for the first sound in each of these words. Find a comparable set of words with bilabial sounds at the end.

2 Labiodental
(Lower lip and upper front teeth.) Most people when saying words such as "fie, vie" raise the lower lip until it nearly touches the upper front teeth.

3 Dental

(Tongue tip or blade and upper front teeth.) Say the words "thigh, thy." Some people have the tip of the tongue protruding below the upper front teeth, others have it close behind the upper front teeth. Both these kinds of sounds are normal in English and both may be called dental.

4 Alveolar

(Tongue tip or blade and the alveolar ridge.) Again there are two possibilities in English, and you should find out which you use. You may pronounce words such as "tie, die, nigh, sigh, zeal, lie" using the tip of the tongue or the blade of the tongue. Feel how you normally make the alveolar consonants in each of these words, and then try to make them in the other way.

5 Retroflex

(Tip of the tongue and the back of the alveolar ridge.) Many speakers of English do not use retroflex sounds at all. But for some, retroflex sounds occur initially in words such as "rye, row, ray." Note the position of the tip of your tongue in these words. Speakers who pronounce r at the ends of words may also have retroflex consonants with the tip of the tongue raised in "ire, hour, air."

6 Palato-Alveolar

(Tongue blade and the back of the alveolar ridge.) Say words such as "shy, she, show." During the consonants the tip of your tongue may be down behind the lower front teeth, or it may be up near the alveolar ridge, but the blade of the tongue is always close to the back part of the alveolar ridge. Try saying "shipshape" with your tongue tip up on one occasion, and down on another. Note the blade of the tongue will always be raised. You may be able to feel the place of articulation more distinctly if you hold the position while taking in a breath through the mouth. The incoming air cools the blade of the tongue and the back part of the alveolar ridge.

7 Palatal

(Front of tongue and hard palate.) Say the name "Hugh" very slowly, so that you can isolate the consonant at the beginning. If you say this consonant by itself you should be able to feel that the front of the tongue is raised towards the hard palate. Try to hold the consonant position and breathe inwards through the mouth. You will probably be able to feel the rush of cold air between the front of the tongue and the hard palate.

8 Velar

(Back of the tongue and soft palate.) The consonants that have the furthest back place of articulation in English are those that occur at the end of "hack, hag, hang." In all these sounds the back of the tongue is raised so that it touches the velum.

To get the feeling of different places of articulation, consider the consonant at the beginning of each of the following words: "fee, theme, see, she." Say these consonants by themselves. Are they voiced or voiceless? Now note that the place of articulation moves back in the mouth in making this series of voiceless consonants, going from labiodental, through dental and alveolar, to palato-alveolar. Try the same thing with the consonants at the ends of "wing, win, whim." When you say these consonants by themselves note whether the air is coming out through the mouth or the nose. In the formation of these sounds the point of articulatory closure moves forward, from velar, through alveolar, to bilabial. The soft palate is lowered—there is no velic closure—so that the air can come out through the nose.

Manners of Articulation

At most places of articulation there are several basic ways in which articulation can be accomplished. The articulators may completely close off the oral tract for an instant or a relatively long period, they may narrow the space considerably, or they may simply modify the shape of the tract by approaching each other.

Stop

(Complete closure of the articulators involved so that the airstream cannot escape through the mouth.) There are two possible types of stop.

Nasal stop   If the air is stopped in the oral cavity but the soft palate is down so that it can go out through the nose, the sound produced is a **nasal stop**. Sounds of this kind occur at the beginning of the words "my" (bilabial closure) and "nigh" (alveolar closure) and at the end of the word "sang" (velar closure). Figure 1.6 shows the position of the vocal organs during the bilabial nasal stop in "my."

Oral stop   If in addition to the articulatory closure in the mouth, the soft palate is raised so that the nasal tract is blocked off, then the airstream will be completely obstructed. Pressure in the mouth will build up and an **oral stop** will be formed. When the articulators come apart the airstream will be released in a small burst of sound. This kind of sound occurs in the consonants in the words "pie, buy" (bilabial closure), "tie, dye" (alveolar closure), and "kye, guy" (velar closure). Figure 1.7 shows the positions of the vocal organs in the bilabial stop in "buy." Apart from the presence of a velic closure, there is no difference between this stop and the one in "my" shown in Figure 1.6. Although both the nasal sounds and the oral sounds can be classified as stops, the term **stop** by itself is almost always used by phoneticians to indicate an oral stop, and the term **nasal** to indicate a nasal stop. Thus the consonants at the ends of the words "bad" and "ban" would be called an alveolar stop and an alveolar nasal respectively.

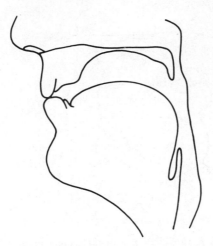

Figure 1.6 *The position of the vocal organs during the bilabial nasal in "my."*

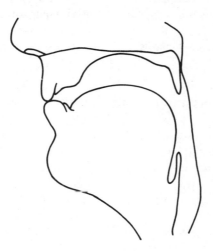

Figure 1.7 *The positions of the vocal organs in the bilabial stop in "buy."*

Fricative

(Close approximation of two articulators so that the airstream is partially obstructed and turbulent airflow is produced.) The mechanism involved in making these slightly hissing sounds may be likened to that involved when the wind whistles around a corner. The consonants in "fie, vie" (labiodental), "thigh, thy" (dental), "sigh, zoo" (alveolar), and "shy" (palato-alveolar) are examples of fricative sounds. Figure 1.8 illustrates one pronunciation of the

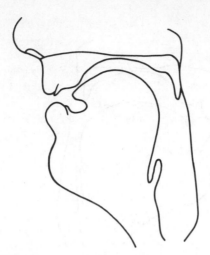

Figure 1.8 *The positions of the vocal organs in the palato-alveolar fricative in "shy."*

palato-alveolar fricative consonant in "shy." Note the narrowing of the vocal tract between the blade of the tongue and the back part of the alveolar ridge. The higher-pitched sounds with a more obvious hiss, such as those in "sigh, shy," are sometimes called **sibilants**, and the others **nonsibilants**.

Approximant

(The approach of one articulator towards another, but without the tract being narrowed to such an extent that a turbulent airstream is produced.) In saying the first sound in "yacht" the front of the tongue is raised toward the palatal area of the roof of the mouth, but it does not come close enough for a fricative sound to be produced. The consonants in the word "we" (approximation between the lips and in the velar region) and, for some people, in the word "raw" (approximation in the alveolar region) are also examples of approximants.

Lateral

(Obstruction of the airstream at a point along the center of the oral tract, with incomplete closure between one or both sides of the tongue and the roof of the mouth.) The sound at the beginning of the word "lip" is an alveolar lateral consonant. Say this word and note the tongue position. You may be able to find out which side of the tongue is not in contact with the roof of the mouth by holding the consonant position while you breathe inward. The tongue will feel colder on the side that is not in contact with the roof of the mouth.

In this preliminary chapter it will not be necessary to discuss all of the manners of articulation used in the various languages of the world—nor, for that matter, in English. But it might be useful to know the terms **trill** (sometimes called roll), and **tap**. Tongue-tip trills occur in some forms of Scottish English in words such as "rye" and "raw." Taps, in which the tongue makes a single tap against the alveolar ridge, occur in the middle of a word such as "letter" in many forms of American English.

The production of some sounds involves more than one of these manners of articulation. Say the word "cheap" and think about how you make the first sound. At the beginning the tongue comes up to make contact with the alveolar ridge to form a stop closure. This contact is then slackened so that there is a fricative at the same place of articulation. This kind of combination of a stop immediately followed by a fricative is called an **affricate**. There is a voiceless affricate at the beginning and end of the word "church." The corresponding voiced affricate occurs at the beginning and end of "judge." In all these sounds the articulators (tongue tip or blade and alveolar ridge) come together for the stop, and then, instead of coming fully apart, separate only slightly, so that a fricative is made at the same place of articulation. Try to feel these movements in your own pronunciation of these words.

To summarize, the consonants we have been discussing so far may be described in terms of five factors: (1) state of the vocal cords (voiced or voiceless); (2) place of articulation; (3) central or lateral articulation; (4) velic closure (oral or nasal); (5) manner of articulatory action. Thus the consonant at the beginning of the word "sing" is a (1) voiceless, (2) alveolar, (3) central, (4) oral, (5) fricative, and the consonant at the end of "sing" is a (1) voiced, (2) velar, (3) central, (4) nasal, (5) stop.

On most occasions it is not necessary to state all these five points. Unless a specific statement to the contrary is made, consonants are usually presumed to be central, not lateral, and oral rather than nasal. Consequently points (3) and (4) may often be left out, so that the consonant at the beginning of "sing" is simply called a voiceless alveolar fricative. When describing nasals, point (4) has to be specifically mentioned and point (5) can be left out, so that the consonant at the end of "sing" is simply called a voiced velar nasal.

The Articulation of Vowel Sounds

In the production of vowel sounds none of the articulators come very close together, and the passage of the airstream is relatively unobstructed. Vowel sounds may be specified in terms of the position of the highest point of the tongue and the position of the lips. Figure 1.9 shows the articulatory position for the vowels in "heed, hid, head, had, father, good, food." As you can see, in all these vowels the tongue tip is down behind the lower front teeth and the body of the tongue is domed upward. Check that this is so in your own pronunciation. In the first four vowels, the highest point of the tongue is in the front of the mouth. Accordingly, these vowels are called **front vowels**. The tongue is fairly close to the roof of the mouth for the vowel in "heed,"

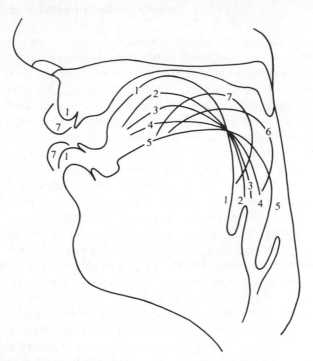

Figure 1.9 *The positions of the vocal organs for the vowels in the words*
1 heed, **2** hid, **3** head, **4** had, **5** father, **6** good, **7** food.

slightly less close for the vowel in "hid," and lower still for the vowels in "head" and "had." If you look in a mirror while saying the vowels in these four words you will find that the mouth becomes progressively more open while the tongue remains in the front of the mouth. The vowel in "heed" is classified as a high front vowel, and the vowel in "had" as a low front vowel. The height of the tongue for the vowels in the other words is between these two extremes, and they are therefore called mid front vowels. The vowel in "hid" is a high mid vowel, and the vowel in "head" is a low mid vowel.

Now try saying the vowels in "father, good, food." Figure 1.9 also shows the articulatory position for these vowels. In all three the tongue is close to the upper or back surface of the vocal tract. These vowels are classified as **back vowels**. The body of the tongue is highest in the vowel in "food" (which is therefore called a high back vowel), and lowest in the first vowel in "father" (which is therefore called a low back vowel). The vowel in "good" is a mid back vowel.

The position of the lips varies considerably in different vowels. They are generally closer together in the mid and high back vowels (as in "good, food"), though in some forms of American English this is not so. Look at the position of your lips in a mirror while you say just the vowels in "heed, hid, head, had, father, good, food." You will probably find that in the last two words there is a movement of the lips in addition to the movement which occurs because of the lowering and raising of the jaw. This movement is called **lip rounding**. Vowels may be described as being **rounded** (as in "who'd") or **unrounded**, or spread (as in "heed").

In summary, therefore, vowels can be described in terms of three factors: (1) the height of the body of the tongue; (2) the front-back position of the tongue; and (3) the degree of lip rounding. The relative positions of the highest points of the tongue are given in Figure 1.10. Say just the vowels in the words given below this figure and check that your tongue moves in the pattern described by the points. It is very difficult to become aware of the position of the tongue in vowels, but you can probably get some impression of tongue height by observing the position of your jaw while saying just the vowels in the four words, "heed, hid, head, had." You should also be able to feel the difference between front and back vowels by contrasting words such as "he" and "who." Say these words silently and concentrate on the sensations involved. You should feel the tongue going from front to back as you say "he, who." You can also feel your lips becoming more rounded.

As you can see from Figure 1.10, the specification of vowels in terms of the position of the highest point of the tongue is not entirely satisfactory for a number of reasons. First, the vowels that are called high do not have the same tongue height. The back high vowel (point 7) has approximately the same tongue height as a mid front vowel (point 2). Second, the so-called back vowels vary considerably in their degree of backness. Third, as you can see by looking at Figure 1.9, this kind of specification disregards considerable differences in the shape of the tongue in front vowels and in back vowels. Furthermore, it does not take into account the fact that the width of the pharynx varies considerably, and to some extent independently of the height of the tongue, in different vowels. We will discuss better ways of describing vowels in Chapters 4 and 9.

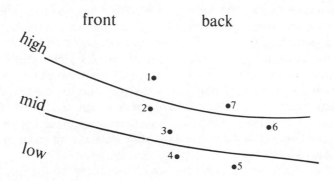

Figure 1.10 *The relative positions of the highest points of the tongue in the vowels in* **1** *heed,* **2** *hid,* **3** *head,* **4** *had,* **5** *father,* **6** *good,* **7** *food.*

Suprasegmentals

Vowels and consonants can be thought of as the segments of which speech is composed. Together they form the syllables, which go to make up utterances. Superimposed on the syllables there are other features known as suprasegmentals. These include variations in stress and pitch. Variations in length are also usually considered to be suprasegmental features, although they can affect single segments as well as whole syllables.

Variations in stress are used in English to distinguish between a noun and a verb, as in "an insult" versus "to insult." Say these words yourself, and check which syllable has the greater stress. Then compare similar pairs, such as "(a) pervert, (to) pervert" or "(an) overflow, (to) overflow." You should find that in the nouns the stress is on the first syllable, but in the verbs it is on the last. Thus, stress can have a grammatical function in English. It can also be used for contrastive emphasis (as in "I want a *red* pen, not a black one"). Variations in stress are caused by an increase in the activity of the respiratory muscles (so that a greater amount of air is pushed out of the lungs) and in the activity of the laryngeal muscles (so that there is a significant change in pitch).

You can usually find where the stress occurs on a word by trying to tap with your finger in time with each syllable. It is much easier to tap on the stressed syllable. Try saying "abominable" and tapping first on the first syllable, then on the second, then on the third, and so on. If you say the word in your normal way you will find it easiest to tap on the second syllable. Many people cannot tap on the first syllable without altering their normal pronunciation.

Pitch changes due to variations in laryngeal activity can occur independently of stress changes. When they do they can affect the meaning of the sentence as a whole. The pitch pattern in a sentence is known as the **intonation**. Listen to the intonation (the variations in the pitch of your voice) when you say the sentence "This is my father." Try to find out which syllable has the highest pitch and which the lowest. In most people's speech the highest pitch will occur on the first syllable of "father" and the lowest on the second. Now observe the pitch changes in the question "Is this your father?" In this sentence the first syllable of "father" is usually on a low pitch, and the last syllable is on a high pitch. In English it is even possible to change the meaning of a sentence such as "That's a cat" from a statement to a question without altering the order of the words. If you substitute a mainly rising for a mainly falling intonation, you will produce a question spoken with an air of astonishment—"That's a *cat*?"

All the suprasegmental features are characterized by the fact that they must be described in relation to other items in the same utterance. It is the relative values of pitch, length, or degree of stress of an item that are significant. You can stress one syllable as opposed to another irrespective of whether you are shouting or talking softly. Children can also use the same intonation patterns as adults, although their voices have a higher pitch. The absolute values are never linguistically important. But they do, of course, convey information about the speaker's age, sex, emotional state, and attitude toward the topic under discussion.

16

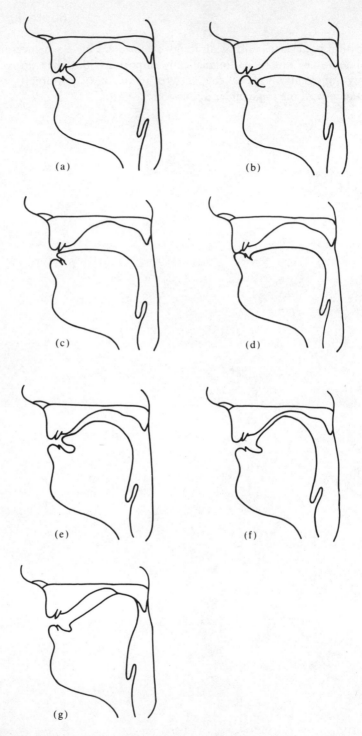

Figure 1.11 *Sounds illustrating all the places of articulation discussed so far except for retroflex sounds.*

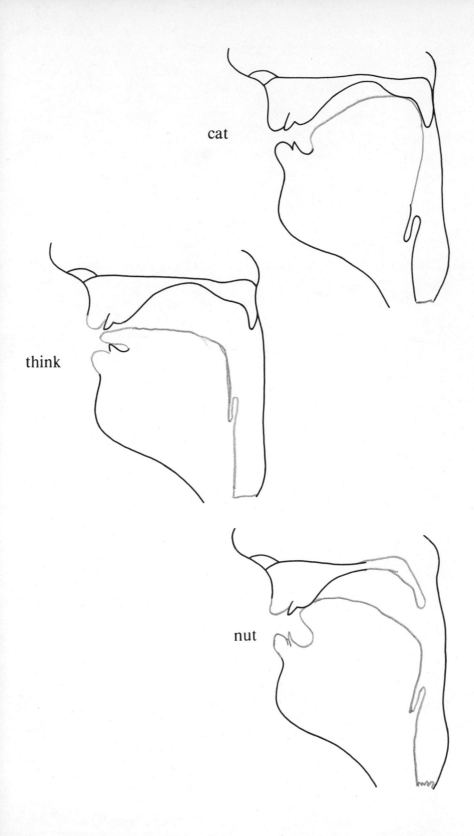

cat

think

nut

Phonology and Phonetic Transcription 2

Many people think that learning phonetics means simply learning to use phonetic transcription. But there is really much more to the subject than learning to use a set of symbols. A phonetician is a person who can describe speech, who understands the mechanisms of speech production and speech perception, and who knows how languages use these mechanisms. Phonetic transcription is no more than a useful tool that phoneticians use in the description of speech.

When phoneticians transcribe an utterance, they usually do so by noting how the sounds convey differences in meaning. For the most part they concern themselves with describing only the significant articulations rather than the total set of movements of the vocal organs. For example, when saying the English word "tie," some people pronounce the consonant with the blade of the tongue against the alveolar ridge, others with the tip of the tongue. This kind of difference in articulation does not affect the meaning of the word and is not usually transcribed.

In order to understand how phonetic transcription works it is necessary to understand the basic principles of phonology. **Phonology** is the description of the systems and patterns of sounds that occur in a language. It involves studying a language to determine its distinctive sounds and to establish a set of rules that describe the set of changes that take place in these sounds when they occur in different relationships with other sounds. The smallest segments of sound that can be distinguished by their contrast within words are called **phonemes**. They are the abstract units that form the basis for writing down a language systematically and unambiguously. We often want to record all and only the variations between sounds that cause a difference in meaning. Transcriptions of this kind are called **phonemic transcriptions**.

The Transcription of Consonants

Let us begin by considering the contrasting consonant sounds in English. Take, for example, all the words that rhyme with "pie" and have only a single consonant at the beginning. A set of words each of which differs from all the others by only one sound is called a **minimal set**. The second column of Table 2.1 lists a minimal set of this kind. There are obviously many additional words that rhyme with "pie," such as "spy, try, spry," but these words begin with sequences of two or more sounds. Some of the words in the list begin with two consonant letters ("thigh, thy, shy"), but they each begin with a single consonant sound. "Shy," for example, does not contain a sequence of two consonant sounds in the way that "spy" and "try" do.

Table 2.1

Symbols for transcribing English consonants.

p	pie	pea	
t	tie	tea	
k	kye	key	
b	by	bee	
d	dye	D	
g	guy		
m	my	me	ra*m*
n	nigh	knee	ra*n*
ŋ			ra*ng*
f	fie	fee	
v	vie	V	
θ	thigh		
ð	thy	thee	
s	sigh	sea	
z		Z	mi*zz*en
ʃ	shy	she	mi*ss*ion
ʒ			vi*s*ion
l	lie	lee	
w	why	we	
r	rye	re	
j		ye	
h	high	he	

Note also the following:

tʃ	chi(me)	chea(p)
dʒ	ji(ve)	G

Some consonants do not occur in words rhyming with "pie." If we allow the names of the letters as words, then we can find a larger set of consonants beginning words rhyming with "pea." A list of such words is shown in the third column of Table 2.1. (Speakers of British English will have to remember that in American English the name of the last letter of the alphabet belongs in this set rather than in the set of words rhyming with "bed.")

Even in this set of words we are still missing some consonant sounds which contrast with others only in the middle or at the ends of words. The letters *ng* often represent a single consonant sound that does not occur at the beginning of a word. You can hear this sound at the end of the word "rang," where it contrasts with other nasals in words such as "ram, ran." There is also a contrast between the consonants in the middle of "mission" and "vision," although there are very few pairs of words that are distinguished by this contrast in English. (One such pair in my English involves the name of a chain of islands—"Aleutian" versus "allusion.") Words illustrating these consonants are given in the fourth column of Table 2.1.

Most of the symbols in Table 2.1 are the same letters we use in spelling these words, but there are a few differences. One variation between spelling and phonetic usage occurs with the letter *c*, which is sometimes used to represent a [k] sound, as in "cup" or "bacon," and sometimes to represent an [s] sound, as in "cellar" or "receive." It may even represent a sequence of these sounds in the same word, as in "accent, access." Another example is the symbol [g], which is used for the sound "guy" and "guess" but never for the sound in "age" or in the letter *g* itself.

A few other symbols are needed to supplement the regular alphabet. The velar nasal at the end of "rang" is written with [ŋ], a letter *n* combined with the tail of the letter *g* descending below the line. The symbol [θ], an upright version of the Greek letter theta, is used for the voiceless dental fricative in words such as "thigh, thin, thimble, ether, breath, mouth." The symbol [ð], derived from an Anglo-Saxon letter, is used for the corresponding voiced sound in words such as "thy, then, them, breathe, mouthe." Both these symbols are ascenders (letters which go up from the line of writing rather than descending below it). The spelling system of the English language does not distinguish between [θ] and [ð]. They are both written with the letters *th* in pairs such as "ether, either."

The voiceless palato-alveolar fricative [ʃ] in "shy, sheep, rash" is both an ascender and a descender. It is like a long, straightened *s* going both above and below the line of writing. The corresponding voiced symbol [ʒ] is like a long *z* descending below the line (on a typewriter, one can use a figure 3 lowered half a line space). This symbol occurs in the middle of words such as "vision, measure, leisure, rouge" and at the beginning of foreign words such as French "Jean, gendarme."

The phonetic symbols used here are part of the set suggested by the International Phonetic Association (IPA), a body founded in 1886 by a group of leading phoneticians from France, Germany, Britain, and Denmark. A more complete set of these symbols will be found on the inside back cover of this book, and a detailed set, along with recommendations for their usage, is given in the booklet *Principles of the International Phonetic Association* (obtainable from the Phonetics Department, University College, London).

Unfortunately, it nevertheless happens that different books on phonetics use different forms of phonetic transcription. This is not because phoneticians cannot agree on which symbols to use, but because different styles of transcription are more appropriate in one circumstance than in another. Thus in this book, where we are concerned with general phonetics, I have used the symbol [j] for the initial sound in "yes, yet, yeast" because I wish to reserve the symbol [y] for another sound, the vowel in the French word "tu." Another reason for using [j] is that in many languages (German, Dutch, Norwegian, Swedish, and others) this letter is used in words such as "ja," which are pronounced with a sound that in our spelling system would be written with the letter *y*. Books that are only concerned with the phonetics of English often use [y] where this one uses [j].

There are also disagreements among texts on phonetics on how to transcribe sounds such as the first and last sounds in both "church" and "judge." I have taken the position that these sounds are each sequences of two other consonants and should be written [tʃ] and [dʒ]. You can see that a word such as "choose" might be said to begin with [tʃ] if you compare your pronunciation of the phrases "white shoes" and "why choose." In the first phrase the [t] is at the end of one word and the [ʃ] at the beginning of the next, but in the second phrase the sounds occur together at the beginning of the second word. The difference between the two phrases is simply one of the timing of the articulations involved rather than the use of different articulations. Other pairs of phrases that demonstrate this point are "heat sheets" versus "he cheats" and "might shop" versus "my chop." There are no pairs of phrases illustrating the same point for the voiced counterpart [dʒ] found in "jar, gentle, age" because no English word begins with [ʒ].

Some other books on phonetics take the view that the sounds [tʃ] and [dʒ] as in "church" and "judge" are really single units and are better transcribed with a single symbols such as [č] and [ǰ]. This view has much to commend it since the consonants [ʃ] and [ʒ] are not like other consonants such as [r] and [l]. Each of the latter pair of consonants can occur as the second element in many clusters (for example, in "priest, tree, cream, play, clay"). But [ʃ] and [ʒ] cluster only with [t] and [d] respectively.

There is one minor matter still to be considered in the transcription of the consonant contrasts of English. In many forms of both British and American English, "which" does not contrast with "witch." Accordingly, both "why" and "we" in Table 2.1 are said to begin simply with [w]. But many speakers of English contrast pairs of words such as "which, witch; why, wye; whether, weather." These speakers will have to transcribe the first of each of these pairs of words with an initial [h]. Note that phonetically the [h] occurs before the [w], whereas in the spelling the *w* occurs before the *h*.

The Transcription of Vowels

The transcription of the contrasting vowels in English is more difficult than the transcription of consonants for two reasons. First, dialects of English differ more in their use of vowels than in their use of consonants. Second, authorities differ widely in their views of what constitutes an appropriate description of vowels.

Taking the same approach in looking for contrasting vowels as we did in looking for consonant contrasts, we might try to find a minimal set of words that differ only in the vowel sounds. We could, for example, look for monosyllables that begin with [h] and end with [d] and supplement this minimal set with other lists of monosyllables that contrast only in their vowel sounds. Table 2.2 shows lists of words in the kind of British English that I speak myself. The reason for starting with this kind of English is that it contrasts a larger number of vowels than many others.

Table 2.2

Symbols for transcribing contrasting vowels in English. Column **1** applies to most speakers of American English, column **2** to most speakers of British English.

1	2					
i	i	heed	he	bead	heat	keyed
ɪ	ɪ	hid		bid	hit	kid
eɪ	eɪ	hayed	hay	bayed	hate	Cade
ɛ	ɛ	head		bed		
æ	æ	had		bad	hat	cad
ɑr	ɑ	hard		bard	heart	card
ɑ	ɒ	hod		bod	hot	cod
ɔ	ɔ	hawed	haw	bawd		cawed
ʊ	ʊ	hood				could
oʊ	oʊ	hoed	hoe	bode		code
u	u	who'd	who	booed	hoot	cooed
ər	ə	herd	her	bird	hurt	curd
ʌ	ʌ	Hudd		bud	hut	cut
aɪ	aɪ	hide	high	bide	height	
aʊ	aʊ		how	bowed		cowed
ɔɪ	ɔɪ		(a)hoy	Boyd		
ir	ɪə		here	beard		
er	ɛə		hair	bared		cared
aɪr	aə	hired	hire			

Note also

ju	ju	hued	hue	Bude		cued

In general, speakers of American English can pronounce [r] sounds after vowels, as well as before them. Consequently they distinguish between words such as "heart" and "hot" not by making a difference in vowel quality (as I do) but by pronouncing "heart" with an [r] and "hot" with the same vowel but without an [r] following it. Similarly they may distinguish between "bud" and "bird" (or "hut" and "hurt") mainly by the absence or presence of the [r] sound. In "here, hair, hire," they use vowels similar to those in "he, hay, high," respectively, but in each case with a following [r]. Most speakers of British English use different diphthongs—movements from one vowel to another within a single syllable.

Even within American English there are variations in the number of contrasting vowels that occur. Many Midwestern speakers and most Far Western speakers do not distinguish between the vowels in pairs of words such as "odd, awed" and "cot, caught." Some forms of American English make additional distinctions not shown in Table 2.2. For example, some speakers (mainly from the East Coast) distinguish the auxiliary verb "can" from the noun "can." But we will have to overlook these small differences in this introductory textbook.

There are several possible ways of transcribing the contrasting vowels in Table 2.2. The two principal forms that will be used in this book are shown in the first and second columns. The first column is suitable for many forms of American English and the second for many forms of British English. The two columns have been kept as similar as possible; as you will see in Chapter 4, I have tried to make the transcriptions compatible with those of well-known authorities on the phonetics of English.

As in the case of the consonant symbols, the vowel symbols in Table 2.2 are used in accordance with the principles of the IPA. Those symbols that have the same shape as ordinary letters of the alphabet represent sounds similar to the sounds these letters have in French or Spanish or Italian. Actually, the IPA usage of the vowel letters is that of the great majority of the world's languages when they are written with the Roman alphabet, including such diverse languages as Swahili, Turkish, and Navaho. The present spelling of English reflects the way it used to sound many centuries ago when it still had vowel sounds with values similar to those of the corresponding letters in all these other languages.

One of the principal problems in transcribing English phonetically is that there are more vowel sounds than there are vowel letters in the alphabet. In a transcription of the English word "sea" as [si], the [i] represents a similar (but not identical) sound to that in the Spanish or Italian "si." But unlike Spanish and Italian, English differentiates between vowels such as those in "seat, sit" and "heed, hid." Because the vowels in "sit, hid" are somewhat like those in "seat, heed," they are represented by the symbol [ɪ], an un-dotted form of the letter *i*.

The vowels in words such as "hay, bait, they" are transcribed with a sequence of two symbols [eɪ], indicating that for most speakers of English these words contain a diphthong. The first element in this diphthong is similar to sounds in Spanish or Italian that use the letter *e*, such as the Spanish word for three, which is written "tres" and pronounced [tres].

Two symbols that are not ordinary letters of the alphabet, [ɛ] and [æ], are used for the vowels in "head" and "had" respectively. The first is based on the Greek letter epsilon, and the second on the letters *a* and *e* joined together. They may be referred to by the names epsilon and digraph.

Most Americans have the same vowel sound in the words "heart" and "hot" and can use one form of the letter *a*. They would transcribe these words as [hɑrt] and [hɑt]. But some East Coast Americans and speakers of British English who do not pronounce [r] sounds after a vowel distinguish between these words by the qualities of the vowels and have to use two different forms of the letter *a*. They would transcribe these words as [hɑt] and [hɒt].

The symbol for use in the words "bawd, bought, law" is [ɔ], an open letter *o* or an inverted letter *c*. Many Midwestern and Far Western American speakers do not need to use this symbol, as they do not distinguish between the vowels in words such as "cot" and "caught."

Another special symbol is used for the vowel in "hood, could, good." This symbol [ʊ] may be thought of as a letter *w* with the ends curled in (or as an inverted heart).

The vowel in "hoe, dough, snow" is regarded as a diphthong, with a first element similar to sounds that are written in Spanish, French, or Italian with the letter *o*. As we will see in Chapter 4, this is obviously an oversimplification for many speakers of British English, who use a very different sound for the first element of the diphthong in these words. The final element of this diphthong is like [ʊ] as in "hood."

The symbol [u], used in transcribing "who, hoot, boot," has a value similar to that of the corresponding letter in the Spanish "uno." Note that it does not by itself represent the word "you" or the name of the letter *u*, which would be transcribed with the consonant [j] at the beginning. The words "cute, few" would be transcribed as [kjut, fju].

Another symbol, [ə], an upside-down letter *e*, is used for the sounds in "pert, bird, curt." It may be referred to by the name schwa. Americans who pronounce the [r] in these words would transcribe them as [pərt, bərd, kərt]. Most speakers of British English would transcribe them in the same way but without the [r]. These British speakers usually distinguish these words from the corresponding words "putt, bud, cut" simply by a difference in vowel quality. They therefore need an additional symbol, [ʌ], an inverted letter *v*, for transcribing these vowels. Many Americans also have very different qualities in the vowels in words such as "pert, putt; bird, bud; curt, cut." Some phoneticians regard the difference in vowel quality as being conditioned by the [r] and transcribe them with [ər] and [ə], but we will use different vowel symbols and transcribe them with [ər] and [ʌ]. A transcription of this kind is slightly redundant in the sense that it uses one more symbol than is necessary for distinguishing words.

The next three words in Table 2.2 contain diphthongs composed of elements that have been discussed already. The vowel in "hide" [haɪd] begins with a sound between that of the vowel in "cat" [kæt] and that in "hard" [hɑd] or [hɑrd], and moves towards the vowel [ɪ] as in "hid" [hɪd]. The symbol [a] is used for the first part of this diphthong. The vowel in "how" [aʊ] begins with a similar sound but moves towards [ʊ] as in "hood." The vowel in "boy" [bɔɪ] is a combination of the sound [ɔ] as in "bawd" and [ɪ] as in "hid."

Most Americans pronounce the remaining words in Table 2.2 with one of the other vowels followed by [r], while most British English speakers have additional diphthongs in these words. Some British English speakers use a diphthong in words like "poor, cure" that can be transcribed as [ʊə], and some differ from my usage in that they pronounce words such as "fire, hire" as two syllables (like "higher" and "liar"), transcribing them as [faɪə, haɪə].

All the words in Table 2.2 are monosyllables. Consequently none of them contains both stressed and unstressed vowels. By far the commonest unstressed vowel is [ə]. It occurs at the ends of words such as "sofa, soda" [ˈsoʊfə, ˈsoʊdə], in the middle of words such as "emphasis, deprecate" [ˈɛmfəsɪs, ˈdɛprəkeɪt], and the beginnings of words such as "around, arise" [əˈraʊnd, əˈraɪz]. (In all these words the symbol [ˈ] is a stress mark which has been placed before the syllable carrying the main stress. Stress should always be marked in words of more than one syllable.)

In British English [ə] is usually the sole component of the "-er" part of words such as "father, brotherhood, simpler" [ˈfɑðə, ˈbrʌðəhʊd, ˈsɪmplə]. In forms of American English in which [r] is pronounced after vowels, these words are usually [ˈfɑðər, ˈbrʌðərhʊd, ˈsɪmplər]. In addition [ə] occurs very frequently in unstressed monosyllables such as the grammatical function words "the, a, to, and, but." In connected speech these words are usually [ðə, ə, tə, ənd, bət].

Some of the other vowels also occur in unstressed syllables, but because of the varieties of English, it is a little more difficult to say which vowel occurs in which word. For example, nearly all speakers of English differentiate between the last vowels in "Sophie" and "sofa" or "pity" and "patter." But some people have the vowel [i] as in "heed" at the end of "Sophie, pity, only, corny." Others have [ɪ] as in "hid." Similarly, most people make the vowel in the second syllable of "taxis" different from that in "Texas." Some have [i] and some have [ɪ] in "taxis." Nearly everybody pronounces "Texas" as [ˈtɛksəs]. (Note that in English the letter *x* often represents the sounds [ks].)

EXERCISES

Find the errors in the transcription of the consonant sounds in the following words. In each word there is one error, indicating an impossible pronunciation of that word for a native speaker of English of any variety. Circle this error, and write the correct symbol in the space provided after the word.

1. "strength" [ˈstrɛŋgθ] should be [ŋ]
2. "crime" [ˈcraɪm] [k]
3. "wishing" [ˈwɪshɪŋ] [ʃ]
4. "wives" [ˈwaɪvs] [z]
5. "these" [ˈθiz] [ð]
6. "hijacking" [ˈhaɪjækɪŋ] [dʒ]
7. "yellow" [ˈjɛlloʊ] [l]
8. "chipping" [ˈtʃɪppɪŋ] [p]
9. "sixty" [ˈsɪxti] [ks]
10. "thesis" [ˈðisɪs] [θ]

Now try another ten words in which the errors are all in the vowels. Again, there is only one possible error; but because of differences in varieties of English, there are sometimes alternative possible corrections.

11. "man-made" [ˈmanmeɪd] should be [æ]
12. "snowball" [ˈsnoʊbol] [ɔ]
13. "tea chest" [ˈtitʃest] [ɛ]
14. "tomcat" [ˈtomkæt] [ɑ]
15. "tiptoe" [ˈtiptoʊ] [ɪ]
16. "avoid" [æˈvoɪd] [ə]
17. "remain" [rəˈman] [eɪ]
18. "roommate" [ˈrommeɪt] [u]
19. "umbrella" [umˈbrɛlə] [ʌ]
20. "manage" [ˈmænædʒ] [ə]

Now correct the following words, again by circling the error and noting the correction. There is still only one per word, but it may be among the vowels, the consonants, or the stress marks.

21. "exclusion" [ɛksˈkluʃən] should be [ʒ]
22. "traffic" [ˈtræfɪc] [k]
23. "simplistic" [ˈsɪmplɪstɪk] [mˈp]
24. "citation" [siˈteɪʃən] [aɪ]
25. "improvement" [ɪmˈproʊvmənt] [u]
26. "improvident" [ɪmˈprɒvɪdənt] [ɛ]

27. "demonstrate"   [ˈdɛmɑnstreɪt]   [ə]
28. "human being"   [hjumən ˈbiɪŋ]   [ju]
29. "appreciate"   [əˈpreʃieɪt]   [i]
30. "joyful"   [ˈdʒɔyfol]   [ɪ]

Finally, transcribe the following words or phrases as you pronounce them. Give a rough label for your accent (e.g., Southern Californian, New York, London, Scottish), and try to make the transcription illustrate your ordinary conversational style. Do not use a reading pronunciation or one that you think you ought to use. Say the words aloud and listen to what you normally do. Be careful to put in stress marks at the proper places.

accent ___Wisc / SE U.S.___

31. chocolate pudding   [ˈtʃaklət pʊdiŋ]

32. modern languages   [ˈmɔdərn leɪŋgwədʒəz]

33. impossibility   [ɪmˈpɔsəbrləti]

34. boisterous   [ˈbɔɪstrəs]

35. youngster   [ˈjʌŋstər]

36. another   [əˈnʌðər]

37. diabolical   [daɪəˈbɔləkəl]

38. nearly over   [ˈnɪrli oʊvər]

39. red riding hood   [red ˈraɪdiŋ hʊd]

40. inexcusable   [ɪn eksˈkjuzəbəl]

Consonant and Vowel Charts

So far we have been using the consonant and vowel symbols simply as ways of representing the contrasts that occur among words in English. But they can also be thought of in a completely different way. We may regard them as shorthand descriptions of the articulations involved. Thus [p] is an abbreviation for "voiceless bilabial stop" and [l] is equivalent to "voiced alveolar lateral approximant." The consonant symbols can then be arranged in the form of a chart as in Figure 2.1. The places of articulation are shown

Place of articulation

	bilabial	labio-dental	dental	alveolar	palato-alveolar	palatal	velar
nasal	m			n			ŋ
stop	p b			t d			k g
fricative		f v	θ ð	s z	ʃ ʒ		
(central) approximant	(w)			r		j	w
lateral (approximant)				l			

(Manner of articulation — vertical axis label)

Figure 2.1 *A chart of the English consonants we have dealt with so far. Whenever there are two symbols within a single cell, the one on the left represents a voiceless sound. All other symbols represent voiced sounds. Note also the consonant [h], which is not on this chart, and the affricates [tʃ, dʒ], which are sequences of symbols on the chart.*

across the top of the chart, starting from the most forward articulation (bilabial) and going toward those sounds made in the back of the mouth (velar). The manners of articulation are shown on the vertical axis of the chart. By convention, the voiced–voiceless distinction is shown by putting the voiceless symbols to the left of the voiced symbols.

The symbol [w] is shown in two places in the consonant chart in Figure 2.1. This is because it is articulated with both a narrowing of the lip aperture, which makes it bilabial, and a raising of the back of the tongue towards the soft palate, which makes it velar. The symbol [h] does not appear anywhere on the chart. In English [h] acts like a consonant, but from an articulatory point of view it is simply the voiceless counterpart of the following vowel.

The symbols we have been using for the contrasting vowels may also be regarded as shorthand descriptions for different vowel qualities. There are problems in this respect, in that we have been using these symbols somewhat loosely, allowing them to have different values for different dialects. But the general values can be indicated by a vowel chart as in Figure 2.2. The symbols have been placed within a quadrilateral, which shows the range of possible vowel qualities. Thus [i] is used for a high front vowel, [u] for a high back one, [ɛ] for a slightly lowered mid-front vowel, and so on.

The simple vowel chart in Figure 2.2 shows only two of the dimensions of vowel quality. It does not show anything about the variations in the degree

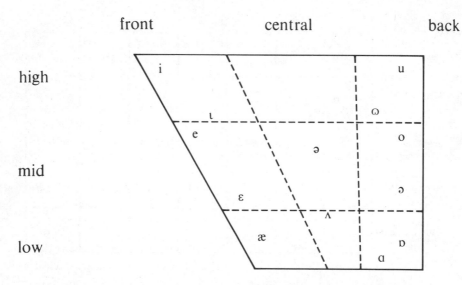

Figure 2.2 *A vowel chart showing the relative vowel qualities represented by some of the symbols used in transcribing English. The symbols [e, a, o] occur as the first elements of diphthongs.*

of lip rounding in the different vowels, nor does it indicate anything about vowel length. It does not show, for example, that in most circumstances [i] and [u] are longer than [ɪ] and [ʊ].

Phonology

There is another reason why it is only approximately true that in our transcriptions of English the symbols have the values shown in Figures 2.1 and 2.2. In the style of transcription we have been using so far, some of the symbols may represent different sounds when they occur in different contexts.

For example the symbol [t] may represent a wide variety of sounds. In "tap" [tæp] it represents a voiceless alveolar stop. But the [t] in "eighth" [eιtθ] may be made on the teeth, because of the influence of the following voiceless dental fricative [θ]. This [t] is more accurately called a voiceless dental stop and we will later use a special symbol for transcribing it. In my form of British English and in many forms of American English, the [t] in "bitten" ['bιtn] is accompanied by a glottal stop, and we will later be using a special symbol for this sound. For most Americans the [t] in "catty" ['kæti] symbolizes a voiced, not a voiceless, stop, and this word might have been transcribed as ['kædi].

Similarly, other symbols represent different sounds in different contexts. The symbols [l] and [r] normally stand for voiced approximants. But in words such as "ply" [plaι] and "try" [traι] they represent voiceless sounds. Vowel sounds may also vary. The [i] in "heed" [hid] is usually very different from the [i] in "heel" [hil].

Many of the variations we have been discussing can be described in terms of simple statements about regular sound patterns. Statements of this kind may be considered rules. In most forms of American English, for example, it is a rule that [t] becomes voiced not only in "catty," but on all occasions when it occurs immediately after a stressed vowel and before an unstressed vowel (for example, in "bitty, matter, utter," etc.). In English of nearly all kinds it is also a rule that [t] is pronounced as a dental stop [t̪] whenever it occurs before a dental fricative. The same is true of [d], as in "width" [wιd̪ð], [n], as in "tenth" [tɛṇθ], and [l], as in "wealth" [wɛl̪θ].

Variations in words that can be described in terms of rules are called **alternations**. There are many rule-governed alternations in English. For example, there are rules that will account for variations in the placement of stress or for alternations in vowel quality. Consider the ways in which the letter o is pronounced in sets of words such as "melody" ['mɛlədi], "melodic" [mə'lɑdιk], and "melodious" [mə'loωdiəs]. In the first word it is [ə], in the second [ɑ] (or [ɒ] in many forms of British English), and in the third word [oω]. Note that the same variations occur for the o in "harmony, harmonic, harmonious." The rules that predict these variations are very general and cover many similar cases.

We can consider words such as "melody, melodic, melodious" to consist of a constant stem "melod-" followed by various affixes. When we describe the sound patterns that occur in English we want to be able to say that in some sense there are always the same underlying sounds in both the stems and the affixes. But these underlying sounds may change when the stems and affixes are put together to form words and sentences. The phonology of a language is the set of rules that describe the changes in the underlying sounds when they occur in speech. The underlying sounds are the abstract units called phonemes at the beginning of this chapter.

When we transcribe a word in a way that shows none of the details of the pronunciation that are predictable by phonological rules, we are making a **phonological transcription**. The phonemic segments are usually placed between slanting lines. Thus we may say that the underlying phonemic segments in "cat" and "catty" are /kæt/ and /kæti/. But the phonetic segments that are actually pronounced are usually [kæt] and [kædi].

The variants of the phonemes that occur in detailed phonetic transcriptions are known as **allophones**. They are generated as a result of applying the phonological rules to the segments in the underlying forms of words. We have already discussed some of the rules that generate different allophones of the segment /t/. For example, we know that, in most varieties of American English, /t/ has an allophone [d] when it occurs between a stressed vowel and an unstressed vowel.

The transcription used in the first part of this chapter is not, strictly speaking, a phonological transcription. The symbols in Tables 2.1 and 2.2 distinguish all the oppositions that occur in actual pronunciations of English words. But these are not the underlying segments. There are several ways in which we could change our transcription into a more abstract one that uses a simpler set of symbols.

One way would be to show the differences in length between pairs of vowels. Our present transcription indicates the difference in quality in the vowels in a pair of words such as "bead, bid" [bid, bɪd] or "fool, full" [ful, fʊl], or "laid, led" [leɪd, lɛd]. But it is also a fact that the vowel in the first word of each pair is longer than the vowel in the second: [i] is longer than [ɪ], [u] than [ʊ], and [eɪ] than [ɛ]. We have presumed that the symbols that indicate differences in quality also indicate differences in length. But we could use the symbol [ː] to indicate greater length and then redefine the phonetic values of the vowel symbols. The symbol [i] can be said to have the value appropriate for the vowel in "bead" when it occurs before a length mark as in [biːd]. But it has the value appropriate for the vowel in "bid" when it occurs without a length mark, which would then be transcribed as [bid]. Remember that there is nothing sacred about the phonetic value of a symbol. Some phoneticians transcribe "bead, bid" as [bid, bɪd] as I have done in this book, while others transcribe these same words as [biːd, bid]. Using the same principle they might transcribe "cooed, could" not as [kud, kʊd], as we do, but as [kuːd, kud]. Finally, "laid, led" would not be [leɪd, lɛd], but [leːd, led]. In this style of transcription the differences in quality are treated as if they depended on the differences in length. The symbols /i/ and /u/ would be said to represent higher vowels when long, and the symbol /e/ would be said to represent a diphthong in these circumstances. This style of transcription uses an additional symbol for length, but it more than compensates for that by eliminating the vowel symbols [ɪ, ɛ, ʊ].

Another way to reduce the number of vowel symbols would be to regard some other combinations of vowels in pairs. It can be shown that there are rules governing the alternations in vowel quality that occur in "line, linear; sign, signal; mine, mineral." In each of these pairs /aɪ/ occurs in the first word and /ɪ/ in the second. Similar rules govern the alternations between

/i/ and /ɛ/, as in "sleep, slept," /eɪ/ and /æ/ as in "mania, manic," /oʊ/ and /ɑ/ as in "tone, tonic," and /ju/ and /ʌ/, as in "punitive, punish." It would be possible to devise a transcription based on differences of this kind instead of differences in length. The English spelling system does this to some extent. Beginning readers are often taught that each of the letters *a, e, i ,o, u,* has two values, exemplified by words such as "made, mad; Pete, pet; hide, hid; robe, rob; cute, cut." Thus the English spelling system is not as nonphonemic as at first it might appear.

We can now see why there are various possible ways of transcribing a language. Even if we consider only one particular dialect of the language, it might be appropriate in some cases to symbolize one aspect of a contrast, such as the length, and in other cases to symbolize another, such as the quality. In addition, we may choose to make a transcription that shows only the underlying phonemes, or we may choose to represent some allophonic differences. The term **broad transcription** is often used to designate a transcription that uses a simple set of symbols. Conversely, a **narrow transcription** is one that shows more phonetic detail. The use of diacritics, small marks that can be added to a symbol to modify its value, is a means of increasing precision. One such diacritic is a small circle [̥] that can be placed under a symbol to make it represent a voiceless sound, so that "ply" and "try," for instance, can be written [pl̥aɪ] and [tr̥aɪ]. Another useful diacritic is the mark [̪] beneath a consonant. This indicates that the sound is dental and not alveolar. We used it to transcribe the example near the beginning of this section, "eighth," more accurately as [eɪt̪θ].

Every transcription should be considered as having two aspects, one of which is often not explicit. There is the text itself, and at least implicitly, there is a set of conventions for interpreting the text. These conventions are usually of two kinds. First, there are the conventions that ascribe general phonetic values to the symbols. It was with these conventions in mind that I said earlier that a symbol could be regarded as an approximate specification of the articulations involved. In the second, there are the rules that specify the allophones that occur in different circumstances. Thus when I transcribe the word "peels" as [pilz], I am assuming that the reader knows a number of the rules of English, including those that make /i/ somewhat lower and more central when it occurs before /l/ and a final /z/ voiceless toward the end.

On a few occasions a transcription cannot be said to imply the existence of rules accounting for allophones. This is at least theoretically possible in the case of a narrow transcription so detailed that it shows *all* the rule-governed alternations among the sounds. A transcription that shows the allophones in this way is called a completely **systematic phonetic transcription**. In practice it is difficult to make a transcription so narrow that it shows every detail of the sounds involved. (The kind of transcription used in this book shows only a few of the major allophones, so it is only a partially systematic phonetic transcription.) On some occasions a transcription may not imply the existence of rules accounting for allophones because, in the circumstances when the transcription was made, nothing was known about the rules. When writing down an unknown language or when transcribing a child or a patient not seen previously, one does not know what rules will apply. In these circumstances the symbols indicate only the general phonetic value of the sounds. This kind of transcription is called an **impressionistic transcription**.

EXERCISES

A   Which of the two transcriptions below is the narrower?
"Betty cried as she left in the red plane."
(a) [ˈbɛti ˈkraɪd əz ʃɪ ˈlɛft ɪn ðə ˈrɛd ˈpleɪn]
(b) [ˈbɛdi ˈkr̥aɪd əz ʃɪ ˈlɛft ɪn̪ ðə ˈr̥ɛd ˈpl̥eɪn]

B   State rules for converting the transcription in (a) into that in (b). Make your rules as general as possible, so that they cover not only this pair of transcriptions but also other similar sentences (for example, [t] → [d] when it occurs after a stressed vowel and before an unstressed vowel).

[r] is voiceless when preceded by a voiceless stop

[n] → [n̪] when followed by a dental fricative

[l] → [l̥] when preceded by a voiceless stop

C   Read the following passages in phonetic transcription. Both passages use a fairly broad style of transcription, showing few allophones. The first represents a form of British English of the kind I speak myself. The second represents an American pronunciation typical of a Midwestern speaker. By this time you should be able to read transcriptions of different forms of English, although you may have difficulty in pronouncing each word exactly as it is represented. Nevertheless, read each passage several times and try to pronounce it as indicated. Take care to put the stresses on the correct syllables, and say the unstressed syllables with the vowels as shown. Note any differences between each transcription and your own pronunciation of the corresponding words.

British English

ɪt ɪz ˈpɒsəbl tə trænˈskraɪb fəˈnɛtɪklɪ ˈɛnɪ ˈʌtrəns, ɪn ˈɛnɪ ˈlæŋgwɪdʒ, ɪn ˈsɛvrəl ˈdɪfrənt ˈweɪz ˈɒl əv ðəm ˈjuzɪŋ ði ˈælfəbɛt ənd kənˈvɛnʃnz əv ði ˈaɪ piˈeɪ. (ðə ˈseɪm ˈθɪŋ ɪz ˈpɒsəbl wɪð ˈmoʊst ˈʌðə ɪntəˈnæʃənl fəˈnɛtɪk ˈælfəbɛts.) ə trænˈskrɪpʃn wɪtʃ ɪz ˈmeɪd baɪ ˈjuzɪŋ ˈlɛtəz əv ðə ˈsɪmpləst ˈpɒsəbl ˈʃeɪps, ənd ɪn ðə ˈsɪmpləst ˈpɒsɪbl ˈnʌmbə, ɪz ˈkɔld ə ˈsɪmpl foʊˈnimɪk trænˈskrɪpʃn.

American English

ɪf ðə ˈnʌmbər əv ˈdɪfrənt ˈlɛdərz ɪz ˈmɔr ðən ðə ˈmɪnəməm æz dəˈfaɪnd əˈbʌv ðə trænˈskrɪpʃn wɪl ˈnat bi ə foʊˈnimɪk, bəd ən æloʊˈfanɪk wʌn. ˈsʌm əv ðə ˈfoʊnimz, ˈðæd ɪz tə ˈseɪ, wɪl bɪ rɛprəˈzɛntəd baɪ ˈmɔr ðən ˈwʌn ˈdɪfrənt ˈsɪmbl. ɪn ˈʌðər ˈwərdz ˈsərtn ˈæloʊfoʊnz əv ˈsərtn ˈfoʊnimz wɪl bɪ ˈsɪŋgld ˈaʊt fər ˈrɛprəzɛnˈteɪʃn ɪn ðə trænˈskrɪpʃn, ˈhɛns ðə ˈtərm æloʊˈfanɪk.

(Both the above passages are adapted from David Abercrombie, *English Phonetic Texts*, Faber & Faber, 1964.)

D Transcribe the following phrases as you would say them yourself using (a) a fairly broad transcription, and (b) a narrower transcription.

accent ___Wisc/NC___

"Please come home."

(a) [ˈpliz ˈkʌm ˈhoɑm]

(b) [ˈpliz ˈkʌm ˈhoɑm]

"He is going by train."

(a)

(b)

"The angry American."

(a)

(b)

"His knowledge of the truth."

(a)

(b)

"I prefer sugar and cream."

(a)

(b)

"Sarah took pity on the young children."

(a)

(b)

PERFORMANCE EXERCISES

As I said in the preface, it is extremely important to develop practical phonetic skills and at the same time learn the theoretical concepts. One way to do this is to transcribe nonsense words which are dictated to you. By using nonsense words you are forced to listen to the sounds that are being spoken. It is also useful to learn to pronounce nonsense words. Accordingly you should find another student to work with, so that you can do the following exercises in pairs.

A Choose an order in which to say the following "words" (for example, say the second word first, the fourth word next, and then the fifth, third, and first words). Write this order down as you dictate the words to your partner—whose task is, of course, to write down the order in which you have said them. Reverse roles and repeat the exercises. You may find it advisable to repeat each word twice.

spoken	heard
piˈsuz	
piˈsus	
piˈzus	
piˈzuz	
piˈzuʒ	

B Repeat this exercise with the following sets of words:

spoken	heard	spoken	heard
tɑˈθɛð		ˈkipik	
tɑˈθɛθ		ˈkɪpik	
tɑˈðɛθ		ˈkipɪk	
tɑˈðɛð		ˈkɪpɪk	
tɑˈfɛð		ˈkɪpɪt	

spoken	heard	spoken	heard
ˈlæmæm		ˈmʌlʌl	
ˈlæmæn		ˈmʌrʌl	
ˈlænæm		ˈmʌwʌl	
ˈlænæn		ˈnʌlʌl	
ˈlænæŋ		ˈnʌrʌl	

C Look at the following nonsense words, and either say these to your partner or (preferably, since your partner has seen these words too) make up a set similar to them, and say these instead. Your words can differ from the sample set in as many sounds as you like. But I suggest that you should not make them much longer at first. You will also find it advisable to write down your words and practice saying them for some time by yourself, so that you can pronounce them fluently when you come to say them to your partner.

ˈskɑnzil

ˈbraɪgbluzd

ˈdʒɪŋsmæŋ

flɔɪʃˈθraɪðz

pjutˈpeɪtʃ

When you have finished saying each word several times, and your partner has written them down, compare notes. Try to decide whether any discrepancies were due to errors in saying the words or in hearing them. If possible, the speaker should try to illustrate discrepancies by pronouncing the word in both ways, saying, for example, "I said [ˈskɑnzil] but you wrote [ˈskɑnsil]."

There is no one best way of doing ear training work of this kind. I find it helpful to look carefully at the speaker while he is pronouncing an unknown word, then try to say the word myself immediately after him, getting as much of it right as possible, but not worrying if I miss some things on first hearing. I then write down all that I can, leaving blanks to be filled in when I hear the word again. It seems important to me to get at least the number of syllables and the placement of the stress correct on first hearing, so that I have a framework in which to fit later observations.

Repeat this kind of production and perception exercise as often as you can. You should do a few minutes' work of this kind every day, so that you spend at least an hour a week doing practical exercises.

The Consonants of English 3

Stop Consonants

Consider the difference between the words in the first column in Table 3.1 and the corresponding words in the second column. This opposition may be said to be between the set of voiceless stop consonants and the set of voiced stop consonants. But the difference is really not just one of voicing

Table 3.1

Words illustrating allophones of English stop consonants.

1	2	3	4	5
pie	buy	spy	nap	nab
tie	die	sty	mat	mad
kye	guy	sky	knack	nag

during the consonant closure, as you can see by saying these words yourself. Most people have very little voicing going on while the lips are closed during either "pie" or "buy." Both stop consonants are essentially voiceless. But in "pie" *after* the release of the lip closure there is a moment of **aspiration**, a period of voicelessness after the stop articulation and before the start of the voicing for the vowel. If you put your hand in front of your lips while saying "pie" you can feel the burst of air that comes out during the period of voicelessness after the release of the stop.

In a narrow transcription, aspiration may be indicated by a small raised h [ʰ]. Accordingly, these words may be transcribed as [pʰaɪ, tʰaɪ, kʰaɪ]. You may not be able to feel the burst of air in "tie, kye" because these stop closures are made well inside the mouth cavity. But listen carefully and notice that you can hear the period of voicelessness after the release of the stop closure in each of them. It is this interval that indicates the fact that the stop is aspirated. The major difference between the words in the first two columns is not that one has voiceless stops and the other voiced stops. It is that the first column has (voiceless) aspirated stops and the second column has (partially voiced) unaspirated stops.

Now consider the words in the third column. Are the stop consonants more like those in the first column or those in the second? As in many cases, English spelling is misleading, and they are in fact more like those in the second column. There is no opposition in English between words beginning with /sp/ and /sb/, or /st/ and /sd/, or /sk/ and /sg/. English spelling arbitrarily uses *p*, *t*, *k*, but the stops that occur after /s/ are really somewhere in between initial /p/ and /b/, /t/ and /d/, /k/ and /g/. Usually, like the so-called voiced stops, they are completely unaspirated. If you can do a simple tape cutting experiment, you can verify this for yourself. Record words such as "spy, sty, sky, spill, still, skill," each said as a separate word. Now by playing the tape very slowly or by pulling it manually past the playback head, find the beginning and end of each /s/. Cut this part out and splice the tape together again. When you play the tape to others and ask them to write down the words that they hear, they will almost certainly write "buy, die, guy, bill, dill, gill."

What about the differences between the words in the fourth and fifth columns? The consonants at the ends of "nap, mat, knack" are certainly voiceless. But again, if you listen carefully to the sounds at the ends of the words "nab, mad, nag," you will find that the so-called voiced consonants /b, d, g/ are also partially voiceless. Try saying these words separately. You can, of course, say each of them with the final consonant exploded and a short vowel-like sound resembling [ə] afterward. But it would be equally normal to say each of them without exploding the final consonants. You could, for example, say "cab" and not open the lips for a considerable period of time, if it were the last word of an utterance. In such circumstances it is quite clear that the final consonants are not fully voiced throughout the closure.

There is, however, a clear distinction between the words in the fourth and fifth columns. Say these words in pairs "nap, nab; mat, mad; knack, nag" and try to decide which has the longer vowel. In these pairs, and in all similar pairs, such as "cap, cab; cat, cad; back, bag" the vowel is much shorter before the voiceless consonants /p, t, k/ than it is before the voiced consonants /b, d, g/. The major difference between such pairs of words is in the vowel length, not in the voicing of the final consonants.

You probably cannot hear the difference in the length of the final consonants in these words. But try saying sentences such as "Take a cap now" and "Take a cab now." If you say both these sentences with a regular rhythm you should be able to observe that the length of time between "Take" and "now" is about the same on both occasions. This is because the whole word "cap" is only slightly shorter than the whole word "cab." The vowel is much shorter in "cap" than in "cab." But the consonant /p/ makes up for this by being slightly longer than the consonant /b/. It is a general rule of English (and of most if not all other languages) that, after a given vowel, syllable final voiceless consonants are longer than the corresponding voiced consonants.

The phrases "Take a cap now" and "Take a cab now" also illustrate another point about English stop consonants at the end of a word (or, in fact, at the end of a syllable). Say each of these phrases without a pause before "now." Do your lips open before the [n] of "now" begins, or do they open during the [n]? If they open before the [n] there will be a short burst of aspiration or a short vowel-like sound between the two words. But for most people final stops are unexploded when the next word begins with a nasal. The same is true if the next word begins with a stop. The final [t] in "cat" is nearly always unexploded in phrases like "the cat pushed . . ." In a narrow transcription we can symbolize the fact that a consonant is unexploded by adding a small raised circle [°]. We could therefore transcribe the phrase as [ðə ˈkʰæt° ˈpʰʊʃt].

The same phenomenon occurs even within a word such as "apt" [æp°t] or "act" [æk°t]. Furthermore, across a word boundary the two consonants involved can even be identical, as in the phrase "white teeth." In order to convince yourself that there are two examples of /t/ in this phrase, try contrasting it with "why teeth (are . . .)." Not only is the vowel in "white" much shorter than the vowel in "why" (because the vowel in "white" is in a syllable with a voiceless consonant at the end), but also the stop closure in "white teeth" is very much longer than the stop in the phrase with only one /t/. In "white teeth" there really are two examples of /t/ involved, the first of which is unexploded.

Other languages do not have this rule. For example, it is a mark of a speaker with an Italian accent (at least as caricatured in films and television) that he explodes all his final stop consonants, producing an extra vowel at the end, as he normally would in his own language. Authors trying to indicate an Italian speaking will write the phrase "It's a big day" as "It's a bigga day." They are presumably trying to indicate the difference between the normal (ɪts ə ˈbɪg° ˈdeɪ] and the foreign accent [ɪts ə ˈbɪgə ˈdeɪ].

It is interesting that words such as "rap, rat, rack" are all distinguishable, even when the final consonants are unexploded. The difference in the sounds must therefore be in the way that the vowels end—after all, the rest is silence. The consonants before and after a vowel always affect it, so that there is a slight but noticeable difference in its quality. Compare your pronunciation of words such as "pip, tit, kick." Your tongue tip is up throughout the word "tit," whereas in "pip" and "kick" it remains behind the lower front teeth. In "kick" it is the back of the tongue that is raised throughout the word, and in "pip" the lip gestures affect the entire vowel. The same is true for words with voiced consonants, such as "bib, did, gig." The consonant gestures are superimposed on the vowel in such a way that their effect is audible throughout much of the syllable.

The sounds [p, t, k] are not the only voiceless stops that occur in English. Many people also pronounce a glottal stop in some words. A **glottal stop** is the sound (or, to be more exact, the lack of sound) that occurs when the vocal cords are held tightly together. The symbol for it is [ʔ], which is similar to a question mark without the dot.

Glottal stops occur whenever one coughs. You should be able to get the sensation of the vocal cords being pressed together by making small coughing noises. Next take a deep breath and hold it with your mouth open. Listen to the small plosive sound that occurs when you let the breath go. Now while breathing out through your mouth, try to check and then release the breath by making and releasing a short glottal stop. Then do the same while making a voiced sound such as the vowel [ɑ]. Practice producing glottal stops between vowels, saying [ɑʔɑ] or [iʔi], so that you get to know what they feel like.

One of the commonest occurrences of a glottal stop is in the utterance meaning "no," which is often spelled "uh-uh." If someone asks you a question, you can reply "no" by saying [ˈʔʌʔʌ]. Note that there is a contrast between the utterance meaning "no" and that meaning "yes" which is dependent on the stress and intonation pattern and on the presence of the glottal stop. If you had meant to say "yes" you might well have said [ˈʌhʌ]. We can tell that it is the stress pattern and the glottal stop that are important in conveying the meaning by the fact that one could be understood equally well saying [ˈmhm] for "yes" and [ˈʔmʔm] for "no." As long as the stress is on the first syllable and there is a glottal stop between the two syllables, the utterance will mean "no," irrespective of what vowel or nasal is used.

Glottal stops frequently occur as allophones of /t/. Probably most Americans and many British speakers have a glottal stop in words such as "beaten, kitten, fatten" [ˈbiʔn̩, ˈkɪʔn̩, ˈfæʔn̩]. London Cockney also has this sound between vowels as in "butter, kitty, fatter" [ˈbʌʔə, ˈkɪʔɪ, ˈfæʔə]. Many speakers in both countries have a glottal stop just before final voiceless consonants in words such as "rap, rat, rack." Usually the articulatory gesture for the other stop is still audible, so these words could be transcribed [ræʔp, ræʔt, ræʔk].

Practice producing words with and without a glottal stop. After you have some awareness of what a glottal stop feels like, try saying the words "rap, rat, rack" in several different ways. Begin by saying them with a glottal stop and a final release [ræʔpʰ, ræʔtʰ, ræʔkʰ]. Next say them without a glottal stop and with the final stops unreleased [ræp°, ræt°, ræk°]. Then say them with a glottal stop and a final unreleased consonant [ræʔp°, ræʔt°, ræʔk°]. Finally, say them with a glottal stop and no other final consonant [ræʔ, ræʔ, ræʔ].

So far, all the examples I have given of stops before nasals have had the stop at the end of one word and the nasal at the beginning of the next. When a stop and a nasal occur in the same word, as in "hidden" [ˈhɪdn], the stop is not released in the usual way. Both the [d] and the [n] are alveolar consonants. The tongue comes up and contacts the alveolar ridge for [d] and stays there for [n]. Consequently, as is shown in Figure 3.1, the air pressure

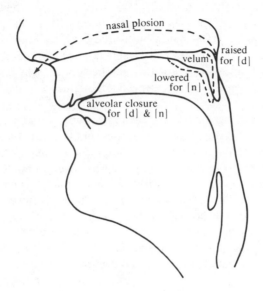

Figure 3.1   *Nasal plosion.*

that is built up behind the stop closure is released through the nose by the lowering of the soft palate (the velum) for the nasal consonant. This phenomenon is known as **nasal plosion**. It is normally used in pronouncing words such as "sadden, sudden, leaden" [ˈsædn, ˈsʌdn, ˈlɛdn]. It is considered a mark of a foreign accent to add a vowel [ˈsædən, ˈsʌdən, ˈlɛdən]. Nasal plosion also occurs in the pronunciation of words with [t] followed by [n] as in "kitten" [ˈkɪtn] for those people who do not have a glottal stop instead of the [t].

When two sounds have the same place of articulation, they are said to be **homorganic**. Thus the consonants [d] and [n], which are both articulated on the alveolar ridge, are homorganic. For nasal plosion to occur within a word there must be a stop followed by a homorganic nasal. Only in these circumstances can there be pressure first built up in the mouth during the stop and then released through the nose by lowering the soft palate. Many forms of English do not have any words with a bilabial stop [p] or [b] followed by the homorganic nasal [m] at the end of the word. Nor in most forms of English are there any words in which the velar stops [k] or [g] are normally followed by the velar nasal [ŋ]. Consequently both bilabial and velar nasal plosion are less common than alveolar nasal plosion in English. But when talking in a rapid conversational style many people pronounce the word "open" as [ˈoʊpm], particularly if the next word begins with [m], as in "open my door, please." Quite frequently when counting, people will pronounce "seven" as [ˈsɛbm], and I have also heard "something, captain, bacon" pronounced [ˈsʌmpm, ˈkæpm, ˈbeɪkŋ]. You should try to pronounce all these words in these ways yourself.

A phenomenon similar to nasal plosion takes place when an alveolar stop [t] or [d] occurs before a homorganic lateral [l], as in "little, ladle" [ˈlɪtl, ˈleɪdl]. The air pressure that is built up during the stop is released by lowering the sides of the tongue, and the effect is called **lateral plosion**. Say the word "middle" and note the action of the tongue. The contact on the alveolar ridge in the center of the mouth is maintained throughout both the stop and the lateral.

No vowel sound occurs in the second syllable of any of the words "bitten, hidden, little, ladle." The final consonants in all these words are themselves syllabic. In a narrow transcription syllabicity can be indicated by the mark [ˌ] under a consonant symbol. These words could therefore be transcribed as [ˈbɪtn̩, ˈhɪdn̩, ˈlɪtl̩, ˈleɪdl̩]. However, many Americans do not pronounce "little" as [ˈlɪtl̩]. Instead of [t] they have a voiced stop [d], and they in fact say [ˈlɪdl̩]. There is a general rule in American English that whenever [t] occurs after a stressed vowel and before an unstressed syllable other than [n̩], it is changed into a voiced sound. In "little" this voiced sound is the stop [d]. But in "city, better, writer" it is not really a stop but a quick tap in which the tongue tip is thrown against the alveolar ridge. This sound can be written with the symbol [ɾ], so that "city" can be transcribed as [sɪɾi]. Many Americans do not distinguish between pairs of words containing this sound, such as "latter, ladder." But some maintain a distinction by having a shorter vowel in words such as "latter" which have a voiceless consonant in their underlying form. It is as if the rule that vowels are shorter before voiceless consonants had applied first, and then a later rule was applied changing [t] into [ɾ] when it occurred between a stressed and an unstressed syllable.

Coarticulation

So far I have discussed variations in the manner of English stop consonants. I have said little about variations in the exact place of articulation. A major problem in describing speech is that all utterances involve **coarticulations**—the overlapping of adjacent articulations. English consonants often vary their place of articulation so that they become more like the next sound. We noted in the previous chapter that /t, d/ are usually alveolar stops but are pronounced with tongue contact on the teeth, so that they become [t̪, d̪] when they occur before dental fricatives as in "eighth" [eɪt̪θ] and "width" [wɪd̪ð]. (Some people pronounce the latter word with voiceless consonants at the end, making it [wɪt̪θ].)

Another noticeable change in the place of articulation occurs in the pronunciation of /k, g/ before a front vowel as in "key, geese" [ki, gis] as compared with a back vowel as in "caw, gauze" [kɔ, gɔz]. The different forms of /k/—the allophones—occur because of the influence of the following vowel. The whole body of the tongue has to be pulled up and forward for [i]. This action begins during the formation of the closure for /k/, which is consequently farther forward than the closure in the allophone of /k/ before /ɔ/. In the latter case the /k/ anticipates the low back position of the body of the tongue in /ɔ/.

You should be able to feel that the place of articulation of /k/ is much farther forward before a front vowel. Check that in your own pronunciation of "key" the articulatory contact is between the tongue and a point on the roof of your mouth near the hard palate. Now compare this with your pronunciation of "caw," in which the articulation is at the back of the mouth fairly low down on the soft palate.

Now try to find out whether there is as much variation in the place of articulation when the /k/ occurs *after* vowels in words such as "peak" [pik] and "hawk" [hɔk]. You will probably discover that there is very little difference between these allophones of /k/. In general, English may be said to be an anticipatory language—that is, one in which the articulations of the sounds yet to come are anticipated to some extent. Other languages, such as French or Italian, are perseverative in that the articulation of one sound tends to persevere, or continue, into the following sound.

We have already seen an example of the tendency of English to anticipate future articulations. We noted that when a stop occurs before another consonant—as in "apt" and "act"—it is unexploded, so that these words are pronounced [æp°t] and [æk°t]. This may be regarded as a case of the articulation of the last consonant being anticipated during the closure of the previous consonant. The [p] in "apt" is unexploded because the closure for the [t] occurs before the lips come apart. In English an articulator that is not necessarily involved in a given sound will nearly always start moving toward its position in the next sound in which it is the primary articulator. This phenomenon is known as **anticipatory coarticulation**.

We can regard those positions of the vocal organs that are specified for a given sound as the **target positions** for that sound. The estimated target for [k] as in "key" or in "caw" is the position for the back of the tongue shown by the heavy line in Figure 3.2. The soft palate is required to be raised (also shown by a heavy line) so as to ensure a velic closure. The position of the rest of the tongue is shown with a dashed line because in the case of [k] the *only* requirement is for the back of the tongue to approach the target shown in Figure 3.2. The targets for [i] and [a] are shown in Figures 3.3 and 3.4 respectively. The increase in the thickness of the line shows that the major

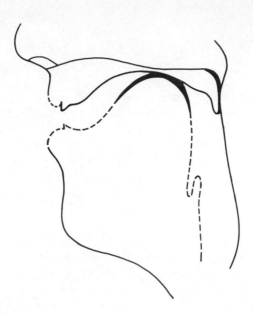

Figure 3.2 *The estimated target position for* [k] *as in "key" or "caw."*

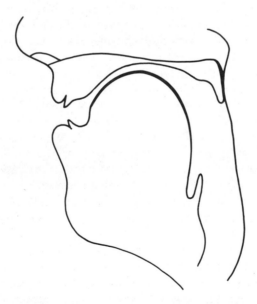

Figure 3.3 *The estimated target position for* [i] *as in "key."*

requirement for a vowel sound is for certain parts of the tongue to be in the correct positions so as to cause constrictions in the vocal tract at the appropriate places.

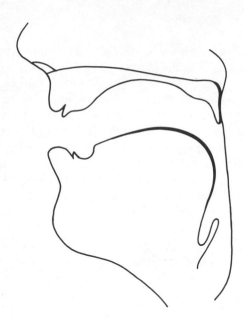

Figure 3.4 *The estimated target position for* [ɔ] *as in "caw."*

We can now see why the positions for [k] in "key" and "caw" are differ-ent. In each case there is the same target, but you do not necessarily hit the target for which you aimed. Even while the back of the tongue is aiming at the target for [k], other parts of the tongue are already moving toward their targets for the following vowel. The result is that the articulation achieved in saying [k] will be considerably influenced by the articulation required for saying the following vowel.

Ideally, the description of an utterance might consist of the specification of the targets and a specification of the rules for moving from one target to the next. We should be able to state the articulatory targets in terms of numerical values of distances between the vocal organs. One of the objects of any science is to express things in terms of verifiable measurements. In a sense, we do not really know anything until it can be stated in terms of numbers. We are now beginning to be able to do this in the description of English utterances.

The data in Figures 3.2, 3.3, and 3.4 represent an attempt to specify graphically, and hence measurably, the articulatory targets for three English sounds. This kind of diagram can be drawn for each of the other English sounds that have separate targets. The extent to which anticipatory coarticu-lation occurs depends in part on the extent to which the position of that part of the vocal tract is specified in the two sounds.

The degree of coarticulation between two sounds also depends on the interval between them. For example, a considerable amount of lip rounding occurs during [k] when the next sound is rounded as in "coo" [ku]. Slightly less lip rounding occurs if the [k] and the [u] are separated by another sound as in "clue" [klu]. And even less occurs if there is also a word boundary between the two sounds, as in the phrase "sack Lou" [ˈsæk lu]. Anticipatory coarticulations have been observed, however, over even longer sequences. In the phrase "tackle Lou" [ˈtækl lu] the lip rounding for the final [u] starts in the [k], which is separated from it by two segments and a word boundary.

There is no simple relationship between the description of a language in terms of phonemes and the description of utterances in terms of targets and conjoining rules. Phonemes are certainly not in a one-to-one relation with targets, even though some allophonic differences (such as those between the [k] in "key" and the [k] in "caw") can be explained in terms of targets and conjoining rules. Similarly, we do not have to specify separate targets for the alveolar [n] in "ten" and the dental [n̪] in "tenth." Both are the result of aiming at the same target, but in the case of [n̪] the articulation is influenced by the target required for the following sound. However, the differences between some allophones are actually the result of aiming at different targets. For example, the [k] at the end of "back" does not have the same target as the [k] at the beginning of "cab." A final [k] is longer than an initial [k]; it is often accompanied by a glottal stop; and it is not followed by a burst of aspiration. These two [k] sounds must therefore have different targets. Similarly, the [l] in "leaf" and the [l] in "feel" differ in ways that cannot be ascribed to coarticulation. The initial and final allophones of /l/ have different vocal tract shapes as the result of aiming at different targets. In my own case, initial [l] involves trying to make an alveolar lateral; but final [l] involves aiming at a back unrounded vowel position, with no requirement for alveolar contact.

To summarize, targets are units that can be used in descriptions of how a speaker produces utterances. Phonemes are more abstract units that can be used in descriptions of languages to show how one word contrasts with another. The two kinds of units overlap to a considerable extent, but they are not completely identical.

Fricatives

The fricatives of English vary less than the stop consonants, yet the major allophonic variations that do occur are in many ways similar to those of the stops. Earlier we saw that when a vowel occurs before one of the voiceless stops /p, t, k/ it is shorter than it would be before one of the voiced stops /b, d, g/. The same kind of difference in vowel length occurs before voiceless and voiced fricatives. The vowel is shorter in the first word of each of the pairs "strife, strive" [straɪf, straɪv]; "teeth, teethe" [tiθ, tið]; "rice, rise" [raɪs, raɪz]; "mission, vision" [ˈmɪʃn̩, ˈvɪʒn̩].

Stops and fricatives are the only English consonants that can contrast by being either voiced or voiceless. Consequently we can revise our rule that vowels are shorter before voiceless stops than before voiced stops. Instead we can say that vowels are shorter before all voiceless consonants than before all voiced consonants. In this way we can capture a linguistically significant generalization that would have been missed if our statements about English had included two separate rules, one dealing with stops and the other dealing with fricatives.

We also saw that a voiceless stop at the end of a syllable (as in "hit") is longer than the corresponding voiced stop (as in "hid"). Similarly, the voiceless fricatives are longer than their voiced counterparts in each of the pairs "safe, save" [seɪf, seɪv], "lace, laze" [leɪs, leɪz], and all the other pairs of words we have been discussing in this section. Again, because fricatives behave like stops, a linguistically significant generalization would have been missed if we had regarded each class of consonants completely separately.

Fricatives are also like stops in another way. Consider the degree of voicing that occurs in the fricative at the end of the word "ooze." In most pronunciations the voicing that occurs during the final [z] does not last throughout the articulation but changes in the last part to a voiceless sound like [s]. In general, voiced fricatives at the end of a word, as in "prove, smooth, choose, rouge" [pruv, smuð, tʃuz, ruʒ], are voiced throughout their articulation only when they are followed by another voiced sound. In a phrase such as "prove it" the [v] is fully voiced because it is followed by a vowel. But in "prove two times two is four" or "try to improve," where the [v] is followed by a voiceless sound [t] or by a pause at the end of the phrase, it is not fully voiced.

Briefly stated, then, fricatives are like stops in three ways: first, vowels before voiceless stops or fricatives are shorter than before voiced stops or fricatives; second, final voiceless stops and fricatives are longer than final voiced stops and fricatives; and third, the final stops and fricatives that are classified as voiced are not actually voiced throughout the articulation unless the next sound is also voiced. All these points are also true of affricates. In addition, all these types of articulation involve an obstruction of the airstream. Because they have an articulatory feature in common and because they act together in phonological rules, we refer to fricatives, stops, and affricates together as a natural class of sounds called **obstruents**.

However, fricatives do differ from stops in that they sometimes involve actions of the lips that are not immediately obvious. Try saying "fin, thin, sin, shin" [fɪn, θɪn, sɪn, ʃɪn]. There is clearly a lip action in the first word as it involves the labiodental sound [f]. But do your lips move in any of the other three words? Most people find that their lips move slightly in any word containing /s/ ("sin, kiss") and quite considerably in any word containing /ʃ/ ("shin, wish"), but that there is no lip action in words containing /θ/ ("thin, teeth"). There is also lip movement in the voiced sounds corresponding to /s/ and /ʃ/, namely /z/ as in "zeal, zest" and /ʒ/ as in "leisure, treasure," but none in /ð/, as in "that, teethe."

The primary articulation in these fricatives is the close approximation of two articulators so that friction can be heard. The lip rounding is a lesser articulation in that the two articulators (the lower lip and the upper lip) approach one another but not sufficiently to cause friction. A lesser degree of closure by two articulators not involved in the primary articulation is called a secondary articulation. This particular one, in which the action of the lips is added to another articulation, is called labialization. The English fricatives /ʃ, ʒ/ are strongly labialized, and the fricatives /s, z/ are slightly labialized.

Nasals

The nasal consonants of English vary even less than the fricatives. There is a slight tendency for initial nasals to be shorter than final nasals. The same kind of difference between initial and final consonants occurs for other sorts of sounds. It is a general rule of English that, other things being equal, syllable initial consonants are shorter than syllable final consonants.

Nasals, together with [r, l], can be syllabic when they occur at the ends of words. As we have seen, the mark [ˌ] under a consonant indicates that it is syllabic. (Vowels, of course, are always syllabic, and therefore need no special mark.) In a narrow transcription we may transcribe the words "sadden, table" as [ˈsædn̩, ˈteɪbl̩]. In most pronunciations "prism, prison" can be transcribed [ˈprɪzm̩, ˈprɪzn̩], as these words do not usually have a vowel between the last two consonants.

The nasal [ŋ] differs from the other nasals in a number of ways. No English word can begin with [ŋ]. This sound can occur only within or at the end of a word, and even in these circumstances it does not behave like the other nasals. It can be preceded only by the vowels /ɪ, ɛ, æ, ʌ, ə, ɑ, ɔ/, and it cannot be syllabic (except in slightly unusual pronunciations, such as "bacon" as [beɪkŋ̩]).

One way to consider the different status of [ŋ] is that it is a sequence of the phonemes /n/ and /g/. Looking at it this way, "sing" would be phonemically /sɪng/. There is a rule saying that /n/ has the allophone [ŋ] whenever it occurs before /g/, turning [sɪng] into [sɪŋg]. Another rule allows for the dropping of /g/ whenever it occurs after [ŋ] at the end of either a word (as in "sing") or a stem followed by a suffix such as "-er" or "-ing" (as in "singing").

Approximants

The approximants are /w, r, j, l/ as in "whack, rack, yak, lack." The first three of these sounds are central approximants, and the last is a lateral approximant. The articulation of each of them varies slightly depending on the articulation of the following vowel. You can feel that the tongue is in a different position in the first sounds of "we" and "water." The same is true for "reap" and "raw," for "lee" and "law," and "ye" and "yaw." Try to feel where your tongue is in each of these words.

These consonants also share the possibility of occurring in consonant clusters with stop consonants. The approximants /r, w, l/ combine with stops in words such as "pray, bray, tray, dray, cray, gray, twin, dwell, quell, Gwen, play, blade, clay, glaze." The approximants are largely voiceless when they follow one of the voiceless stops /p, t, k/, as in "pry, try, cry." Using the diacritic [₀] to indicate a voiceless sound, we may transcribe these words as [pr̥aɪ, tr̥aɪ, kr̥aɪ]. The approximant /j/ in "you" [ju] can also occur in similar consonant clusters, but usually with the restriction that the following vowel is [u], as in "pew, beauty, cue" [pju, ˈbjuti, kju], and for speakers of British English, "tune, dune" [tjun, djun]. In many ways, the sequence [ju] is more like a special kind of diphthong rather than a consonant followed by a vowel.

Lip rounding is an essential part of /w/. Accordingly, stops are slightly rounded when they occur in clusters in which /w/ is the second element, as in "twice, dwindle, quick" [tw̥aɪs, ˈdwɪndl̩, kw̥ɪk]. This is another example of the general principle of anticipatory coarticulation.

In many people's speech /r/ also has some degree of lip rounding. Try saying words such as "read" and "heed." Do you get some movement of the lips in the first word but not in the second? Note also whether you get anticipatory lip rounding so that the stops [t, d] are slightly labialized in words such as "tree, dream."

In most forms of British English there is a considerable difference in the articulation of /l/ before a vowel, as in "leaf," as compared with after a vowel, as in "feel." Americans also make a difference between these two sounds, but it is usually less noticeable. You should compare these two words in your own pronunciation. Try to feel where the tongue is during the /l/ in "leaf." You will probably find that the tip is touching the alveolar ridge, and one or both sides are near the upper side teeth, but not quite touching. The front of the tongue will be raised towards the hard palate (quite considerably in British English, less so in many forms of American English). Now compare this articulation with the /l/ in "feel." Most (but not all) speakers make this sound with the tongue tip touching the alveolar ridge. But in both British and American English the back of the tongue is considerably raised towards the soft palate. If there is contact on the alveolar ridge it is, of course, the primary articulation. When the back of the tongue is raised in this way, we may say that there is the secondary articulation called velarization. In most forms of British English syllable final [l] is strongly velarized. The symbol for velarization is the mark [˜] through the middle of the symbol. Accordingly a narrow transcription of "feel" would be [fiɫ]. In my own speech the whole body of the tongue is drawn up and back in the mouth so that the tip of the tongue no longer makes contact with the alveolar ridge. Strictly speaking, therefore, this sound is not an alveolar consonant but more like some kind of back vowel in the speech of some English speakers.

Finally we must consider the approximant /h/. As I mentioned before, /h/ is simply the voiceless counterpart of the following sound. When saying "he" [hi], all you do is assume the vowel position for [i], pronounce this first as a voiceless sound, then add vocal cord vibrations to turn it into a voiced sound. In many accents of English /h/ can occur only before vowels, or before the approximant /j/ as in "hue" [hju]. Some speakers of English also sound /h/ before /w/, so that they contrast "which" [hwɪtʃ] and "witch" [wɪtʃ].

EXERCISES

A The sequence of annotated diagrams below illustrates the actions that take place during the consonants at the end of the word "branch." Fill in the blanks.

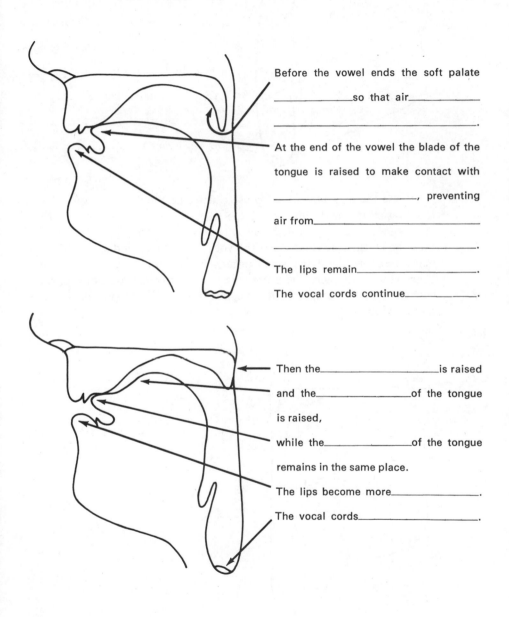

Before the vowel ends the soft palate _____ so that air_____ _____.

At the end of the vowel the blade of the tongue is raised to make contact with _____, preventing air from_____ _____.

The lips remain_____.

The vocal cords continue_____.

Then the_____is raised and the_____of the tongue is raised,

while the_____of the tongue remains in the same place.

The lips become more_____.

The vocal cords_____.

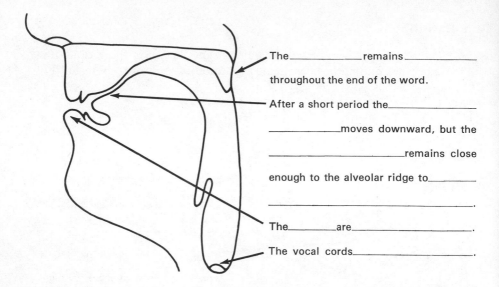

The_____remains_____
throughout the end of the word.

After a short period the_____

_____moves downward, but the

_____remains close

enough to the alveolar ridge to_____

_____.

The_____are_____.

The vocal cords_____.

B Annotate the diagram below so as to describe the actions required for the consonants in the middle of the word "implant." Make sure that your annotations mention the action of the lips, the different parts of the tongue, the soft palate, and the vocal cords in each diagram. Try to make clear which of the vocal organs moves first in going from one consonant to another. The pronunciation illustrated is that of a normal conversational utterance; note the position of the tongue during the bilabial stop.

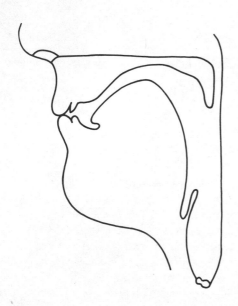

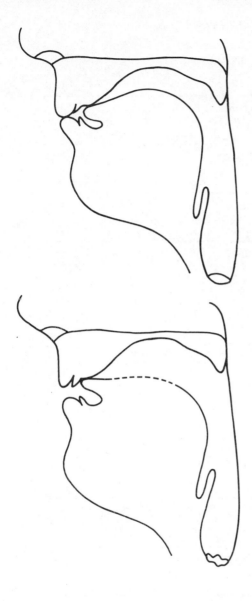

C Draw and annotate diagrams similar to those in the previous exercises, but this time illustrate the actions that occur in pronouncing the consonants in the middle of the phrase "thick snow." Make sure that you show clearly the sequence of events, noting what the lips, tongue, soft palate, and vocal cords do at each moment. Say the phrase over to yourself several times at a normal speed before you begin. Note especially whether the back of your tongue lowers before or after the tip of the tongue forms the articulation for subsequent consonants.

D Make a broad transcription of the following paragraph:

The earliest phoneticians were the

[_____

Indian grammarians who wanted to

[_____

preserve what they thought to be the

[_____

correct pronunciation of Sanskrit.

[_____

Their motives were religious in that

[_____

it was very important to them that

[_____

their holy scriptures should be pronounced

[_____

in the traditional way. Their accounts

[_____

of the sound pattern of Sanskrit are

[_____

still highly regarded by linguists.

[_____

The Greeks were responsible for

[_____

the greatest phonetic invention of

[_____

all time, the development of a writing

[_____

system in which syllables are

[_____

represented in terms of their

[————————————————————————

components. The realization that each

[————————————————————————

vowel and each consonant could be

[————————————————————————

systematically represented by a separate

[————————————————————————

symbol made it possible to write

[————————————————————————

down any word that was said using a

[————————————————————————

comparatively small inventory of symbols.

[————————————————————————

PERFORMANCE EXERCISES

A Learn to produce some non-English sounds. First, in order to recall the sensation of adding and subtracting voicing while maintaining a constant articulation, repeat the exercise saying [ssszzzssszzz]. Now try a similar exercise saying [mmmm̥m̥m̥mmmmm̥m̥m̥]. Make sure that your lips remain together all the time. During [m̥] you should be producing exactly the same action as when breathing out through the nose. Now say [m̥] in between vowels, producing sequences such as [am̥a, im̥i], etc. Try not to have any gap between the consonant and the vowels.

B Repeat this exercise with [n, ŋ, l, r, w, j], learning to produce [aṇa, aŋa, al̥a, ar̥a, aw̥a, aj̊a] and similar sequences with other vowels.

C Make sure that you can differentiate between the English words "whether, weather; which, witch," even if you do not normally do so.

Say:

[hwɛðə(r)]	"whether"
[wɛðə(r)]	"weather"
[hwɪtʃ]	"which"
[wɪtʃ]	"witch"

D Learn to produce the following Burmese words. (You may for the moment neglect the tones, indicated by accents above the vowels.)

mà	healthy	nà	pain	ŋâ	fish
m̥à	order	n̥à	nostril	ŋ̊â	rent
		la	moon		
		l̥á	beautiful		

E Working with a partner, produce and transcribe *several* sets of nonsense words. You should use slightly more complicated sets than previously. Make up your own sets on the basis of the illustrative set given below, including glottal stops, nasal and lateral plosion, and some combinations of English sounds that could not occur in English. Remember to mark the stress.

'kl̥antʃɷps'kweɪdʒ
'ʒiʒm̥'spobm̥
'tsɪʔɪ'bɛʔɪdl̩
mbu'tr̥igŋ
'tw̥aɪbrɛʔɪp

F In order to increase your memory span in perceiving sounds, include some simpler but longer words in your production-perception exercises. A set of possible words is given below. You may find words such as the last two, which have eight syllables each, too difficult at the moment. But try to push your hearing ability to its limit. When you are listening to your partner dictating words, remember to try to (1) look at the articulatory movements; (2) repeat, to yourself, as much as you can immediately afterwards; (3) write down as much as you can, including the stress, as soon as possible.

'kiputu'pikitu
'bɛgɪ'gɪdɛ'dɛdɪ
tr̥i'tʃɪʔitʃu'drudʒi
'rilɛ'tolɛ'manu'dɷli
'faɪθiði'vɔɪðuvu'θifi

English Vowels and Phonological Rules 4

The Transcription of English Vowels

One way of discussing the properties of English vowels is to compare the different ways in which they have been symbolized by different authors. Table 4.1 shows the set of symbols we have been using and a number of other systems used by well-known authorities. The first set is that used by J. S. Kenyon and T. A. Knott in *A Pronouncing Dictionary of American English* (Springfield: G. & C. Merriam, 1953). This work, which was first published in 1935, is a little out of date but well worth consulting for an account of some of the major varieties of American English pronunciation. The second set was used by G. Trager and H. L. Smith in their influential book *An Outline of English Structure* (Norman, Oklahoma: Battenberg Press, 1951). This style of transcription was very popular in the 50's and 60's and is still used in many textbooks. The third set is from C. Prator and B. Robinette, *A Manual of American English Pronunciation*, 3rd ed. (New York: Holt, Rinehart and Winston, 1973). It is a good example of a set of symbols useful for teaching the pronunciation of American English to speakers of other languages. The fourth set was used by the well-known English phonetician Daniel Jones in his *English Pronouncing Dictionary* (London: Dent, 1956), which is undoubtedly the major work on the pronunciation of the prestige form of British English. Finally, there is the transcription used in Webster's *New International Dictionary*, 3rd ed. (Springfield: G. & C. Merriam, 1961).

Table 4.1

A comparison of some systems for transcribing vowel sounds.

This book		Kenyon & Knott	Trager & Smith	Prator & Robinette	Jones	Webster's
i	beat	i	iy	iy	iː	ē
ɩ	bit	ɪ	i	ɪ	i	i
eɩ	bait	e	ey	ey	ei	ā
ɛ	bet	ɛ	e	ɛ	e	e
æ	bat	æ	æ	æ	æ	a
ɑ	father	ɑ	a	a	ɑ	ä
ɒ	bother	ɑ	a	a	ɔ	ä
ɔ	bought	ɔ	ɔh	ɔ	ɔː	ȯ
oɷ	boat	o	ow	ow	ou	ō
ɷ	put	ʊ	u	ʊ	u	u̇
u	boot	u	uw	uw	uː	ü
ʌ	butt	ʌ	ə	ə	ə	ə
aɩ	bite	aɪ	ay	ay	ai	ī
aɷ	bout	aʊ	aw	aw	au	au̇
ɔɩ	boy	ɔɪ	ɔy	ɔy	ɔi	ȯi

The symbols I have been using are very like those of Kenyon and Knott, differing in only two ways. First, I use [ɩ] and [ɷ] where they use [ɪ] and [ʊ]. This is purely a typographical change. Some years ago the IPA decided that [ɪ] and [ʊ] were unsatisfactory shapes and not so distinct as [ɩ] and [ɷ]. I am therefore simply following contemporary usage in making this change. Second, I have chosen to symbolize the vowels in "bait, boat" as [eɩ, oɷ] rather than [e, o] in order to emphasize the fact that they are diphthongs.

The Trager and Smith style of transcription shown in the next column has a fundamentally different aim from mine. I am trying to give a systematic phonetic transcription that is in accord with the principles of the IPA. Trager and Smith, however, attempt to describe English in terms of the smallest number of vowel sounds that can occur as single vowels on their own or with semivowels after them to form what we have been calling diphthongs. Thus in addition to the vowels that we have been calling diphthongs, they claim that the vowels in "beat" and "boot" can also be regarded as combinations of simple vowels followed by changes in quality that they consider to be vowel-like. It is perhaps worth noting that Trager and Smith came from the Eastern part of the United States where the vowels in "beat, boot" are more diphthongal than they are in the Midwest or Far Western states or in most forms of British English.

Trager and Smith transcribe these and other diphthongs with the appropriate vowel symbol followed by [y] or [w]. In this way they make the point that the second element of these diphthongs is a glide very like the consonantal glides at the beginning of "yes" and "we," but in the reverse direction. Thus in a Trager–Smith transcription the words "say" [sey] and "yes" [yes] are the reverse of one another. This is a valid observation for the style of speech they are representing. Speakers of English from much of the

Eastern part of the United States can hear this by playing a recording of "say, yes" in reverse. Apart from small differences in timing, the recording will sound almost the same in either direction.

The Trager–Smith transcription represents the vowel in "bought" as [ɔh]. In this case the transcription seems to depart considerably from phonetic reality. The reasons Trager and Smith give for using these symbols are fairly involved, and need not be considered in detail here. Basically they argue that the phoneme /h/ is like the phonemes /w, y/ in that it has one set of allophones that occur before vowels and another set that occur as glides after vowels. In this way they can say that there is a small number of simple vowels in English, each of which can occur on its own or with one of a small set of glides in a variety of diphthongs.

The next column shows the set of vowel symbols used by Prator and Robinette. This is an overdifferentiated style of transcription. These authors mark both the quality differences between vowels, as is done by Kenyon and Knott, and the diphthongal character where they consider it to be important. They have chosen not to worry about using just the simplest possible set of symbols that would show all the linguistic oppositions (which was Trager and Smith's aim). Instead Prator and Robinette have a style of transcription that should be maximally helpful for foreign learners of English.

Daniel Jones, in his transcription for the *English Pronouncing Dictionary*, avoids unusual letter shapes as far as possible. He marks the vowels in "beat" and "boot" as longer than those in "bit" and "put." In this way he avoids using the symbols [ɪ] and [ʊ]. Because he transcribes a form of British English, he differentiates among a greater number of vowels than occur in American English, including some not shown in Table 4.1. In his (and my) English there are different vowels in "cart, cot, caught." Or, to give another set of examples, none of the words "father, bother, author" has the same vowel. Jones transcribes these vowels as [ɑ, ɔ, ɔː]. In transcriptions of British English in this book they are transcribed as [ɑ, ɒ, ɔ].

The Webster's transcriptions are not in accordance with the principles of the IPA. They are devised for showing English readers the pronunciation of English words rather than for comparative phonetic purposes.

Table 4.1 once again makes the point that there is no such thing as a single correct form of transcription of English; different styles are appropriate for different purposes. But it is, of course, essential to keep within one style of transcription on any one occasion. It is important to be consistent.

Vowel Quality

In the discussion so far I have deliberately avoided making precise remarks about the quality of the different vowels. This is because, as I said in Chapter 1, the traditional articulatory descriptions of vowels are not very satisfactory. Try asking people who know as much about phonetics as you do to describe where the tongue is at the beginning of the vowel in "boy," and you will get a variety of responses. Can you describe where your own tongue is in a set of vowels?

It is difficult to give a meaningful answer to requests to describe the tongue position of a vowel in one's own speech. Very often people can only repeat what the books have told them, because they cannot find out for themselves where their tongue is. It is quite easy for a book to build up a set of terms that are not really descriptive but are in fact only labels. I started introducing terms of this kind for vowel qualities in Chapters 1 and 2 and will continue with this procedure here. But it is important for you to remember that the terms we are using are simply labels that describe how vowels sound in relation to one another. They are not absolute descriptions of the position of the body of the tongue.

Part of the problem in describing vowels is that there are no distinct boundaries between one type of vowel and another. When talking about consonants the categories are much more distinct. A sound may be a stop or a fricative, but it cannot be half way between the two. But it is perfectly possible to make a vowel that is half way between a high vowel and a mid vowel. In theory (as opposed to what a particular individual can do in practice), it is possible to make a vowel at any specified distance between any two other vowels.

In order to appreciate the fact that vowel sounds form a continuum, try gliding from one vowel to another. Say [æ] as in "had" and then try to move gradually to [i] as in "he." Do not say just [æ–i], but try to spend as long as possible on the sounds in between them. If you do this correctly you should pass through sounds that are something like [ɛ] as in "head" and [eɪ] as in "hay." If you have not achieved this effect already, try saying [æ–ɛ–eɪ–i] again, slurring slowly from one vowel to another.

Now do the same in the reverse direction, going slowly and smoothly from [i] as in "he" to [æ] as in "had." Take as long as possible over the in-between sounds. You should learn to stop at any point in this continuum so that you can make, for example, a vowel like [ɛ] as in "head," but slightly closer to [æ] as in "had."

Next try going from [æ] as in "had" slowly towards [ɑ] as in "father." When you say [æ–ɑ] you probably will not pass through any other vowel of your own speech. But there is a continuum of possible vowel sounds between these two vowels. You may be able to hear sounds between [æ] and [ɑ] that are more like those used by other accents in "had" and "father." Some forms of Scottish English, for example, do not distinguish between the vowels in these words. Speakers of these dialects pronounce both "had" and "father" with a vowel about half way between the usual Midwestern American pronunciation of these two vowels.

Last, in order to appreciate the notion of a continuum of vowel sounds, glide from [ɑ] as in "father" to [u] as in "who." In this case it is difficult to be specific as to the vowels that you will go through on the way, because English accents differ considerably in this respect. But you should be able to hear that the movement from one of these sounds to the other covers a range of vowel qualities that have not been discussed so far in this section.

The vowel [i] in "heed" is traditionally called a high front vowel, and the vowel [æ] in "had" is a low front vowel. The vowel [ɑ] as in "father" is a low back vowel, and the vowel [u] in "who" is a high, fairly back vowel. These four vowels, therefore, give us something like the four corners of a vowel space which may be drawn as in Figure 4.1.

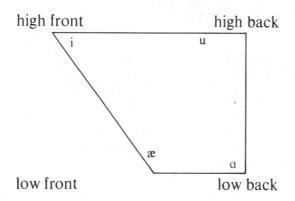

Figure 4.1 *The vowel space.*

None of the vowels has been put in an extreme corner of the space in Figure 4.1. It is possible to make a vowel that sounds more back than the vowel [u], which most people use in "who." You should be able to find this fully back vowel for yourself. Start by making a long [u], then round and protrude your lips a bit more. Now try to move your tongue back in your mouth, while still keeping it raised towards the soft palate. The result should be a fully back [u]. Another way of making this sound is to whistle the lowest note that you can, and then while retaining the same tongue and lip position, voice this sound. Again, the result will be an [u] sound that is further back than the vowel in "who." Try saying [i] as in "heed," [u] as in "who," and then this new sound, which we may symbolize with an added underline [u̠]. It you say the series [i, u, u̠], you should be able to hear that [u] is intermediate between [i] and [u̠], but—for most speakers—much nearer [u̠].

Similarly, it is possible to make vowels with a more extreme quality than the usual English vowels [i, æ, ɑ]. If, for example, while saying [æ] as in "had," you lower your tongue or open your jaw slightly further, you will produce a vowel that sounds relatively further from [i] as in "heed." It will probably also sound a little more like [ɑ] as in "father."

Given a notion of a vowel space of this kind, we can plot the relative quality of the different vowels. Remember that the labels high–low and front–back should not be taken as precise descriptions of tongue positions. They are simply indicators of the way one vowel *sounds* in relation to another. They describe the relative auditory qualities, not the articulations.

Most of the vowels of a typical Midwestern speaker of American English are shown in Figure 4.2. The solid points represent the vowels that we are

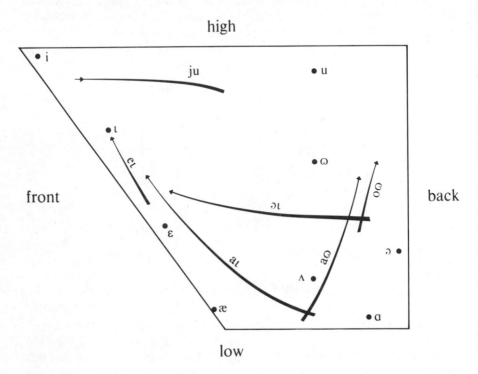

Figure 4.2 *The relative auditory qualities of some of the vowels of American English.*

treating as monophthongs, and the lines represent the movements involved in the diphthongs. There is good scientific basis for placing the vowels exactly as shown here. The precise positions of both monophthongs and diphthongs are not just the result of my own listening. The data are taken from the acoustic analyses of a number of authorities. We will return to this point in Chapter 8 when we discuss acoustic phonetics. Meanwhile if you are able to listen to a speaker of Midwestern American English, you should be able to hear that the relative vowel qualities are as indicated. Other varieties of English will differ in some respects, but you should find that in most dialects—even in British English—the majority of the relationships are the same. We will note the cases in which there are substantial differences as we discuss the individual vowels.

Listen first of all to the vowels [i, ɪ, ɛ, æ] as in "heed, hid, head, had." Do they sound as if they differ by a series of equal steps? Make each vowel about the same length (although in actual words they differ considerably), saying just [i, ɪ, ɛ, æ]. Now say them in pairs, first [i, ɪ], then [ɪ, ɛ], then [ɛ, æ]. In many forms of English [i] sounds about the same distance from [ɪ] as [ɪ] is from [ɛ], and as [ɛ] is from [æ]. Some Eastern American speakers make a distinct diphthong in "heed" so that their [i] is really a glide starting from almost the same vowel as that in "hid." Other forms of English, for example, as spoken in the Midlands and the North of England, make a lower and more back vowel in "had," making it sound a little more like the [ɑ] in "father." This may result in the distance between [ɛ] and [æ] being greater than that between [ɛ] and [ɪ]. But speakers who have a lower [æ] may also have a slightly lower [ɛ], thus keeping the distances between the four vowels [i, ɪ, ɛ, æ] approximately the same.

The remaining front vowel in English is [eɪ] as in "hay." We will discuss this vowel after we have discussed some of the back vowels. The back vowels vary considerably in different forms of English, but no form of English has them evenly spaced like the front vowels. Say for yourself [ɑ, ɔ, ʊ, u] as in "father, author, good, food." As before, make each vowel about the same length, and say just [ɑ, ɔ, ʊ, u]. Consider pairs of vowels as you did the front vowels, saying the distances between each of these vowels, and compare them with those shown in Figure 4.2.

We have already noted that some Midwestern and Californian speakers do not distinguish [ɑ] and [ɔ] as in "cot" and "caught." They usually have a vowel intermediate in quality between the two points shown on the chart. On the other hand, most speakers of British English have an additional vowel in this area. They distinguish between the vowels [ɑ, ɒ, ɔ] as in "balm, bomb, bought." Their vowels [ɑ, ɔ] have roughly the same quality as that shown in Figure 4.2. The additional vowel [ɒ] is lower, more back, and slightly more rounded than [ɑ].

The vowels [ʊ, u] as in "good, food" also vary considerably. Many speakers have a very unrounded vowel in "good" and a rounded but central vowel in "food." Look in a mirror and observe your own lip positions in these two vowels.

The most central of the low vowels on the chart in Figure 4.2 is [ʌ] as in "bud." Try saying the series of vowels in "bet, but, bought" [ɛ, ʌ, ɔ] and note that [ʌ] has a quality in between [ɛ] and [ɔ]. Compare also other series such as the vowels in "bat, but, bought" [æ, ʌ, ɔ]. Again, you will probably find that [ʌ] is in between the other two vowels.

We must now consider the diphthongs shown in Figure 4.2. Each of these sounds involves a change in quality within the one vowel. As a matter of convenience, they can be described as movements from one vowel to another. The first part of the diphthong is usually more prominent than the last. In fact, the last part is often so brief and transitory that it is difficult to determine its exact quality. Furthermore, contrary to the traditional transcriptions, the diphthongs often do not begin and end with any of the sounds that occur in simple vowels.

As you can see from Figure 4.2, both of the diphthongs [aɪ, aʊ] as in "high, how" start from more or less the same low central vowel position, midway between [æ] and [ɑ] and slightly closer to [ʌ] than to any of the other vowels. Say the word "eye" very slowly and try to isolate the first part of it. Compare this sound with the vowels [æ, ʌ, ɑ] as in "bad, bud, father." Now make a long [ɑ] as in "father," and then say the word "eye" as if it began with this sound. The result should be something like some forms of New York or London Cockney English pronunciation of "eye." Try some other pronunciations, starting, for example, with the vowel [æ] as in "bad." In this case the result is a somewhat affected pronunciation.

The diphthong [aɪ] as in "high, buy" moves toward a high front vowel, but in most forms of English it does not go much beyond a mid front vowel. Say a word such as "buy," making it end with the vowel [ɛ] as in "bed" (as if you were saying [baɛ]). A diphthong of this kind probably has a smaller change in quality than occurs in your normal pronunciation. Then say "buy," deliberately making it end with the vowel [ɪ] as in "bid." This vowel is usually slightly higher than the normal Midwestern ending of this diphthong. Finally say "buy" with the vowel [i] as in "heed" at the end. This is a much larger change in quality than normally occurs in this word. But some speakers of Scottish English and of Canadian English have a diphthong of this kind in words such as "sight," which is different from the more usual diphthong in "size."

The diphthong [aʊ] in "how" usually starts with a slightly more front quality than that in "high." But most speakers do not begin this diphthong with a fully front vowel such as [æ] as in "had." Try to say "owl" as if it started with [æ] as in "had," and note the difference from your usual pronunciation. Some speakers have a complicated movement in this diphthong, making a sequence something like the qualities of [ɛ] as in "bed," [ʌ] as in "bud," and [u] as in "food." Say [ɛ–ʌ–u] in quick succession. Now say the phrase "how now brown cow" using a diphthong of this type.

The diphthong [eɪ] as in "hay" varies considerably in different forms of English. Some speakers have a diphthong starting with a vowel very like [ɛ] in "head" (as in Figure 4.2). Others (such as myself) have a much smaller diphthong, starting much closer to [ɪ] as in "hid." Yet others (including many Scots) have an even higher vowel which is a monophthong that can be written [e]. Check your own pronunciation of "hay" and try to decide how it should be represented on a chart as in Figure 4.2.

The diphthong [oʊ] as in "hoe" may be regarded as the back counterpart of [eɪ]. But note that because it is mainly a movement in the low–high dimension, [oʊ] ends in a vowel very different from [ʊ] as in "hood." In most forms of British English and in many forms of American English, this diphthong goes over a wider range of vowel quality than in the Midwestern American English in Figure 4.2. It may start from about half way between [ʊ] and [ɛ] and end a little higher than [ʊ]. Say each part of this diphthong and compare it with other vowels.

The remaining diphthong moving in the upward direction is [ɔι] as in "boy." Again, this diphthong does not end in a very high vowel. Note how it begins with a very similar vowel to that in "hoe" and ends with a vowel similar to that in "bed." I might well have transcribed "boy" as [boε], but I decided it was preferable to keep the style of transcription used in this book as similar as possible to other widely used transcriptions.

The last diphthong, [ju] as in "cue," differs from all the other diphthongs in that the more prominent part occurs at the end. Because it is the only vowel of this kind, many books on English phonetics do not even consider it as a diphthong; they treat it as a sequence of a consonant followed by a vowel. I have followed this traditional view only in symbolizing it as [ju] rather than using two vowel symbols and writing it as [iu]. Figure 4.2 shows that this sound begins with a high front vowel, and moves towards a high central (rounded) vowel.

The only common vowel of American English not shown in Figure 4.2 is [ər] as in "sir, her, fur." This vowel does not fit on the chart because it cannot be described simply in terms of the features high–low, front–back, and rounded–unrounded. The vowel [ər] involves an additional feature called **rhotacization**. Just like high–low and front–back, the feature rhotacization describes an auditory property, the so-called r–coloring, of a vowel. When we describe the height of a vowel, we are saying something about how it sounds rather than something about the tongue position necessary to produce it. Similarly, when we describe a sound as a rhotacized vowel, we are saying something about how it sounds.

Rhotacized vowels are often called retroflex vowels, but there are at least two distinct ways in which a rhotacized quality can be produced. Some speakers have the tip of the tongue raised, as in a retroflex consonant, but others keep the tip down and produce a high bunched tongue position. These two gestures produce a very similar auditory effect. Recent x-ray studies of speech have shown that in both these ways of producing a rhotacized quality there is usually a constriction in the pharynx caused by retraction of the part of the tongue below the epiglottis.

In many forms of American English rhotacization occurs when any of the vowels [i, eι, ɑ, ɔ, u, aι, aɷ] are followed by [r], as in "beard, bared, bard, board, poor, tire, hour." In these circumstances the rhotacization of the vowel is often not so evident at the beginning of the vowel, and something of the quality of the individual vowel remains. But in "sir, here, fur" the whole vowel is rhotacized. Insofar as the quality of this vowel can be described in terms of the features high–low and front–back, it appears to be a mid-central vowel and would be designated by a point that might be labeled [ə] in the middle of the chart. In the systematic phonetic transcription of Midwestern American English that we are using, [ə] does not occur in stressed syllables except before [r].

English accents can be divided into those that are rhotic, or having rhotacized vowels, and those that are nonrhotic. Speakers of many forms of

British English do not have rhotacized vowels. Instead, they distinguish between the vowels in "cut, curt" by making a vowel in "curt" that is slightly higher than the [ʌ] in "cut." They would transcribe the words "cut, curt" as [kʌt, kət]. Again, in a diagram of this particular form of English the symbol [ə] would be placed almost exactly in the center of the chart.

Unstressed Syllables

In all forms of English, the symbol [ə], which is not shown in Figure 4.2, may be used to specify a range of mid-central vowel qualities. Vowels of this kind often occur in unstressed syllables as well as before /r/. As the vowel chart in Figure 4.2 represents a kind of auditory space, vowels near the outside of the chart are more distinct from one another than vowels in the middle, and differences in vowel quality become progressively reduced among vowels nearer the center. The symbol [ə] may be used to designate vowels that have a reduced vowel quality.

We will be considering the nature of stress in English in the next chapter, but we can note here that all the English vowels can occur in unstressed syllables. Many of them can occur in three forms, as shown in Table 4.2. In

Table 4.2

Examples of vowels in stressed and unstressed syllables and in reduced syllables. The dark type shows the syllable in which the vowel occurs.

	stressed syllable	unstressed syllable	reduced syllable
i	depreciate	create	deprecate
ɪ	implicit	simplistic	implication
eɪ	explain	chaotic	explanation
ɛ	allege	tempestuous	allegation
æ	emphatic	fantastic	emphasis
ɑ,ɒ	demonstrable	prognosis	demonstration
ɔ	cause	causality	
oʊ	invoke	vocation	invocation
ʊ	hoodwink	neighborhood	
u	acoustic	acoustician	
ʌ	confront	umbrella	confrontation
ər	confirm	verbose	confirmation
aɪ	recite	citation	recitation
aʊ	devout	outsider	
ɔɪ	exploit	exploitation	
ju	compute	computation	circular

this table the vowel to be considered is in boldface. The words in the first column illustrate the full forms of the vowels. The second column gives an example of the same vowel in an unstressed syllable. The last column illustrates the same vowel in what we will call a reduced syllable. For many people the reduced vowels in this last column are all very similar. Some people have slightly different qualities in some of these words, but all still within the range of a mid-central vowel that can be symbolized by [ə]. Others have [ɪ] in some of these words, such as "recitation," or perhaps a high central vowel, which may be symbolized by [ɨ]—a letter *i* with a bar through it. Say all these words yourself and find out which vowels you have.

There are some widely applicable rules of English relating the pronunciation of the words in the first column to that of the words in the third column. Consequently we are able to say that the same underlying vowels occur in the words in the first and third columns. If we were making a phonemic transcription, we could transcribe the vowels in the different columns with the same symbols and allow the rules to make it clear that different allophones occurred. Thus we could transcribe "emphatic" as /ɛmfætɪk/ and "emphasis" as /ɛmfæsɪs/ as long as we also have a rule that makes /æ/ into [ə] in the second word.

The rules accounting for the allophones are very general in the sense that they account for thousands of similar alternations among English words. But they are also very complicated. They have to account for the blanks in the third column, which show that some vowels can be completely reduced but that others cannot. There is, for example, a completely reduced vowel in "explanation, demonstration, recitation," but not, for most people, in the very similar words "exploitation, computation." As you can also see from an examination of Table 4.2, the vowels [ɔ, u, aʊ] do not fit into this scheme of alternations in the same way as the other vowels. Because the rules are so complicated we will not use completely phonemic transcriptions of English in this elementary textbook. Instead, we will continue to use [ə] or [ɪ] in reduced syllables.

Tense and Lax Vowels

The vowels of English can be divided into what may be called tense and lax sets. These terms are really just labels that are used to designate two groups of vowels that behave differently in English words. There are phonetic differences between the two groups, but they are not simply a matter of "tension."

The difference between the two sets can be discussed in terms of the different kinds of syllables in which they can occur. Table 4.3 shows some of the restrictions for one form of American English. The first column of words illustrates a set of **closed syllables**—those that have a consonant at the end. All of the vowels can occur in these circumstances. The next column shows that in **open syllables**—those without a consonant at the end—only a restricted set of vowels can occur.

None of the vowels [ɪ, ɛ, æ, ɔ, ʌ] as in "bid, bed, bad, good, bud" can appear in stressed open syllables. This is the set of vowels that may be called lax vowels as opposed to the tense vowels in the other words. In order to

Table 4.3

The distribution of tense and lax vowels in stressed syllables in American English.

Tense Vowels	Lax Vowels	most closed syllables	open syllables	syllables closed by [r]	syllables closed by [ŋ]	syllables closed by [ʃ]
i		beat	bee	beer		(leash)
	ι	bit			sing	wish
eι		bait	bay	bare		
	ɛ	bet			length	fresh
	æ	bat			hang	crash
ɑ		hot	ah	bar		slosh
ɔ		bought	saw	bore	long	(wash)
oω		boat	low	(boar)		
	ω	good				push
u		boot	boo	tour		
	ʌ	but			hung	crush
aι		bite	buy	fire		
aω		bout	bough	hour		
ɔι		void	boy	(coir)		
ju		cute	cue	pure		

Note also the reduced vowel ə   purr

characterize the differences between tense and lax vowels we can consider some of them in pairs, each pair consisting of a tense vowel and the lax vowel which is nearest to it in quality. Three pairs of this kind are: [i, ι] as in "beat, bit"; [eι, ɛ] as in "bait, bet"; and [u, ω] as in "boot, foot." In each of these pairs the lax vowel is shorter, lower, and slightly more centralized than the corresponding tense vowel. There are no vowels that are very similar in quality to the remaining two lax vowels in most forms of American English, [æ] as in "hat, cam" and [ʌ] as in "hut, come." But both these low lax vowels are shorter than the low tense vowel [ɑ] as in "spa." Speakers of most forms of British English have an additional lax vowel. They have the tense vowel [ɑ] as in "calm, car, card" in both open and closed syllables; and they also have a lax vowel [ɒ] in "cod, common, con" [kɒd, ˈkɒmən, kɒn], which occurs only in closed syllables.

The next column shows the vowels that can occur in syllables closed by /r/ in American English. In general, all the tense vowels can occur in these circumstances, but all the lax vowels have been replaced by the reduced vowel [ə] as in "purr." There is no contrast between a tense vowel and the lax vowel nearest to it in quality in a syllable closed by /r/. Consequently, as often happens in contexts in which there is no opposition between two sounds, the actual sound produced is somewhere between the two. (We have already observed another example of this tendency. We saw that after /s/ at the beginning of a word there is no contrast between /p/ and /b/, or /t/ and /d/, or /k/ and /g/. Consequently the stops that occur in words such as "spy, sty, sky" are in between the corresponding voiced and voiceless stops.)

I put the words "boar" and "coir" in parentheses in this column because for many people [oʊ] and [ɔɪ] do not occur before /r/. The word "coir" [kɔɪr], which is the only word I have heard pronounced with [ɔɪr], is not in many people's vocabulary; and many people make no difference between "bore" and "boar." But some speakers do contrast [ɔ] and [oʊ] in these two words, or in other pairs such as "horse" and "hoarse."

The next column shows the vowels that occur before [ŋ]. In these circumstances again there is no possible contrast between tense and lax vowels. But, generally speaking, it is the lax vowels that occur. However, I have heard some people pronounce "sing" with a vowel a little closer to that in "beat" rather than to that in "bit." And in some dialects "length" is regularly pronounced with virtually the same vowel as that in "bait" rather than that in "bet." The pronunciation of "long" varies. It is [lɑŋ] or [lɔŋ] in most forms of American English and [lɒŋ] in most forms of British English.

The last column shows that there are similar restrictions in the vowels that can occur before [ʃ]. By far the majority of words ending in /ʃ/ have lax vowels. In my own speech the only word containing the tense vowel /i/ is "leash." Some speakers have tense vowels in a few new or unusual words such as "creche, gauche," which may be [kreɪʃ, goʊʃ]. The pronunciation of "wash" varies in much the same way as that of "long." Both [wɑʃ] and [wɔʃ] occur in American English.

If we were going to make a completely phonemic transcription we would have to take into account some other facts about vowels. There are a number of circumstances in which one vowel alternates phonetically with another in a predictable way. Table 4.4 shows some pairs of related words in which the vowel changes are completely rule governed. There is a tense vowel in the stressed syllable in the stem when no suffix follows (as in the left column of each pair). In each case this same syllable has a lax vowel when there is a following suffix (as in the right column of each pair).

Table 4.4

Some predictable alternations among English vowels. The dark type shows the vowel that changes.

[aɪ]	↔	[ɪ]	[i]	↔	[ɛ]	[eɪ]	↔	[æ]
divine		divinity	serene		serenity	insane		insanity
derive		derivative	supreme		supremacy	explain		explanatory
reside		residual	redeem		redemption	mania		manic

[aʊ]	↔	[ʌ]	[u]	↔	[ɒ] or [ɑ]	[oʊ]	↔	[ɒ] or [ɑ]
profound		profundity	school		scholar	verbose		verbosity
abound		abundance	fool		folly	depose		deposit
south		southern	goose		gosling	tone		tonic

It is possible to state a rule that shows the circumstances in which the tense vowel in a stem becomes a lax vowel with a different quality. Accordingly, in a phonemic transcription we could write both "divine" and "divinity" with the same vowel in the second syllable. The rule would show that "divine" is related to "divinity" in the same way as "serene" is related to "serenity" or "insane" to "insanity." But the rules for these alternations are very complicated, so we will have to continue to use a transcription that is not fully phonemic in this way.

Rules for English Allophones

A good way of summarizing all that I have said about English phonology so far is to list a set of rules describing the allophones. These rules are simply *descriptions* of language behavior. They are not the kind of rules that prescribe what people ought to do. Like most phoneticians, I would not presume to set myself up as an arbiter of fashion and declare what constitutes "good" speech. To the extent that phonetics is part of an exact scientific discipline, I would like to be able to formalize my description of speech in terms of a set of precise statements. But these statements should be regarded as descriptive, not prescriptive, rules.

The rules can be stated conveniently in terms of the classes of sounds to which they apply. The classes of sounds can be described in terms of the features of which they are composed. For example, the class of stops /p, t, k, b, d, g/ can be specified simply as:

$$[+\text{stop}]$$

The voiceless stops /p, t, k/ require a statement about two features. They will be:

$$\begin{bmatrix} -\text{voiced} \\ +\text{stop} \end{bmatrix}$$

This is a shorthand way of specifying the complete set of sounds that are, first, voiceless (or [−voiced], as we will say in these rules), and, second, stop consonants (or, more simply, [+stop]). If we wanted to specify all the sounds that are both voiced and stops (that is, /b, d, g/) we could write:

$$\begin{bmatrix} +\text{voiced} \\ +\text{stop} \end{bmatrix}$$

The nasal consonants can be specified simply as:

$$[+\text{nasal}]$$

We do not in this case have to specify whether they are voiced or voiceless, for there is no opposition between voiced and voiceless nasals in English.

We can write a rule saying that voiceless stops (/p, t, k/) are aspirated when they are syllable initial, as in words such as "pipped, testy, kicked" [pʰɪp°t, ɪtʰɛsti, kʰɪk°t], by saying:

(1) $\begin{bmatrix} -\text{voiced} \\ +\text{stop} \end{bmatrix} \rightarrow$ [+aspirated] when syllable initial.

This is a convenient way of saying that any sound that is [−voice, +stop] will become [+aspirated] in addition to being [−voice, +stop] when it is syllable initial.

Now consider how we might formulate a rule stating that the obstruents —the stops and fricatives—classified as voiced, that is, (/b, d, g, v, ð, z, ʒ/) are not in fact fully voiced when they occur at the end of an utterance or before a voiceless sound (as the /v/ in "try to improve" or the /d/ in "add two"). This rule would be:

(2) $\begin{bmatrix} +\text{voiced} \\ +\text{obstruent} \end{bmatrix} \rightarrow$ partially voiced when syllable final except when followed by a voiced sound.

We can also write a similar rule for stops that accounts for the fact that they are often not fully voiced when syllable initial:

(2a) $\begin{bmatrix} +\text{voiced} \\ +\text{stop} \end{bmatrix} \rightarrow$ partially voiced when syllable initial except when preceded by a voiced sound.

These two rules can be combined in a more precise account of English phonology.

Some of the rules apply to all the consonants of English. This class of sounds can be called simply [+consonantal]. One of the rules dealing with consonant length is:

(3) [+consonantal] → longer when at the end of a word.

You can see the application of this rule by comparing the consonants in words such as "bib, did, don, nod."

Next consider the rule that accounts for the devoicing of /w, r, j, l/ after initial /p, t, k/, as in "play, twin, cue" [pl̥eɪ, tw̥ɪn, kju]. This rule is very easy to state because we have simple ways of describing these classes of sounds. We can write:

(4) [+approximant] → [−voiced] after $\begin{bmatrix} +\text{aspirated} \\ +\text{stop} \end{bmatrix}$

We could also have a rule dealing with the fact that /p, t, k/ are unaspirated in words such as "spew, stew, skew." This would be:

(5) $\begin{bmatrix} -\text{voiced} \\ +\text{stop} \end{bmatrix} \rightarrow$ [−aspirated] after /s/ at the beginning of a syllable.

This rule might not be necessary in a formal set of rules accounting for the pronunciation of English. Rule (1) stated where in an utterance voiceless stops are aspirated, so one might presume them to be unaspirated elsewhere. But I have included rule (5) because the object of listing these rules is not to account for the allophones of English in the most rigorous and economical set of rules possible, but simply to review what I have said about the consonants of English.

Other rules would include:

(6)   [+vowel] → shorter before voiceless sounds in the same syllable.

(7)   [−voiced] → longer when at the end of a syllable.

Words exemplifying these two rules are "cap" as opposed to "cab," and "back" as opposed to "bag." Try contrasting these words in sentences, and you may be able to hear the differences more clearly.

Next we must account for the fact that sounds such as /p/ and /k/ are unexploded in words such as "apt" [æp°t] and "act" [æk°t]. The rule for this is:

(8)   [+stop] → unexploded before [+stop].

As we have seen, this is really part of a much more general rule about anticipatory coarticulation in English. We should perhaps have begun our set of rules with a statement of two general principles: First, when two consecutive sounds have a feature in common, that feature will be retained throughout the transition between them; second, articulators not involved in the primary articulation will take up or tend toward the articulation of the following item.

We may now list the rule that adds glottal stops before syllable final /p, t, k/, as in pronunciations of "tip, pit, kick" as [tɪʔp, pɪʔt, kɪʔk]. Because this rule turns one segment into a sequence of two segments, it will have the following form:

$$
(9) \quad \begin{bmatrix} -\text{voiced} \\ +\text{stop} \end{bmatrix} \rightarrow [+ \text{ glottal stop}] + \begin{bmatrix} -\text{voiced} \\ +\text{stop} \end{bmatrix} \begin{array}{l} \text{when after a vowel} \\ \text{and at the end of a} \\ \text{syllable.} \end{array}
$$

This rule does not apply to all varieties of English. Some people do not have any glottal stops in these circumstances, and others have glottal stops completely replacing some or all of the voiceless stops. In any case, even for those who simply add a glottal stop, the rule is not completely accurately stated. Many people will have a glottal stop at the end of "cat" in phrases such as "that's a cat" or "the cat sat on the mat," but they will not have this allophone of /t/ in "The cat is on the mat." An accurate statement of this rule would require my giving a much better account of what is meant by a syllable, but I cannot do this because it is not possible to give a phonetic definition of a syllable. We will return to this point in Chapter 10.

The next rule also does not apply to all varieties of English. This is the one that states that /t/ may be completely replaced by a glottal stop in "beaten" [ˈbiʔn].

(10) $\begin{bmatrix} -\text{voiced} \\ +\text{alveolar} \\ +\text{stop} \end{bmatrix}$ → [+ glottal stop] when it occurs before a nasal in the same word.

We also need a rule accounting for the syllabicity of the nasal in "leaden, chasm" ['lɛdn̩, 'kæzm̩], which would be stated:

(11)   [+nasal] → [+syllabic] when at the end of a word and after [+ obstruent].

Note that we cannot say that nasals become syllabic whenever they occur at the end of a word and after a consonant. The nasals in "kiln, film" are not syllabic in most dialects of English. We can, however, state a rule accounting for the syllabicity of /l/ by saying simply:

(12)   [+lateral] → [+syllabic] when at the end of a word and after another consonant.

This rule summarizes the fact that /l/ is syllabic not only after stops and fricatives (as in "paddle, whistle" ['pædl̩, 'wɪsl̩]) but also after nasals (as in "kennel, channel" ['kɛnl̩, 'tʃænl̩]). If we regard /r/ as a consonant, rule (12) would be invalidated in most forms of American English by words such as "curl, snarl" [kɜrl, snɑrl]. In classifying sounds for the purpose of these rules, we will have to regard /r/ not as a true consonant but as some kind of semivowel. Like the other central approximants, we might classify it as [+vowel, −syllabic].

On the other hand /r/ is like /l/ in most forms of American English in that it, too, can be syllabic when it occurs at the end of a word and after a consonant, as in "sabre, razor, hammer, tailor" ['seɪbr̩, 'reɪzr̩, hæmr̩, 'teɪlr̩]. If we introduce a new term, **liquid**, which is used simply as a cover term for the consonants /l, r/, we may describe these dialects by a rule:

(12a)   [+liquid] → [+syllabic] when at the end of a word and after a consonant.

The next rule also applies more to American English than to British English. It accounts for the /t/ in "fatty, data" ['færi, 'dærə]. It must also apply to /t/ after a stressed vowel and before unstressed syllables containing nonnasal syllabic consonants, as in "Peter, little." Accordingly it may be worded:

(13) $\begin{bmatrix} -\text{voice} \\ +\text{alveolar} \\ +\text{stop} \end{bmatrix}$ → $\begin{bmatrix} +\text{voiced} \\ +\text{tap} \end{bmatrix}$ when between a stressed vowel and an unstressed syllable (other than a syllabic nasal).

This rule does not apply to /t/ before syllabic [n] as in "mutton" ['məʔn̩] because the /t/ there has become a glottal stop, in accordance with rule (10). In addition, there is a great deal of variation among speakers. Some people have [ɾ] after lax vowels in words such as "litter, better" but not after tense vowels as in "writer, later." Some have [ɾ] in "motto" but not in "veto."

Try to formulate rule (13) in a way that describes your own speech.

The rule accounting for the dental consonants in "sixth, eighth, tenth, wealth" (sɪks̪θ, eɪt̪θ, tɛn̪θ, ˌwɛl̪θ] is as follows:

(14)   [+alveolar] → [+dental] before [+dental]

In a more rapid style of speech some of these dental consonants tend to be omitted altogether. Say these words first slowly and then more rapidly, and see what you do yourself.

We also need a rule to describe the increasingly more front articulation of /k/ in "cap, kept, kit, key (kæp, kɛpt, kɪt, ki] and of /g/ in "gap, get, give, geese" [gæp, gɛt, gɪv, gɪs]. You should be able to feel the more front position of your tongue contact in the latter words of these series. The rule is:

(15)   [+velar] → more front before more front vowels.

The rule that describes the difference in the quality of /l/ in "life" [laɪf] and "file" [faɪɫ], or "clap" [klæp] and "talc" [tæɫk] is:

(16)   [+lateral] → velarized when after a vowel and before another consonant or the end of a word.

There are also a number of simple phonological rules that apply to vowels. Thus we saw that a given vowel is longer in syllables closed by voiced consonants than in syllables closed by voiceless consonants. If you compare words such as "sea, seed, seat" or "sigh, side, site" you will hear that the vowel is longer still in the syllable without any consonant at the end. Accordingly we may add a rule:

(17)   [+vowel] → longer in open syllables.

Note that this rule is part of the general tendency in English to equalize the lengths of syllables that differ in the segments they contain. This same tendency is also reflected by the fact that the lax vowels, which are shorter than the corresponding tense vowels, cannot occur in open stressed syllables.

Not all syllables are the same length. Stressed syllables are longer than the corresponding unstressed syllables. Compare words such as "cite" and "citation." You will find that the vowel [aɪ] in the stressed syllable in the first word is longer than the same vowel in the second word where it occurs in an unstressed syllable. We will therefore have a rule:

(18)   [+vowel] → longer in stressed syllables.

Another kind of length variation is exemplified by sets of words such as "speed, speedy, speedily." Here the vowel in the stressed syllable gets progressively shorter as a result of adding extra syllables in the same word. The reasons for this phenomenon will be dealt with in the next chapter.

Other rules can be used to specify some anticipatory coarticulations that affect vowels. The most obvious is that vowels tend to become nasalized before nasal consonants. In a word such as "ban" the soft palate often lowers for the nasal considerably before the tongue tip rises to make the articulatory contact. As a result much of the vowel is nasalized. Nasalization is shown by the diacritic [~] over a symbol. This is the same diacritic as is used to denote velarization. When describing velarization it is placed in the middle of the symbol, but for nasalization it is placed above the symbol. In a narrow transcription "ban" might be transcribed [bæ̃n]. We could write the required general rule as:

(19) [+vowel] → [+nasal] before [+nasal]

Finally we must note the allophones produced when vowels occur in syllables closed by /l/. Compare your pronunciation of /i/ in "heed" and "heel," of /eɪ/ in "paid" and "pail," and [æ] in "pad" and "pal." In each case you should be able to hear a noticeably different vowel quality before the velarized [ɫ]. All the front vowels become considerably retracted in these circumstances. It is almost as if they became diphthongs with [ʊ] as the last element. In a narrow transcription we could transcribe this element so that "peel, pail, pal" would be [pʰiʊɫ, pʰeʊɫ, pʰæʊɫ]. Note that I omitted the usual second element of the diphthong [eɪ] in order to show that in these circumstances the vowel moved from a mid-front to a mid-central rather than to a high front quality.

Back vowels, as in "haul, pull, pool," are usually less affected by the final [ɫ] because they already have a tongue position similar to that of [ɫ]. But there is often a great difference in quality in the vowels in "hoe" and "hole." As we have seen, many people, myself included, have a fairly front vowel as the first element in the diphthong [oʊ]. This vowel becomes considerably retracted before /ɫ/ at the end of the syllable. You can observe the change by comparing words such as "holy," where there is no final [ɫ], and "wholely," where the first syllable is closed by [ɫ].

The exact form of the rule for specifying vowel allophones before [ɫ] will vary from speaker to speaker. But, so that we can include a rule in our set summarizing some of the main allophones of English, we may say:

(20) $\begin{bmatrix} +\text{front} \\ +\text{vowel} \end{bmatrix}$ → [+retracted] before syllable final /l/

Some speakers have a similar rule that applies to vowels before /r/, as in "hear, there" which might be [hiᵊr, ðeᵊr]. Note again how /l, r/ may act together in rules, as they did in rule (12a).

These rules are far from a complete set specifying the behavior of vowels in English. I have already mentioned the fact that it is possible to write rules describing the alternations in "divine, divinity" and all similar pairs and the vowel reduction in "explain, explanation" and all similar pairs. It is also possible to write rules that account for there being no opposition between tense and lax vowels before any of the consonants /r, ʃ, ŋ/. But all these rules would get us beyond the limits of an introductory textbook.

Again let me emphasize that these rules roughly specify only some of the major aspects of the pronunciation of English. They do not state everything about English consonants and vowels that is rule governed, nor are they completely accurately formulated. There are problems, for example, in saying exactly what is meant by a word or a syllable, and it is possible to find both exceptions to these rules and additional generalizations that can be made.

EXERCISES

A Put your own vowels in this chart, using a set of words such as that given in Table 4.1. Listen to each vowel carefully and try to judge how it sounds relative to the other vowels. You will probably find it best to say each vowel as the middle vowel of a three-member series, with the vowels on either side forming the first and last vowels in the series. In the case of the diphthongs you should do this with both the beginning and the ending points.

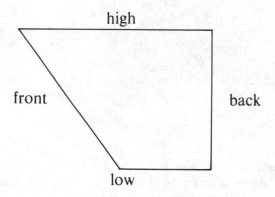

B Try to find a speaker of a dialect different from your own (or perhaps a foreigner who speaks English with an accent) and repeat Exercise **A**, using this blank chart.

accent:

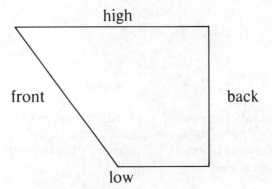

C   List words illustrating the occurrence of vowels in syllables closed by /p/. Do not include names of foreign origin. You will find that some vowels cannot occur in these circumstances.

    i

    ɩ

    eɩ

    ɛ

    æ

    ɑ

    ɔ

    oω

    ω

    u

    ʌ

    aɩ

    aω

    ɔɩ

D   Considering only the vowels that *cannot* occur in syllables closed by /p/ as in **C** above, give words, if possible, illustrating their occurrence in syllables closed by the following consonants.

    /b/

    /m/

    /f/

    /t/

    /n/

    /l/

    /s/

    /z/

    /k/

    /g/

E   Which vowel occurs before the smallest number of consonants? Also, which class of consonants occurs after the largest number of vowels? (Define the class in terms of the place of articulation at which these consonants are made.)

F Look at Table 4.2. Find additional examples illustrating the relationship between the words in the first and third columns. Transcribe each pair of words as shown below for the vowel /i/.

vowel	stressed syllable	reduced syllable
i	secrete [səˈkrit]	secretive [ˈsikrətɪv]
ɪ		
eɪ		
ɛ		
æ		
ɑ or ɒ		
oɷ		
aɪ		

G Look at Table 4.4. Find two additional pairs of words for each alternation. Transcribe each pair of words.

[aɪ] ↔ [ɪ]   [i] ↔ [ɛ]   [e] ↔ [æ]

[taɪp]   [ˈtɪpəkḷ]   _____   _____   _____   _____

_____   _____   _____   _____   _____   _____

[aɷ] ↔ [ʌ]   [u] ↔ [ɒ] or [ɑ]   [oɷ] ↔ [ɒ] or [ɑ]

_____   _____   _____   _____   _____   _____

_____   _____   _____   _____   _____   _____

H Make up and transcribe a sentence containing at least eight different vowels.

_____

_____

I Make a broad transcription of the following passage:
   In Renaissance times Leonardo da Vinci

   [_____

made numerous observations on the

[_____

physiology of speech. But apart

[_____
from a few individual pieces of work,

[_____

which did not have much influence on

[_____
the development of phonetic knowledge,

[_____
there were no systematic descriptions

[_____
of speech until the seventeenth century.

[_____
Then grammarians such as John Wallis

[_____
(1616–1703) included lengthy

[(1616–1703)_____
sections on speech in their work:

[_____
and several publications by teachers

[_____
of pronunciation and spelling reformers

[_____
show that the method of production

[_____
of most speech sounds was becoming

[_____
generally understood.

[_____

J Give a number of examples for each of rules (1) through (16) by making a narrow transcription of some additional words that fit the rules. Your examples should not include any words that have been transcribed in this book so far. They should also use several of the different sounds covered by each rule. Thus when exemplifying rule (1) do not give just words beginning with /p/, but include also words with /t/ and /k/. Remember to mark the stress on words of more than one syllable.

Rule   (1)   three examples

_____   _____   _____

Rule   (2)   seven examples

_____   _____   _____

_____   _____   _____

_____

Rule   (3)   three examples

_____   _____   _____

Rule   (4)   nine examples

_____   _____   _____

_____   _____   _____

_____   _____   _____

Rule   (5)   three examples

_____   _____   _____

Rules (6) and (7)   seven contrasting pairs

_____   _____

_____   _____

_____   _____

_____   _____

_____   _____

_____   _____

_____   _____

Rule (8) six examples

_____   _____   _____

_____   _____   _____

Rule (10) one example

_____

Rule (11) six examples

_____   _____   _____

_____   _____   _____

Rule (12) six examples

_____   _____   _____

_____   _____   _____

Rule (13) three examples

_____   _____   _____

Rule (14) six examples

_____   _____   _____

_____   _____   _____

Rule (15) three examples

_____   _____   _____

Rule (16) three examples

_____   _____   _____

K   As a more challenging exercise, try to list two exceptions to some of these rules.

Rule ( )——————————————————————

Rule ( )——————————————————————

L   Write a rule that describes the allophones of /h/.

——————————————————————————————

——————————————————————————————

——————————————————————————————

——————————————————————————————

——————————————————————————————

M   Write a pair of rules that describes the allophones of /n/ in words such as "sin, sing, singer, finger." Try to formalize the rules in the conventional way, using terms such as [+ nasal] and [+ alveolar] and the symbol →.

——————————————————————————————

——————————————————————————————

PERFORMANCE EXERCISES

A   Learn to produce only the first part of the vowel [eι] as in "hay." This will be a monophthong [e]. Try saying this sound in place of your normal diphthong in words such as "they came late." Similarly learn to produce a mid-high back vowel [o], and say it in words that you have been transcribing with the diphthong [oσ], such as "don't go home."

B   Incorporate [e] and [o] in nonsense words for production and perception exercises. These words might also now include the voiceless sounds [m̥, n̥, ŋ̊, l̥, r̥, w̥, j̥]. Remember to practice saying the words by yourself, so that you can say them fluently to your partner. Start with easy words such as:

> maˈŋɑ
> ˈŋeme
> ˈŋɑle
> ˈmoʔi
> ˈl̥ele

Then go on to more difficult words like:

heˈm̩aɲe
ˈŋambm̩beɭ
ˈspoʔetn̩ʔɪ
ˈw̥oθʃoˈɾesfi
ˈtlepɾidʒiˈkuʒ

C Again working with a partner, write the numbers 1 through 5 somewhere on a vowel chart as, for example, shown below.

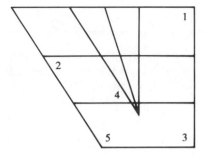

Now say vowels corresponding to these numbered positions in nonsense monosyllables, saying, for example, something like [dub]. Your partner should try to plot these vowels on a blank chart. When you have pronounced five words compare notes, and discuss the reasons for any discrepancies between the two charts. Then reverse roles and repeat the exercise.

D Repeat the exercise in **C** above with as many different partners as you can. It is difficult to make perceptual judgments of the differences among vowels, but you should be able to find a rough consensus of opinion.

E In addition to nonsense words of the kind given in **B** above, continue practicing with words to increase your auditory memory span. Say each word only two or three times. Remember that you should be spending at least one hour a week on production and perception exercises.

θeˈmifeˈðim̩e
ˈserapoˈsapofiˈpos
moˈpretepleteˈki
ɲaˈkotoˈtakpoto
laˈkimitiˈnoneʔe

English Words and Sentences 5

Strong and Weak Forms

The form in which a word is pronounced when it is considered in isolation is called its **citation form**. At least one syllable is fully stressed and has no reduction of the vowel quality. But in connected speech, many changes may take place. Some smaller words such as "and, to, him" may be considerably altered. They will usually be completely unstressed, the vowel may be reduced to [ə] or may disappear altogether, and one or more of the consonants may be dropped or altered. Thus "and" in its reduced form may be pronounced as [ənd] or [ən] or [n̩]. Try to pronounce it in these three different ways in a phrase such as "Bread and butter."

Many words are like "and" in that they seldom maintain their citation form in conversational speech. These words may be said to have two different forms of pronunciation. There is a **strong form** that occurs when the word is stressed, as in sentences such as "I want money *and* happiness, not money *or* happiness." There is also a **weak form**, which occurs when the word is in an unstressed position. Table 5.1 lists a number of common English words which have strong and weak forms.

Several of the words in Table 5.1 have more than one weak form. Sometimes, as in the case of "and," there are no clear rules as to when one as opposed to another of these forms is likely to occur. After a word ending with an alveolar consonant I have a tendency to drop the vowel and say [n̩] or [nd] (in phrases such as "cat and dog" or "his and hers"). But this is far from invariable.

Table 5.1

Strong and weak forms of some common English words. Over five times as many could easily have been listed.

word	strong form	weak form	example of a weak form
a	eɪ	ə	a cup [ə 'kʌp]
and	ænd	ənd, nd, ən, n̩	you and me ['ju ən 'mi]
as	æz	əz	as good as [əz 'gʊd əz]
at	æt	ət	at home [ət 'hoʊm]
can	kæn	kən, kn̩	I can go [aɪ kn̩ 'goʊ]
has	hæz	həz, əz, z, s	he's left [hɪz 'lɛft]
he	hi	i, hɪ, ɪ	will he go? [wɪl ɪ 'goʊ]
must	mʌst	məst, məs, m̩s	I must sell [aɪ m̩s 'sɛl]
she	ʃi	ʃɪ	did she go? ['dɪd ʃɪ 'goʊ]
that	ðæt	ðət	he said that it did. [hɪ 'sɛd ðət ɪt 'dɪd]
to	tu	tʊ, tə	to Mexico [tə 'mɛksɪkoʊ]
would	wʊd	wəd, əd, d	it would do ['ɪt əd 'du]

For some words, however, there are rules that are nearly always applicable. The alternation between "a" [ə] before a consonant and "an" [ən] before a vowel is even recognized in the spelling. Similar alternations occur with the words "the, to," which are [ðə, tə] before consonants and are often [ði, tu] or [ðɪ, tʊ] before vowels. Listen to your own pronunciation of these words in the sentence "The [ðə] man and the [ði] old woman went to [tə] Britain and to [tu] America."

Some of the words in Table 5.1 are confusing in that the spelling represents two different words (two homonyms). Thus the spelling "that" represents a demonstrative pronoun in a phrase such as "that girl and this man," but it represents a relative pronoun in "he said that girls were better." Only the relative pronoun has a weak form. The demonstrative "that" is always pronounced [ðæt]. Similarly, when "has" indicates past tense, it may be [z], as in "she's gone," but it is [həz] or [əz] when it indicates possession, as in "she has nice eyes."

There is another way in which words can be affected when they occur in connected speech. As you already know, sounds are often affected by adjacent—sounds for example, the [n] in "tenth" is articulated on the teeth because of the following dental fricative [θ]. Similar effects commonly occur across word boundaries, so that in phrases such as "in the" and "on the" the [n] is realized as a dental [n̪] because of the following [ð].

When one sound is changed into another because of the influence of a neighboring sound, there is said to be a process of **assimilation**. There is an assimilation of [n] to [n̪] because of the [ð] in the phrase "in the." Anticipatory coarticulation is by far the commonest cause of assimilations in English. But perseverative assimilations do occur, for example, in the pronunciation of the phrase "It is" [ɪt ɪz] as "it's" [ɪts] as a result of the perseveration of the voicelessness of [t].

There is, of course, nothing slovenly or lazy about using weak forms and assimilations. Only people with artificial notions about what constitutes so-called good speech could use adjectives such as these to label the kind of speech I have been describing. Weak forms and assimilations are common in the speech of every sort of speaker in both Britain and America. Foreigners who make insufficient use of them sound stilted.

Intonation

Listen to just the pitch of voice while someone says a sentence. You will find that it is changing continuously. The difference between speaking and singing is that in singing you hold a given note for a noticeable length of time and then jump to the pitch of the next note. But when one is speaking, there are no steady-state pitches. Throughout every syllable in a normal conversational utterance the pitch is going up or down. (Try talking with steady-state pitches and notice how odd it sounds.)

The intonation of a sentence is the pattern of pitch changes that occurs. The part of a sentence over which a particular pattern extends is called a **tone group**. A short sentence often forms a single tone group, while longer ones are made up of two or more. We show the major pitch changes in a tone group by lines placed above the sentence. In this chapter the sentence itself will be given in ordinary spelling, but with IPA stress marks added.

(1) The ˈgirl gave the ˈmoney to her ˈfather.

Within the tone group there is usually a single syllable that stands out because it carries the major pitch change. A syllable of this kind is called the **tonic syllable**. In sentence (1) the first syllable of "father" is the tonic syllable. It is said to receive the tonic accent.

The tonic accent often occurs on the last stressed syllable in a tone group. But it may occur earlier:

(2) He ˈwanted to go to ˈ*Germany* on ˈMonday.

The pitch changes that start on the tonic syllable are continued on the following syllables. In the examples given above, the fall in pitch continues (but at a slower rate) until the end of the sentence. Sometimes there are two or more tone groups within a sentence.

(3) She ˈsat by the ˈwindow, ‖ ˈreading a ˈletter.

In these cases the beginning of a new tone group may be marked, as in (3), by ‖. The pitch changes that begin on the tonic syllable continue only until the beginning of the next tone group.

There is no syntactic unit exactly corresponding to a tone group. When speaking slowly in a formal style, a speaker may choose to break a sentence up into a large number of tone groups. One could, for example, split sentence (1) into three separate tone groups, so that it becomes:

(1a) The ˈgirl ‖ gave the ˈmoney ‖ to herˈ father.

The way in which a speaker breaks up a sentence depends largely on what that person considers to be the important information points in the sentence. A tone group is a unit of information rather than a syntactically defined unit. It is only in rapid conversational style that there is likely to be one tone group per sentence.

It is also usually impossible to predict which syllable will be the tonic syllable in a tone group. Again, it depends on what the speaker considers to be important. In general, new information is more likely to receive a tonic accent than material that has already been mentioned. The topic of a sentence is less likely to receive the tonic accent than the comment which is made on that topic. Thus, if I were discussing the properties of water I might say:

(4) ˈWater is a ˈliquid.

In this case the topic of the sentence is water, and the comment on that topic is that it is a liquid. But if I were discussing liquids and considering that as the topic, I might say:

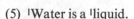

(5) ˈWater is a ˈliquid.

Various pitch changes are possible within the tonic accent. In sentences (1) through (5) the intonation may be simply described as falling. The tonic syllable in all these cases may be said to be [+ falling], with the understanding that the falling feature continues over all the remaining syllables in the tone group.

Another possibility is that the tonic syllable is the start of an upward glide of pitch. This kind of pitch change, which we will simply refer to as rising, is typical in questions requiring the answer "yes" or "no," such as:

(6) Do you ˈwant some ˈcoffee?

As with [+falling], the syllable that is marked [+rising] is not necessarily the last stressed syllable in a tone group. It occurs earlier in:

(7) Do you take ˈcream in your ˈcoffee?

Now consider what you do in questions that cannot be answered "yes" or "no," such as:

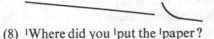

(8) ˈWhere did you ˈput the ˈpaper?

Of course, there are many possible ways of saying this sentence. But probably the most neutral is with [+falling] on the final stressed syllable. Questions that begin with *wh*-question words such as "where, when, who, why, what"–are usually pronounced with a falling intonation.

A rising intonation often occurs in the middle of sentences, a typical circumstance being at the end of a clause, as in:

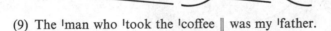

(9) The ˈman who ˈtook the ˈcoffee ‖ was my ˈfather.

A list of items is often given in a similar way:

(10) I ˈwant some ˈapples, ‖ ˈoranges, ‖ and ˈpeaches.

Note that yes–no questions can nearly always be reworded so that they fit into this pattern:

(11) Do you ˈwant some ˈcoffee ‖ or ˈnot?

In detailed studies of intonation it may be useful to distinguish between two kinds of rising intonation. In the one, which typically occurs in yes–no questions, there is a large upward movement of pitch. In the other, which usually occurs in the middle of sentences, there is a smaller upward movement. Some people may use these two intonations contrastively. Thus, if I have a low rising intonation on an utterance, it seems to me to mean that I am expecting to hear or say something more. I might have a slightly rising intonation in:

(12) Perˈhaps   or   (13) I ˈmight

This means "Yes, it's possible, but I don't want to say anything definite for the moment." Whereas, if I have a larger rise in pitch and say:

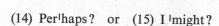

(14) Per'haps?   or   (15) I 'might?

It means "Did you say perhaps?" or "Did you say I might?" However, people are not entirely consistent in the way they use this difference in intonation.

Both rising and falling intonations can occur within the same tonic accent. The pitch changes that result depend on which occurs first. If the fall occurs before the rise, there will be the kind of intonation that commonly conveys doubt. If you tell me someone's name and I do not believe you, I might well say:

(16) His 'name is 'Peter?

This is, of course, quite different from the straightforward statement:

(17) His 'name is 'Peter.

Or the polite question:

(18) His 'name is 'Peter?

The combination [+falling] followed by [+rising] commonly occurs with a lengthened vowel in phrases expressing doubt such as:

(19) I 'think 'so–o.

The opposite possibility, [+rising] followed by [+falling], is far less common. It seems to convey certainty as opposed to doubt. If you tell me someone's name and I doubt it, you might reply:

(20) His 'name is 'Peter.

To summarize, all the intonation patterns we have discussed so far start on the tonic syllable and continue till the end of the tone group. The possible patterns may all be demonstrated on a single word, as in (21) below:

(21) Yes ⌣   falling   = "The answer is yes."

Yes   high   ⎫   = "Did you say 'yes'?"

                     ⎬rising

Yes   low   ⎭   = "Please go on, I'm listening."

Yes   falling–rising = "I'm doubtful."

Yes   rising–falling = "I'm certain."

There are no large rising or falling changes in pitch on any of the syllables other than the tonic syllable in a tone group. In the examples I have given all these syllables have a neutral intonation. In most forms of English this means that they are on a slowly descending line of pitch changes. But, as is the case for much that one can say about intonation, there are numerous other ways in which they can be used to signal a speaker's attitude. For example, it seems to me that the speaker considers himself slightly superior to the person he is talking to if he uses small rises on the unstressed syllables in the pre-tonic part of the tone group, as in:

(22) What is the ˈobject of ˈwriting a ˈletter?

This kind of intonation is either condescending or menacing. It is certainly not at all friendly.

Stress

A stressed syllable is produced by pushing more air out of the lungs. A stressed syllable thus has an increase in respiratory activity. It may also have an increase in laryngeal activity. Stress can always be defined in terms of something a speaker does.

It is difficult to define stress from a listener's point of view. A stressed syllable is often, but not always, louder than an unstressed syllable. It is usually, but not always, on a higher pitch. The most reliable thing for a listener to detect is that a stressed syllable frequently has a longer vowel. But, as stress can be correlated with something a speaker does, you will find that it is always easier to tap on a stressed syllable. This is because it is always easier to produce one increase in muscular activity—a tap—exactly in time with an existing increase in activity. When as listeners we perceive the stresses that other people are making, we are probably putting together all the cues that are available in a particular utterance in order to deduce how we would produce the appropriate increases of activity. It seems as if a listener sometimes perceives an utterance by reference to his or her own motor activities, considering what he or she herself would have to do in order to make similar sounds. This notion is called the motor theory of speech perception.

Stress has several different functions in English. In the first place, it can be used simply to give special emphasis to a word or to contrast one word with another. As we have seen, even a word such as "and" can be given a contrastive stress. The contrast can be implicit rather than explicit. For example, if someone else says, or if I had even thought that someone else might possibly say

ˈJohn or ˈMary should ˈgo

I might, without any prior context actually spoken, say

ˈI think ˈJohn ˈand ˈMary should ˈgo.

Another major function of stress in English is to indicate the syntactic relationships between words or parts of words. There are many noun–verb oppositions, such as "an ˈinsult, to inˈsult; an ˈoverflow, to overˈflow; an ˈincrease, to inˈcrease." In all these pairs of words the noun has the stress on the first syllable, the verb has it on the last. The placement of the stress indicates the syntactic function of the word.

Similar oppositions occur in cases where two word phrases form compounds such as "a ˈwalkout, to ˈwalk ˈout; a ˈput-on, to ˈput ˈon; a ˈpushover, to ˈpush ˈover." In these cases, there is a stress only on the first element of the compound for the nouns but on both elements for the verbs. Stress also has a syntactic function in distinguishing between a compound noun, such as "a ˈhot dog" (a form of food), and an adjective followed by a noun, as in the phrase "a ˈhot ˈdog" (an overheated animal). Compound nouns have a single stress on the first element, and the adjectival phrases have stresses on both elements.

Many other variations in stress can be associated with the grammatical structure of the words. Table 5.2 exemplifies the kind of alternations that can occur. All the words in the first column have the main stress on the first syllable. When the noun-forming suffix "-y" occurs, the stress in these words shifts to the second syllable. But as you can see in the third column, the adjectival suffix "-ic" moves the stress to the syllable immediately preceding it, which in these words is the third syllable. If you make a sufficiently complex set of rules, it is possible to predict the location of the stress in the majority of English words.

Table 5.2

English word stress alternations.

ˈ＿ ＿ ＿	＿ ˈ＿ ＿ ＿	＿ ＿ ˈ＿ ＿
diplomat	diplomacy	diplomatic
photograph	photography	photographic
monotone	monotony	monotonic

Degrees of Stress

In some longer words it might seem as if there is more than one degree of stress. For example, say the word "multiplication" and try to tap on the stressed syllables. You will find that you can tap on the first and the fourth syllables "ˈmultipliˈcation." The fourth syllable seems to have a higher degree of stress. The same is true of other long words such as "ˈmagnifiˈcation, ˈaristoˈcratic, ˈpscholinˈguistics." But this apparently higher degree of stress on the later syllable only occurs when the word is said in isolation or at the end of a phrase. Try saying a sentence such as "The ˈaristoˈcratic ˈrider ˈgalloped aˈway." If you tap on each stressed syllable you will find that there is no difference between the first and fourth syllables of "aristocratic." If you have a higher degree of stress on the fourth syllable in "aristocratic," this word will be given a special emphasis, as though you were contrasting an ordinary rider with an aristocratic rider. The same is true of the word "magnification" in a sentence such as "The deˈgree of ˈmagnifiˈcation deˈpends on the ˈpower of the ˈlens." The word "magnification" will not have a larger stress on the fourth syllable as long as you do not break the sentence into two parts and leave this word at the end of the first tone group.

Why does it seem as if there are two degrees of stress in a word when it occurs at the end of a phrase or when it is said alone—which is, of course, at the end of a phrase? The answer is that in these circumstances another factor is present. As we have seen, the last stressed syllable in a tone group usually carries the tonic accent. In longer words containing two stresses, the apparent difference in the levels of the first and the second stress is really due to the superimposition of an intonation pattern. When these words occur within a sentence in a position where there are no intonation effects, then there are no differences in the stress levels.

A lower level of stress may also seem to occur in some English words. Compare the words in the two columns in Table 5.3. The words in both columns have the stress on the first syllable. The words in the first column might seem to have a second, weaker, stress on the last syllable as well, but this is not so. The words in the first column differ from those in the second by having a full vowel in the final syllable. This vowel is always longer than the reduced vowel—usually [ə] or [ɪ]—in the final syllable of the words in the second column. The result is that there is a difference in the rhythm of the two sets of words. This is due to a difference in the vowels that are present; it is not a difference in stress. There is not a strong increase in respiratory activity

Table 5.3

Three syllable words exemplifying the difference between an unreduced vowel in the final syllable (first column) and a reduced vowel in the final syllable (second column).

'multiply	'multiple
'regulate	'regular
'copulate	'copula
'circulate	'circular
'criticize	'critical
'minimize	'minimal

on the last syllable of the words in the first column. Both sets of words have increases in respiratory activity only on the first syllable.

In summary, we can say that English syllables are either stressed or unstressed. If they are stressed, they may or they may not be the tonic syllables, which carry the major pitch change in the tone group. If they are unstressed, they may or may not have a reduced vowel.

As an aid to understanding the difference between these processes, consider the set of words "explain, explanation, exploit, exploitation." If each of these words is said in its citation form, as a separate tone group, the set will be pronounced as shown below:

Intonation	—◡	—◡	—◡	—◡
Stress	ex'plain	'expla'nation	ex'ploit	'exploi'tation
Segments	[ɪkspleɪn	ɛkspləneɪʃən	ɪksplɔit	ɛksplɔɪteɪʃən]

Another way of representing some of these same facts is shown in Table 5.4. This table shows just the presence (+) or absence (−) of a tonic accent, a stress, and a full vowel in each syllable in these four words. Considering first the stress (in the middle row), note that the two syllable words are marked [+stress] on the second syllable, and the four syllable words are marked [+stress] on both the first and third syllables.

Table 5.4

The combination of stress, intonation, and vowel reduction in a number of words.

	explain	explanation	exploit	exploitation
tonic accent	− +	− − + −	− +	− − + −
stress	− +	+ − + −	− +	+ − + −
full vowel	− +	+ − + −	− +	+ + + −

As you can see by comparing the middle row with the top row, the last [+stress] syllable in each word has been marked [+tonic accent]. There is a [+] in the third row if the vowel is not reduced. Note that the difference between "explanation" and "exploitation" is that the second syllable has a reduced vowel in the first word, but a full vowel in the second word. As we saw in the last chapter, there are a number of vowels that do not occur in reduced syllables.

Now, without looking at Table 5.4, try to mark the values of the syllables in Table 5.5. You should find that they fall into the same pattern as those in Table 5.4, except that the words are in the reverse order. Check this for yourself when you have completed the table.

Table 5.5

Words with the same stress, intonation, and vowel reduction possibilities as those in Table 5.4, but in the reverse order. Try to fill in the plus and minus signs yourself, and then compare your answer with the values shown in Table 5.4.

	computation	compute	inclination	incline (verb)
tonic accent				
stress				
full vowel				

Some other books do not make the distinctions described here, maintaining instead that there are several levels of stress in English. The greatest degree of stress is called stress level one, the next is level two, the next level three, a lower level still is level four, and so on. Note that in this system a smaller degree of stress has a larger number.

You can easily convert our system into a multilevel stress system by adding the number of [+] marks on a syllable in a table of the sort just used and subtracting this number from four. If there are three [+] marks it is stress level one; if two, stress level two; if one, stress level three; and if none, it is stress level four. Try this for yourself with the data in Tables 5.4 and 5.5. Writing the stress levels above the syllables, you will find that "explanation" and "exploitation" are "ex$\overset{2}{}$pla$\overset{4}{}$na$\overset{1}{}$tion$\overset{4}{}$" and "ex$\overset{2}{}$ploi$\overset{3}{}$ta$\overset{1}{}$tion$\overset{4}{}$." For somewhat obscure reasons, it is sometimes said that stress level two does not occur within a word. Accordingly this stress level is considered to be reduced to level three, and if there is a level three in the word it and any level fours are each reduced one degree more. In this way "explanation" and "exploitation" become "ex$\overset{3}{}$pla$\overset{4}{}$na$\overset{1}{}$tion$\overset{4}{}$" and "ex$\overset{3}{}$ploi$\overset{4}{}$ta$\overset{1}{}$tion$\overset{5}{}$."

I personally do not consider it useful to think of stress in terms of a multilevel system. Descriptions of this sort are not in accord with the phonetic facts. But as it is so commonly said that there are many levels of stress in English, I thought I should explain how these terms are used. In this book, however, we will continue to regard stress as something that either does or does not occur on a syllable in English, and we will view vowel reduction and intonation as separate processes.

We can sometimes predict by rules whether a vowel will be reduced to [ə] or not. For example, we can formalize a rule stating that [ɔɪ] never reduces. But other cases seem to be simply a matter of frequency of usage. There is no other reason why there should be reduced vowels at the end of "bacon" and "gentleman" but not at the end of "moron" and "superman."

Sentence Stress

The stresses that can occur on words sometimes become modified when the words are part of sentences. The most frequent modification is the dropping of some of the stresses. There is a stress on the first syllable of each of the words "Mary, younger, brother, wanted, fifty, chocolate, peanuts" when these words are said in isolation. But there are normally fewer stresses when they occur in a sentence such as "Mary's younger brother wanted fifty chocolate peanuts." Tap with your finger at each stressed syllable while you say this phrase in a normal conversational style. You will probably find it quite natural to tap on the first syllables marked with a preceding stress mark in "ˈMary's younger ˈbrother wanted ˈfifty chocolate ˈpeanuts." Thus the first syllables of "younger," "wanted," and "chocolate" are pronounced without stresses (but with their full vowel qualities).

The same kind of phenomenon can be demonstrated with monosyllabic words. Say the sentence "The big brown bear ate ten white mice." It sounds unnatural if you put a stress on every word. Most people will say "The ˈbig brown ˈbear ate ˈten white ˈmice." As a general rule English tries to avoid having stresses too close together. Very often, stresses on alternate words are dropped in sentences where they would otherwise come too near one another.

The tendency to avoid having stresses too close together may cause the stress on a polysyllabic word to be on one syllable in one sentence and on another in another. Consider the word "clarinet" in "He had a ˈclarinet ˈsolo" and in "He ˈplays the clariˈnet." The stress is on the first or the third syllable, depending on the position of the other stresses in the sentence. Similar shifts occur in phrases such as "ˈVice-president ˈJones" versus "ˈJones, the vice-ˈpresident." Numerals such as 14, 15, 16 are stressed on the first syllable when counting, but not in phrases such as "She's ˈonly sixˈteen." Read all these phrases with the stresses as indicated and check that it is natural to tap on the stressed syllables. Then try tapping on the indicated syllables while you read the next paragraph.

ˈStresses in ˈEnglish ˈtend to reˈcur at ˈregular ˈintervals of ˈtime. (ˈ) It is ˈperfectly ˈpossible to ˈtap on the ˈstresses in ˈtime with a ˈmetronome. (ˈ) The ˈrhythm can ˈeven be ˈsaid to deˈtermine the ˈlength of the ˈpause between ˈphrases. (ˈ) An ˈextra ˈtap can be ˈput in the ˈsilence, (ˈ) as ˈshown by the ˈmarks withˈin the paˈrentheses. (ˈ)

Of course, not all sentences are as regular as those in the preceding paragraph. I said that stresses *tend* to recur at regular intervals. It would be quite untrue to say that there is always an equal interval between stresses in English. It is just that English has a number of processes which act together to maintain the rhythm. I have already mentioned two of these processes. First, we saw that some words that might have been stressed are nevertheless often unstressed so as to prevent too many stresses coming together. Thus, to give another example, both "wanted" and "pretty" are stressed in "She ˈwanted a ˈpretty ˈparrot" but they may not be in "My ˈaunt wanted ˈten pretty ˈparrots." Second, we saw that some words have variable stress; compare "the ˈunknown ˈman" with "the ˈman is unˈknown."

We can also consider some of the facts mentioned in the previous chapter as part of this same tendency to reduce the variation in the interval between stresses. We saw that the vowel in "speed" is longer than that in "speedy," and this in turn is longer than that in "speedily." This can be interpreted as a tendency to minimize the variation in the length of words containing only a single stress, so that adjacent stresses remain much the same distance apart.

Taking all these facts together, along with others that will not be dealt with here, it is as if there were a conspiracy in English to maintain a regular rhythm. However, this conspiracy is not strong enough to completely override the irregularities caused by variations in the number and type of unstressed syllables. In a sentence such as "The ˈred ˈbird flew ˈspeedily ˈhome," the interval between the first and second stresses will be far less than that between the third and fourth. Stresses tend to recur at regular intervals. But the sound pattern of English does not make this an overriding necessity, adjusting the lengths of syllables so as to enforce complete regularity. The interval between stresses is affected by the number of syllables within the stress group and by the number and type of vowels and consonants within each syllable.

EXERCISES

A List the strong and weak forms of ten words not mentioned in this chapter. For each word transcribe a short utterance illustrating the weak form (as in Table 5.1).

word	strong form	weak form	example of weak form
____	____	____	_____
____	____	____	_____
____	____	____	_____
____	____	____	_____
____	____	____	_____
____	____	____	_____
____	____	____	_____
____	____	____	_____
____	____	____	_____
____	____	____	_____

B Give two new examples of each of the following kinds of assimilations, one of the examples involving a change within a word, the other involving a change across word boundaries. (Even if you yourself do not say assimilations of the kind illustrated, make up plausible examples. I myself have heard all the examples given.)

A change from an alveolar to a bilabial consonant.

| *impatient* | [ɪmˈpeɪʃn̩t] | *Saint Paul's* | [sm̩ˈpɔlz] |

A change from an alveolar consonant to a dental consonant.

| *tenth* | [tɛn̪θ] | *In this* | [ɪn̪ ðɪs] |

A change from an alveolar consonant to a velar consonant.

| *synchronous* | [ˈsɪŋkrənəs] | *within groups* | [wɪðˈɪŋ grups] |

_____ _____ _____ _____

A change from a voiceless consonant to a voiced consonant.

| catty | [ˈkædi] | sit up | [sɪˈdʌp] |

_____ _____ _____ _____

C Give five more examples of assimilation. Choose examples as different as possible from any that have been given before.

_____   [_____]

_____   [_____]

_____   [_____]

_____   [_____]

_____   [_____]

D Indicate the stress and intonation patterns that might occur in the situations described for the following utterances.

1. "Can you pass me that book?" (said politely to a friend)

2. "Where were you last night?" (angry father to daughter)

3. "Must it be typewritten?" (polite question)

4. "Who is the one in the corner?" (excitedly, to a friend)

5. "He's very nice . . . " (but I don't like him)

E Make up pairs of phrases or sentences that show how each of the following words can have two different stress patterns.
Example: continental
It's a ˈcontinental ˈbreakfast.
She's ˈvery contiˈnental.

afternoon

_____

_____

artificial

_____

_____

diplomatic

_____

_____

absent-minded

_____

_____

New York

_____

_____

F List five other pairs of sentences showing a variable stress pattern in five words not previously mentioned in this book.

_____

_____

_____

_____

_____

_____

_____

_____

_____

_____

G About 100 years ago all the following words had stress as shown. Some of them still do for some people. But many of them (in my speech, all of them) are stressed differently nowadays. Transcribe these words and show the stress on each of them in your own speech. Then state a general rule describing this tendency for the position of the stress to change to a particular syllable.

an'chovy _____

ab'domen _____

'applicable _____

'controversy _____

'nomenclature _____

tra'chea _____

eti'quette _____

re'plica _____

va'gary _____

blas'phemous _____

PERFORMANCE EXERCISES

A Pronounce the following phrases exactly as they have been transcribed, with all the assimilations and elisions. (Each of these transcriptions is a record of an utterance that I have actually heard in normal conversations between educated speakers.)

"What are you doing?"   ['wɑdʒə'duɪn]

"I can inquire."   ['aɪkŋŋ'kwaɪə]

"Did you eat yet?"   ['dʒitjɛʔ]

"I don't believe him."   [aɪ'doɷmbə'livɪm]

"We ought to have come."   [wi'ɔtʃ'kʌm]

B Working with a partner, try to transcribe the intonation of a few sentences. You may find it difficult to repeat a sentence over and over again with the same intonation. If you do, try to work from a tape recording. In any case, write down the sentence and the intonation you intend to produce. Practice saying it in this way before you say it to your partner.

C Take turns saying nonsense words such as those shown below, transcribing them and comparing transcriptions.

> ʃkeɪʒdʒ'minʒe
> 'ŋoļipɼə'bredn
> 'ʔaŋkliθuntθ
> sfeɪ'eʔɛɱa
> grɔɪpst'braɪgz

D Also make up lists of words for improving your memory span. These words are more difficult if the stress is varied and if the sounds are mainly of the same class (stops, front vowels, voiceless fricatives, etc.).

> tipe'kiketi'pe
> θɔɪ'saɪθaɷ'fɔɪʃaɷθaɷ
> 'monaŋu'ŋonəma
> wo'ʔɔɪlaɷra'rəlojə
> bəbdɪg'bɛdgɪbdɛd'bɛbdəd

Airstream Mechanisms and Phonation Types 6

In order to describe the various languages of the world, we need to consider the total range of the phonetic capabilities of man. There are several ways in which the sets of terms that we have been using to describe English must now be enlarged. In the first place, all English sounds are initiated by the action of lung air going outwards; other languages may use additional ways of producing an airstream. Second, all English sounds can be categorized as voiced or voiceless; in some languages additional states of the glottis are used. This chapter will describe the general phonetic categories needed to describe the airstream mechanisms and phonation types that occur in other languages. Subsequent chapters will survey other ways in which languages differ.

Airstream Mechanisms

Air coming out of the lungs is the source of power in nearly all speech sounds. When this body of air is moved we say that there is a **pulmonic airstream mechanism**. The air in the lungs is forced out by a downward movement of the rib cage and/or an upward movement of the diaphragm. These two movements are the **initiators** of the pulmonic airstream.

In the description of most sounds, we take it for granted that the pulmonic airstream mechanism is the source of power. But in the case of stop consonants (e.g., [b, d, g, p, t, k]) other airstream mechanisms may be involved. Stops that use only an egressive, or outward-moving, pulmonic airstream are called **plosives**. Stops made with other airstream mechanisms will be specified by other terms.

In some languages, speech sounds are produced by moving different bodies of air. If you make a glottal stop, so that the air in the lungs is contained below the glottis, then the air in the vocal tract itself will form a body of air that can be moved. An upward movement of the closed glottis will move this air out of the mouth. A downward movement of the closed glottis will cause air to be sucked into the mouth. When either of these actions occurs there is said to be a **glottalic airstream mechanism**.

An egressive glottalic airstream mechanism occurs in many languages. Hausa, the principal language of Northern Nigeria, uses this mechanism in the formation of a velar stop that contrasts with the voiceless and voiced velar stops [k, g]. The movements of the vocal organs are shown in Figure 6.1. These are estimated, not drawn on the basis of x-rays.

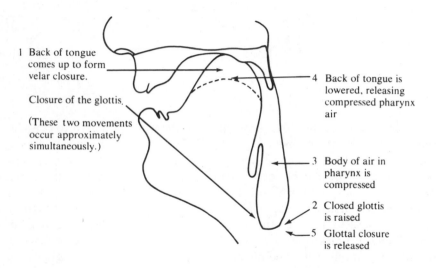

1 Back of tongue comes up to form velar closure.

Closure of the glottis.

(These two movements occur approximately simultaneously.)

4 Back of tongue is lowered, releasing compressed pharynx air

3 Body of air in pharynx is compressed

2 Closed glottis is raised

5 Glottal closure is released

Figure 6.1 *The sequence of events that occurs in a glottalic egressive velar stop* [k'].

As far as I can tell, in Hausa the velar closure and the glottal closure are formed at about the same time. Then, when the vocal cords are tightly together, the larynx is pulled upward, about one cm. In this way it acts like a piston, compressing the air in the pharynx. The compressed air is released by lowering the back of the tongue while the glottal stop is maintained. This produces a sound with a quality different from that in an English [k]. Very shortly after the release of the velar closure the glottal stop is released, and the voicing for the following vowel begins.

Stops made with a glottalic egressive airstream mechanism are called **ejectives**. The diacritic indicating an ejective is an apostrophe ['] placed after a symbol. The Hausa sound I have just described is a velar ejective, symbolized [k'], as in the Hausa word for "song," [wàk'á]. (The accents over the vowels indicate significant pitches which we will have to disregard for the moment.) Other languages have ejectives made at other places of articulation. Some languages also use this mechanism in the production of fricatives as well as stops. Of course, a fricative made in this way can continue only for a short length of time, for there is a comparatively small amount of air that can be moved by raising the closed glottis. Ejectives of different kinds occur in a wide variety of languages, including American Indian languages, African languages, and languages spoken in the Caucasus. Table 6.1 gives examples

Table 6.1

Contrasts involving ejective stops and fricatives in Amharic. An ejective airstream mechanism is shown by a following apostrophe. The vowel [ɨ] denotes a high central vowel. Note also that some of the consonants are doubled.

t'ɨl	quarrel	tɨl	worm	dɨl	victory
k'ir	stay away	kɨrr	thread	gərr	innocent
mətʃ'	one who comes	mətʃ	when	mədʒ	grinding stone
s'əgga	grace	səgga	he worried	zəgga	he closed

of ejectives and contrasting sounds made with a pulmonic airstream mechanism in Amharic, the principal language of Ethiopia. The sounds of Amharic differ from those of English in many ways in addition to having contrastive ejectives. Consequently the data in Table 6.1 include some phonetic possibilities that we have not discussed so far and can ignore for the time being. But you might like to note that the symbol [ɨ] is used for a high central unrounded vowel, something like the vowel that often occurs in the adverb "just" when it is said quickly in a phrase such as "He's just gone."

Learn to make ejective stops. By now you should be fully able to make a glottal stop in a sequence such as [aʔa], so the next step is to learn to raise and lower the glottis. You can recognize what it feels like to raise the glottis by singing a very low note and then moving to the position for singing the highest note that you possibly can. If you do this silently you will find it easier to concentrate on feeling the muscular sensations involved. It will also help you to realize what you are doing if you put your fingers on your throat above the larynx so that you can feel the movements. Repeat (silently) this sequence—low note–very high note—until you have thoroughly experienced the sensation of raising your glottis. Now try to make this movement with a closed glottis. There will, of course, be no sounds produced by these movements alone.

The next step is to learn to superimpose this movement on a velar stop. Say the sequence [ɑk]. Then say this sequence again, very slowly, holding your tongue in the position for the [k] closure at the end for a second or so. Now say it again, and while maintaining the [k] closure, do three things: (1) make a glottal stop; (2) if you can, raise your larynx; and (3) release the

[k] closure while maintaining the glottal stop. Don't worry about step (2) too much. The important thing to concentrate on is having a glottal stop and a velar closure going on at the same time, and then releasing the velar closure *before* releasing the glottal stop. The release of the velar closure will produce only a very small noise, but it will be an ejective [k'].

Next try to produce a vowel after the ejective. This time start from the sequence [ɑkɑ]. Say this sequence slowly, with a long [k] closure. Then, during this closure, make a glottal stop and raise the larynx. Then release the [k] closure while still maintaining the glottal stop. Finally release the glottal stop and follow it with a vowel. You should have produced something like [ɑk'ʔɑ]. When this sequence becomes more fluent, so that there is very little pause between the release of the velar closure and of the glottal stop, it can be considered simply an ejective followed by a vowel—[ɑk'ɑ]. There is, of course, still a glottal stop after the release of the velar stop and before the vowel, but unless it is exceptionally long, we may consider it to be implied by the symbol for the ejective.

Another way of learning to produce an ejective is to start from the usual American (and common British) pronunciation of "button" as [ˈbʌʔn̩]. Try starting to say "button" but finishing with a vowel [ʌ] instead of the nasal [n]. If you make sure that you do include the [t], the result will probably be [ˈbʌʔtʌ]. If you say this slowly you should be able to convert it first into [ˈbʌʔt'ʔʌ], then into [ˈbʌt'ʌ], and finally, altering the stress, into [bəˈt'ʌ].

You should eventually be able to produce sequences such as [p'ɑ, t'ɑ, k'ɑ] and perhaps [tʃ'ɑ, s'ɑ] as well. Practice producing ejectives before, after, and between a wide variety of vowels. You should also try to say the Amharic words in Table 6.1. But if you find ejectives difficult to produce, don't worry. It took my wife twenty years to learn to say them.

It is also possible to use a downward movement of the larynx to suck air inwards. Stops made with an ingressive glottalic airstream mechanism are called **implosives**. In the production of implosives, the downward moving larynx is not usually completely closed. The air in the lungs is still being pushed out, and some of it passes between the vocal cords, keeping them in motion so that the sound is voiced. Figure 6.2 shows the movements in a voiced bilabial implosive of a kind that occurs in Sindhi (a language spoken in India and Pakistan).

In all the implosives I have measured, the articulatory closure—in this case, the lips coming together—occurs first. The downward movement of the glottis, which occurs next, is like that of a piston that would cause a reduction of the pressure of the air in the oral tract. But it is a leaky piston in that the air in the lungs continues to flow through the glottis. As a result, the pressure of the air in the oral tract is not affected very much. (In an ordinary—plosive—[b] there is, of course, an increase in the pressure of the air in the vocal tract.) When the articulatory closure is released, there is neither an explosive nor, in a literal sense, an implosive action. Instead, the peculiar

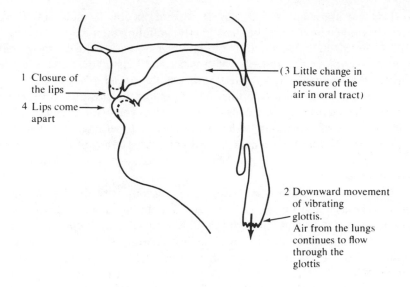

1 Closure of
the lips

4 Lips come
apart

(3 Little change in
pressure of the
air in oral tract)

2 Downward movement
of vibrating
glottis.
Air from the lungs
continues to flow
through the
glottis

Figure 6.2 *Estimated sequence of events in a Sindhi bilabial implosive* [ɓ].

quality of the sound arises from the complex changes in the shape of the vocal tract and in the vibratory pattern of the vocal cords.

In many languages, such as Sindhi and several African and American Indian languages, implosives contrast with plosives. However, in some languages, (e.g., Vietnamese) implosives are simply variants (allophones) of voiced plosives and not in contrast with those sounds. In order to illustrate some words in which a range of airstream mechanisms occur, Table 6.2 lists

Table 6.2

Contrasts involving plosives, ejectives, and implosives in Uduk (a Nilo-Sharan language). The symbols [ɓ, ɗ] denote voiced bilabial and alveolar implosives respectively. The accents over the vowels are tone marks, which will be explained later.

pál	to try	tèr	to collect
ɓáʔ	back of neck	ɗek'	to lift
baʔ	to be something	déɗ	to shiver
		t'èɗ	to lick

some words in Uduk, a language spoken in Southern Sudan, that has contrasting ejectives, implosives, and voiced and voiceless plosives. The symbols [ɓ, ɗ] denote voiced bilabial and alveolar implosives respectively. The symbol [ɠ] may be used for a voiced velar implosive, but this sound does not occur in Uduk.

I do not know any simple way of teaching people to make implosives. Some people can learn to make them just by imitating their instructor; others can't. (I, incidentally, was one of the latter group. I did not learn to make implosives until nearly the end of a year studying phonetics.) The best suggestion I can make is to start from a fully voiced plosive. Say [aba], making sure that the voicing continues throughout the closure. Now say this sequence slowly, making the closure last as long as you can while maintaining strong vocal cord vibrations. Release the closure (open the lips) *before* the voicing stops. If you put your fingers on your throat above the larynx while doing this, you will probably be able to feel the larynx moving down during the closure.

There are straightforward mechanical reasons why the larynx moves down in these circumstances. In order to maintain voicing throughout a [b], air must continue to flow through the glottis. But it cannot continue to flow for very long, because while the articulatory position of [b] is being held, the pressure of the air in the vocal tract is continually increasing. In order to keep the vocal cords vibrating, the air in the lungs must be at an appreciably higher pressure than the air in the vocal tract. One of the ways of maintaining the pressure drop across the glottis is to lower the larynx and thus increase the space available in the vocal tract. Consequently, there is a natural tendency when saying a long [b] to lower the larynx. If you try to make a long, fully voiced [b], very forcibly, but opening the lips before the voicing stops, you may end up by producing [ɓ].

Historically, languages seem to develop implosives from plosives that have become more and more voiced. As I mentioned earlier, in many languages voiced implosives are simply allophones of voiced plosives. Often, as in Vietnamese, these languages have voiced plosives that have to be fully voiced in order to keep them distinct from two other sets of plosives that we will discuss in the next section. In languages such as Sindhi for which we have good evidence of the earlier stages of the language, we can clearly see that the present implosives grew out of older voiced plosives in this way, and the present contrasting voiced plosives are due to later influences of neighboring languages.

There is one other airstream mechanism that is used in a few languages. This is the mechanism which is used in producing **clicks**, such as the interjection expressing disapproval or the noise used to signal horses. Another click in common use is the gentle, pursed-lips type of kiss that one might drop on one's grandmother's cheek. Clicks occur in words (in addition to interjections or nonlinguistic gestures) in several African languages. Zulu, for example, has a number of clicks, including one that is very similar to our expression of disapproval.

The easiest click to start studying is the gentle-kiss-with-pursed-lips type. Say this sound while holding a finger lightly along the lips. You should be able to feel that air rushes into the mouth when your lips come apart. Note that while you are making this sound you can continue to breathe in or out through your nose. This is because the back of the tongue is touching the velum, so that the air in the mouth used in making this sound is separated from the airstream flowing in and out of the nose.

Now say the click expressing disapproval. There is no simple way of writing this as an ordinary English word. Authors sometimes write "tsk-tsk" or "tut-tut" when they wish to indicate a click sound; they do not, of course, mean [tɪsk tɪsk] or [tʌt tʌt]. Say a single click of this kind and try to feel how your tongue moves. The estimated positions of the vocal organs in the corresponding Zulu sound are shown in Figure 6.3. At the beginning of this sound there are both dental and velar closures. As a result, the body of air shown in the shaded area in Figure 6.3 is totally enclosed. When the back

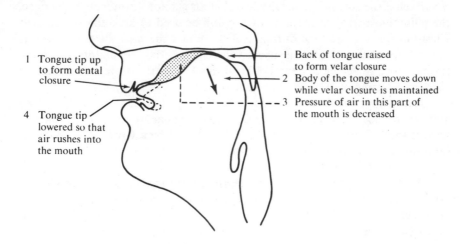

1 Tongue tip up
   to form dental
   closure

4 Tongue tip
   lowered so that
   air rushes into
   the mouth

1 Back of tongue raised
   to form velar closure
2 Body of the tongue moves down
   while velar closure is maintained
3 Pressure of air in this part of
   the mouth is decreased

Figure 6.3 *Estimated sequence of events in a Zulu dental click* [ǀ].

and central parts of the tongue move down, this air becomes rarefied. A click is produced when this partial vacuum is released by lowering the tip of the tongue. The phonetic symbol for a dental click is [ǀ] (an upside-down letter *t*).

Movement of the body of air in the mouth is called a **velaric airstream mechanism**. Clicks are stops made with an ingressive velaric airstream mechanism (as shown in Figure 6.3). It is also possible to use this mechanism to cause the airstream to flow outward by raising the tongue and squeezing the contained body of air, but this latter possibility is not actually used in any known language.

The sound described in Figure 6.3 is a dental click. If the partial vacuum is released by lowering the side of the tongue, a lateral click—the sound sometimes used for encouraging horses—is produced. The phonetic symbol is [ʖ] (a 5 with the top line omitted). Clicks can also be made with the tongue touching the back part of the alveolar ridge. The phonetic symbol for post-alveolar clicks of this kind is [ʗ]. These three possibilities all occur in Zulu and the neighboring language Xhosa. Some of the aboriginal South African languages, such as Hottentot, have an even wider variety of click articulations.

In the production of click sounds there is a velar closure, and the body of air involved is in front of this closure (that is, in the front of the mouth). Consequently, it is possible to produce a velar sound with a glottalic or pulmonic airstream mechanism while a click is being made. You can demonstrate this for yourself by humming continuously while producing clicks. The humming corresponds to a long [ŋ], a voiced velar nasal. We may symbolize the co-occurrence of a nasal and a click by writing a tie-bar [⁀] over the two symbols. Thus a dental click and a velar nasal would be written [ŋ͡ǀ].

Even if the soft palate is raised so that air cannot flow through the nose, the pulmonic airstream mechanism can still be used to keep the vocal cords vibrating for a short time during a click. When the back of the tongue is raised for a click and there is also a velic closure, the articulators are in the position for [g]. A voiced dental click of this kind is therefore a combination of [g] and [ǀ], and may be symbolized [g͡ǀ].

It is perhaps not necessary for a beginning student in phonetics to be able to produce all sorts of different clicks in regular words. But one should be able to produce at least a simple click followed by a vowel. Try saying [ǀ] followed by [a]. Make a vowel as soon after the click as possible, so that it sounds like a single syllable [ǀa].

As a more challenging exercise, learn to produce clicks between vowels. Start by repeating [ǀa] a number of times, so that you are saying [ǀaǀaǀa]. Now say dental, lateral, and post-alveolar clicks in sequences such as [aǀa, aǁa, aʗa]. Make sure that there are no pauses between the vowels and the clicks. Now try to keep the voicing going throughout the sequences, so that you produce [ag͡ǀa, ag͡ǁa, ag͡ʗa]. Last produce nasalized clicks, perhaps with nasalized vowels on either side [ãŋ͡ǀã, ãŋ͡ǁã, ãŋ͡ʗã]. Repeat with other vowels.

The spelling system regularly used in books and newspapers in Zulu and Xhosa employs the letters c, x, q for the dental, lateral, and post-alveolar clicks for which we have been using the symbols [ǀ, ǁ, ʗ] respectively. The name of the language Xhosa should therefore be pronounced with a lateral click at the beginning. The h following the x indicates a short burst of aspiration following the click. Try saying the name of the language with an aspirated lateral click at the beginning. Phonetic transcriptions of some words in Zulu are given in Table 6.3.

Table 6.4 summarizes the principal airstream mechanisms. Note that pulmonic sounds can be voiced or voiceless. Glottalic egressive sounds—ejectives—are always voiceless. Glottalic ingressive sounds—implosives—are nearly always voiced by being combined with a pulmonic egressive airstream, but voiceless glottalic ingressive sounds (voiceless implosives) have been reported in one or two languages. Velaric ingressive sounds (clicks) are

Table 6.3

Contrasting clicks in Zulu. All these items are imperative forms of verbs, all
with the tone pattern low-high.

	Dental	Alveolar lateral	Post-alveolar
Voiceless unaspirated	ǀaǀa climb	ǁoǁa narrate	ǃaǃa explain
Voiced	ɡ͡ǀaɡ͡ǀa dance at wedding	ɡ͡ǁoba pound	ɡ͡ǃoka dress up
Voiced nasal	ŋ͡ǀoŋ͡ǀa gather unripe corn	ŋ͡ǁaŋ͡ǁa coax	ŋ͡ǃala tie tightly

Table 6.4

The principal airstream processes.

Airstream	Direction	Brief description	Specific name for stop consonant	Examples	Vocal cords
Pulmonic	egressive	lung air pushed out under the control of the respiratory muscles.	plosive	p t k b d g	voiceless or voiced
Glottalic	egressive	pharynx air compressed by the upward movement of the closed glottis.	ejective	p' t' k'	voiceless
Glottalic	ingressive	downward movement of the vibrating glottis; pulmonic egressive airstream may also be involved.	implosive	ɓ ɗ ɠ	usually voiced by pulmonic airstream
Velaric	ingressive	mouth air rarefied by the backward and downward movement of the tongue.	click	ǀ ǁ ǃ	combine with pulmonic airstream

combined with pulmonic egressive sounds so that the resulting combination
can be voiced or voiceless. These combinations can also be oral or nasal.

States of the Glottis

So far we have been considering sounds to be either voiceless, with the
vocal cords apart, or voiced, with them nearly together so that they will
vibrate. But in fact the **glottis** (which is defined as the space between the vocal

cords) can assume a number of other shapes. Some of these glottal states are important in the description of other languages.

Photographs of four states of the glottis are shown in Figure 6.4. These

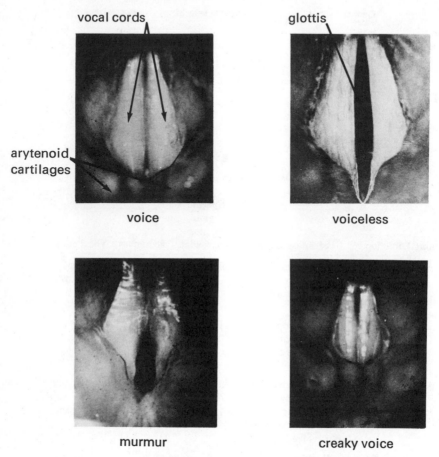

Figure 6.4 *Four states of the glottis.*

photographs were taken by placing a small mirror at the back of the mouth, so that it was possible to look straight down the pharynx towards the larynx. The vocal cords are the white bands running vertically in each picture. Their position can be adjusted by the movements of the arytenoid cartilages, which are underneath the small protuberances visible in the lower part of the pictures.

In a voiced sound the vocal cords are vibrating. In a voiceless sound they are pulled apart so that they cannot be set into vibration by the airstream. Two other intermediate positions are shown in the lower half of Figure 6.4. The position called **murmur**, or **breathy voice**, occurs when the vocal cords are only slightly apart; they can still vibrate, but at the same time a great deal of air passes through the glottis. Murmured sounds are sometimes made as in Figure 6.4 , with the glottis fairly open at one end. They can also be made with a narrower opening extending over nearly the whole length of the vocal cords, so that when they vibrate they do not actually come completely together, but instead appear to be simply flapping in the airstream.

Murmured sounds occur in English in the pronunciation of /h/ in between vowels as in "ahead, behind." In most of the speakers of English I have been able to observe, the /h/ in these words is made with the vocal cords slightly apart along their entire length, but still continuing to vibrate as if they were waving in the breeze. The term "voiced *h*" is sometimes used for this sound, but it is somewhat confusing as there is certainly no voicing in the usual sense. The term "murmured *h*" is preferable. The symbol for this sound is [ɦ].

Learn to distinguish between the murmured sound [ɦ] as in "aha" and the voiceless sound [h] as at the beginning of an English word such as "heart." The murmured sound is like a sigh produced while breathing heavily. Take a deep breath and see how long you can make first [ɦ] and then [h]. In the voiceless sound [h] the air from the lungs escapes very rapidly, so that this sound cannot be prolonged to any great extent. But you can make the murmured sound [ɦ] last much longer, as the flow of air from the lungs is slowed down by the vibrating vocal cords. Note that [ɦ] can be said on a range of different pitches.

Now say [ɦ] before a vowel. When you say [ɦɑ] you will probably find that the breathiness extends into the vowel. But try to make only the first part of the syllable breathy and produce regular voicing at the end. Finally try to produce the sequence [ɦɑ] after a stop consonant. Murmured stops of this kind occur in Hindi and many other languages spoken in India.

In **creaky voice**, which is the other state of the glottis illustrated in Figure 6.4, the arytenoid cartilages are tightly together, so that the vocal cords can vibrate only at the other end. This is a very low pitched sound that occurs at the ends of falling intonations for some speakers of English. You can probably learn to produce it by singing the lowest note that you can— and then trying to go even lower. Creaky-voiced sounds may also be called **laryngealized**.

In some languages laryngealization is used to distinguish one sound from another. Hausa and many other Chadic languages of Northern Nigeria distinguish between two forms of [j]. One has regular voicing, rather like the English sound at the beginning of "yacht," and the other has creaky voice. There is no IPA diacritic to indicate the use of creaky voice, but I have sometimes used [̰] placed under the symbol. Hausa orthography uses an apostrophe (') before the symbol for the corresponding voiced sound, thus contrasting *y* and *'y*. The Hausa letter *y* corresponds to IPA [j]. Try differentiating between the laryngealized and nonlaryngealized sounds in the Hausa words "'ya'ya" (children) and "yaro" (boy).

A slightly more common use of laryngealization is to distinguish one stop from another. Hausa and many other West African languages have voiced stops [b, d] contrasting with laryngealized stops [ɓ, ɗ]. In these sounds the creaky voice is most evident not during the stop closure itself but during the first part of the following vowel. Similar sounds occur in some American Indian languages.

Voice Onset Time

We saw earlier that the terms voiced and voiceless refer to the state of the glottis during a given articulation. We also saw that the terms aspirated and unaspirated refer to the presence or absence of a period of voicelessness during and after the release of an articulation. The combinations of these terms specify the voice onset time—that is, the moment at which the voicing starts relative to the release of a closure. This point can be explained most easily by reference to the diagram in Figure 6.5. The top line indicates the

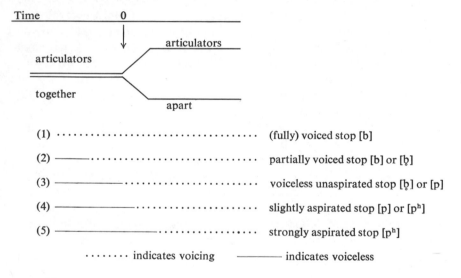

Figure 6.5   *A diagrammatic representation of stops differentiated by voice onset time.*

position of two articulators, such as the lips. They begin together, and at a moment marked time 0, they come apart. The remaining lines indicate five different voice onset times. In (1) the dotted line indicates that the vocal cords are vibrating throughout the closure, the release, and the whole of the following sound, which might be a vowel, such as [ɑ]. This is a diagram for a syllable beginning with a (fully) voiced stop. The next example, (2), begins with a straight line that is used to symbolize a voiceless position of the vocal cords. This example indicates a partially voiced stop in which the vocal cords are vibrating during only part of the closure. In (3) the stop itself is completely voiceless, but the voicing starts at the moment of release of the closure. This is therefore a voiceless stop; and, since there is no period of voicelessness after the release, it is also an unaspirated stop. In (4) and (5) the voicing starts slightly and considerably after the release of the closure. These voiceless stops may therefore be called slightly and considerably aspirated stops.

Some of the sounds shown in Figure 6.5 can be symbolized in more than one way. As often, the choice of symbol depends in part on the reason for making the transcription. In broad transcriptions of English it is sufficient just to use [b, p]. But if one wants to show more phonetic detail, one can specify that the phoneme /b/ is a voiceless [b̥] in, for instance, "*That* boy" [ˈðæʔtb̥ɔɪ] in my English. Similarly one might, or might not, want to show phonetic details such as the aspiration of /p/ which occurs in "pie" [pʰaɪ], but not in "spy" [spaɪ].

Obviously there is a continuum of possible voice onset times. I could have drawn any number of lines just as easily as five. Different languages choose different points along this continuum in forming oppositions among stop consonants. This point is illustrated in Figure 6.6, in which the rows are numbered in the same way as in Figure 6.5, and some of the possibilities that

(fully) voiced	(1) English initial /b/	French /b/		Thai /b/
partially voiced	(2)			
voiceless unaspirated	(3) English /p/ after initial /s/	French /p/	Gaelic /b/	Thai /p/
(voiceless) aspirated	(4) English stressed initial /p/			Thai /pʰ/
(voiceless) strongly aspirated	(5)		Gaelic /p/	

Figure 6.6 *Differences in voice onset time in different languages on a scale equivalent to that shown in Figure 6.5.*

occur in different languages are shown with reference to this scale. English stops at the beginning of an utterance usually have voice onset timings similar to those in (2) and (4). But English stops after initial /s/ (as in "spy, sty, sky") have voice onset timing as in (3). French and Spanish typically use timings more like those in (1) and (3). Gaelic corresponds more to the timings in (3) and (5). What counts in Gaelic as /b/ is more or less the same as what counts in Spanish as /p/. Some languages contrast three different voice onset times. Thai has voiced, voiceless unaspirated, and aspirated stops, corresponding roughly to (1), (3), and (4). Additional examples are given in Table 6.5.

Table 6.5

Stops in Thai.

Voiced	bàa	shoulder	dam	black		
Voiceless unaspirated	pàa	forest	tam	to pound	kàt	to bite
Aspirated stops	pʰàa	to split	tʰam	to do	kʰàt	to interrupt

Many Indian languages, such as Hindi, have not only the three possibilities that occur in Thai, but also murmured stops as well. When murmur (breathy voice) occurs on stop consonants, it often extends into the adjacent vowel. In the Hindi murmured stops, the vocal cords are in the position for murmur during the closure. After the release of the closure there is a period of murmur before the regular voicing starts. Some illustrative Hindi words are given in Table 6.6.

Table 6.6

Hindi stop consonants.

	Voiceless unaspirated	Voiceless aspirated	Voiced	Breathy voiced
bilabial	pal (take care of)	pʰal (edge of knife)	bal (hair)	bɦal (forehead)
dental	t̪an (mode of singing)	t̪ʰan (roll of cloth)	d̪an (charity)	d̪ɦan (paddy)
retroflex	ʈal (postpone)	ʈʰal (place for buying wood)	ɖal (branch)	ɖɦal (shield)
post-alveolar affricate	tʃəl (go)	tʃʰəl (deceit)	dʒəl (water)	dʒɦəl (glimmer)
velar	kan (ear)	kʰan (mine)	gan (song)	gɦan (kind of bundle)

The Hindi murmured stops are sometimes called voiced aspirated sounds. But this is not a very good name for them, as they are neither voiced (in the sense of having regular vibrations of the vocal cords) nor aspirated (in the sense of having a period of voicelessness during and after the release of the closure). The voice onset time of these sounds cannot be represented on a diagram as in Figure 6.5 without some indication that the state of the glottis during the closure and the release is neither voiced nor voiceless but murmured. There is no IPA diacritic for murmur. I have used [..] underneath the symbol for the voiced sound to indicate murmur during the stop and have marked the murmur that occurs after the release of the stop by a raised [ʰ].

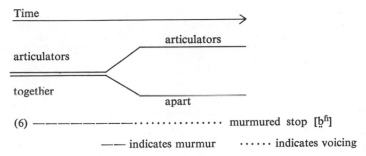

Figure 6.7 *A diagrammatic representation of the voice onset time of a murmured stop.*

Hindi has stops corresponding to lines (1), (3), and (5) of Figure 6.5 and (6) of Figure 6.7.

Learn to produce a series of sounds with different voice onset times. Start by producing fully voiced stops [b, d, g]. See how long you can make the voicing continue during each of these sounds. You will find that you can make it last longer during [b] than during [d] or [g] because in [b] there is a fairly large space above the glottis. Air from the lungs can flow through the glottis for a relatively longer period of time before the pressure above the glottis begins to approach that of the air in the lungs. The vocal cords can be kept vibrating throughout this period. But in [g] there is only a small space above the glottis into which air can flow, so that the voicing can be maintained only briefly. Languages often fail to have fully voiced velar stops. Note that Thai does not have a voiced stop contrasting with a voiceless unaspirated stop at this place of articulation.

When you can produce fully voiced stops satisfactorily try saying voiceless unaspirated [p, t, k]. You may find it easiest to start with words like "spy, sty, sky." Say these words very slowly. Now say words like them, but without the initial [s].

You will have less difficulty in making aspirated stops, because they occur in most forms of English—in words such as "pie" [pʰaɪ] and "tie" [tʰaɪ]. But do try pronouncing all of the Thai and Hindi words in Tables 6.5 and 6.6.

EXERCISES

A Label the diagram below so as to show the sequence of events involved in producing a voiced alveolar implosive.

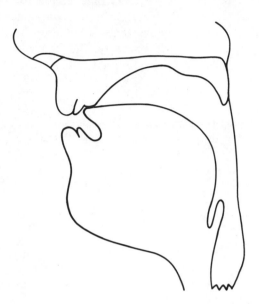

B Complete the diagram below so as to show the positions of the vocal organs in producing [ŋ͡ɔ]. Add labels so that the sequence of events is clear.

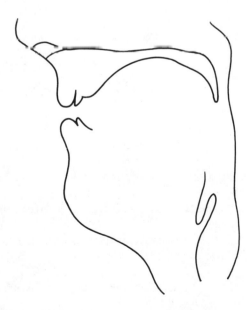

C The diagram below shows the timing of the opening and closing of the lips in the phrase "You may pamper a baby puppy." In the space beneath the transcription, show the states of the glottis that occur. Use a straight line to indicate periods of voicelessness, a dotted line to indicate voicing. Indicate the voice onset time relative to the lip movements as carefully as you can. (In this and the following question, the relative timing of the articulatory movements is based on instrumental records and has been shown fairly precisely. But the relative size of each movement is shown merely diagrammatically.)

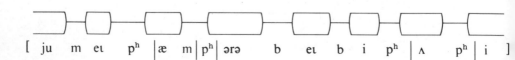

[ju   m eɪ   pʰ │æ m│pʰ│ərə   b   eɪ   b   i   pʰ│ʌ   pʰ│ i]

D Repeat exercise **C** with the phrase "He started to tidy it," but in this case begin by transcribing the phrase. Then add lines beneath the transcription to represent the state of the glottis. (The answer to this question will depend to some extent on the accent of the speaker.)

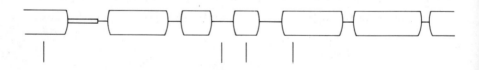

E Fill in the blanks in the following passage.

There are three principal airstream mechanisms: the_____ airstream mechanism, the _____ airstream mechanism, and the _____ airstream mechanism. In normal utterances in all the languages of the world, the airstream is always flowing outwards if the _____ airstream mechanism is involved. Stops made with this mechanism are called _____. The only mechanism that is used in some languages to produce some sounds with inward

going air and some sounds with outward going air is the _____ airstream mechanism. Stops made with this mechanism acting ingres-

sively are called _____. Stops made with this mechanism

acting egressively are called _____. The mechanism which is used in language to produce sounds only with inward going air is the

_____ airstream mechanism. Stops made with this mecha-

nism are called _____.

Stops may vary in their voice onset time. In this respect, [b, d, g]

are _____ stops, [p, t, k] are _____ stops, and

[pʰ, tʰ, kʰ] are _____ stops. The stops [bɦ, dɦ, gɦ], which

occur in Hindi, are called _____ stops. The stops [ɓ, ɗ],

which occur in African languages such as Hausa, are called _____ stops.

F Make a systematic phonetic transcription of your normal pronunciation of the following passage.

The leading phonetician during the

[_____ _____]
first half of the twentieth century

[_____]
was Daniel Jones, who started

[_____]
teaching in 1907 and retired as

[_____]1907[_____]
Professor of Phonetics, University

[_____]

College, London, in 1949. He was

[—————————————————————]1949[—————————
president of the International

[—————————————————————————————————
Phonetic Association from 1950 till

[———————————————————————]1950[——————
his death in 1967 at the age of

[—————————————————]1967[————————————
eighty-six. His numerous publications,

[—————————————————————————————————
particularly those on the pronunciation

[—————————————————————————————— ————
of the British accent known as RP,

[—————————————————————————————————
served as models for phoneticians

[—————————————————————————————————
all over the world. His influence

[—————————————————————————————————
can be seen in the phonetic aspects

[—————————————————————————————————
of the work of American linguists

[—————————————————————————————————
such as Leonard Bloomfield, Bernard

[—————————————————————————————————
Bloch, and many other leading figures

[blɑk————————————————————————————
in the period before the recent work

[—————————————————————————————————
of Chomsky and Halle.

[——————— ˈtʃɑmski ——————— ˈhælɪt] ——————————

PERFORMANCE EXERCISES

There were a large number of non-English sounds discussed in this chapter. About the same number of additional sounds will be considered in the following chapter. Beginning with the exercises given below, you should spend more time doing practical phonetic work. Try to double the time you spend doing work of this kind. If possible you should spend about twenty minutes a day working with a partner reviewing the material in the chapter and going through the exercises given below.

A   Review the different types of phonation. Start by simply differentiating voiced and voiceless sounds, saying:

      (1) [aaa̯g̊g̊aaa̯g̊g̊]

Now add breathy voiced (murmured) sounds to the sequence:

      (2) [aaa̤g̈g̈g̈g̈]

Next add creaky voiced (laryngealized) sounds:

      (3) [g̰g̰aaa̰g̰g̰g̰g̰]

Then make the sequence begin with a glottal stop:

      (4) [ʔg̰g̰aaa̰g̰g̰g̰g̰]

Finally practice saying this sequence in the reverse order:

      (5) [g̰g̰g̰g̰aaa̰g̰g̰ʔ]

B   Try to go in one smooth movement through all these states of the glottis, saying, fairly quickly:

      (1) [ʔg̰ag̈g̊]

and the reverse sequence:

      (2) [g̊g̈ag̰ʔ]

C   Repeat exercises **A** and **B** slowly, quickly, reversed, etc., with other articulations, for example:

      (1) [ʔm̰mm̤m̥]
      (2) [ʔn̰nn̤n̥]
      (3) [ʔŋ̰ŋŋ̤ŋ̥]
      (4) [ʔl̰ll̤l̥]
      (5) [ʔj̰jj̤j̥]

D   Try to superimpose breathy voice (murmur) onto intervocalic consonants, saying:

    [am̤a, an̤a, al̤a]

Do not worry if the breathy voice is also evident on the adjacent vowels.

E   Now try adding breathy voice to stops. The release of the closure should be followed by a period of murmur extending into the vowel:

    [abʱa, adʱa, agʱa]

F   Similarly add creaky voice (laryngealization) to intervocalic consonants, saying:

    [am̰a, an̰a, al̰a]

G Then produce stops with creaky voice (laryngealization):
[aḇa, aḏa, aga]
Again, do not worry if the creaky voice is most evident in the adjacent vowels.

H Say [aba], making sure that you have a fully voiced intervocalic stop. Now repeat this sequence a number of times, each time increasing the length of the consonant closure. Try to make the consonant closure as long as you can while maintaining the voicing.

I Repeat exercise **H** with the sequences [ada] and [aga].

J Produce long, fully voiced stops before vowels: [ba, da, ga]. Make sure that there is a velic closure, and that you are *not* saying [mba, nda, ŋga] but are correctly saying a long, fully voiced, oral stop.

K Produce voiceless unaspirated stops before vowels: [pa, ta, ka]. You may find it helpful to imagine that there is a preceding [s] as in "spar, star, scar."

L Say a series of stops with more aspiration than usual: [pʰa, tʰa, kʰa]. Make sure that there is a really long period of voicelessness after the release of the closure and before the start of the vowel.

M Practice saying sequences of voiced, voiceless unaspirated, and aspirated plosives: [ba, pa, pʰa], [da, ta, tʰa], and [ga, ka, kʰa].

N Try to produce as many intermediate stages as you can in each of these series. You should be able to produce each series with

    (1) a long, fully voiced, stop.
    (2) a slightly less long, partially voiced stop.
    (3) a completely voiceless, but unaspirated stop.
    (4) a slightly aspirated stop.
    (5) a strongly aspirated stop.

O Practice these exercises until you are certain that you can reliably produce a distinction between at least (1) voiced, (2) voiceless unaspirated, and (3) aspirated stops at each place of articulation.

P Extend this series by beginning with a laryngealized stop and ending with a murmured stop. Say:

(1)		(2)		(3)	
	ḇa		ḏa		ga̰
	ba		da		ga
	pa		ta		ka
	pʰa		tʰa		kʰa
	ḇʱa		ḏʱa		ga̰ʱa

Q Incorporate all these sounds into simple series of nonsense words. If you are making up your own series to say to someone else, do not make them too difficult. Try saying something like the following:

	(1)	(2)	(3)
	ˈtemas	ˈbɛkal	ˈgodeŋ
	ˈdemas	ˈbɦɛgal	ˈgɦoteŋ
	ˈtʰemas	ˈpʰɛkʰal	ˈkotʰeŋ
	ˈḍemas	ˈb̰egal	ˈkʰodeŋ
	ˈdɦemas	ˈpɛb̰ɦal	ˈgodɦeŋ

R Review the description of ejectives. When making an ejective you should be able to *feel* that you (1) make an articulatory closure (for example, bringing your lips together); (2) make a glottal stop (feel that you are holding your breath by closing your glottis); (3) raise the larynx (place your fingers on your throat to feel this movement); (4) release the articulatory closure (open your lips); and (5) release the glottal closure (let go of your breath).

S If you cannot produce the sequences [pʼa, tʼa, kʼa] re-read the section on ejectives in hope of finding some useful hints that might help you.

T Review the description of voiced implosives. Starting from a fully voiced stop, try to feel the downward movement of your larynx. Try to say [ɓa, ɗa, ɠa].

U Review the description of clicks. Try to say [ʄa, ʖa, ʘa].

V Incorporate all these sounds into simple series of nonsense words such as:

ˈpʼetag	ˈgopetʼ	ˈʄoko
ˈɗeɗuk	ˈtiɓʼuk	ˈkʼoʈo
ˈpetʼak	ˈbagʼod	ˈɓeʃa
ˈɓedag	ˈɗukapʼ	ˈʘaʈo
ˈkʼebap	ˈtʼedugʼ	ˈtʼiʈi

Place and Manner of Articulation 7

There is a wide variety of consonants in the languages of the world. The places of articulation employed in speaking English do not represent all of the possibilities. Different manners of articulation also occur in other languages. This chapter will consider the place and manner of articulation of a number of different consonants.

Places of Articulation

Most of the possible places of articulation that are used in the languages of the world were defined in Chapter 1. Figure 7.1 is the same as Figure 1.5 except for the inclusion of arrows indicating two additional places that will be discussed below. The terms for all the places of articulation are not just names for particular locations on the roof of the mouth. As is indicated by the numbered arrows, each term specifies two things: first, the part of the upper surface of the vocal tract that is involved, and second, the articulator on the lower surface that is involved.

There are a large number of non-English sounds to be found in other languages, but the majority of them involve using different manners of articulation at the same places of articulation as in English. We will illustrate this point by considering how each place of articulation is used in English and other languages for making stops, nasals, and fricatives. The numbers in the following paragraphs refer to the numbered arrows in Figure 7.1.

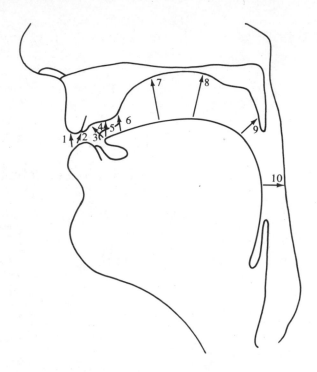

Figure 7.1   *Places of articulation.*

(1) English has bilabial stops and nasals [p, b, m] but no bilabial fricatives. When these fricatives do occur in English, they are simply allophones of the labiodental sounds [f, v]. But in some languages (for example, Ewe of West Africa) bilabial fricatives contrast with labiodental fricatives. The symbols for the voiceless and voiced bilabial fricatives are [ɸ, β]. These sounds are pronounced by bringing the two lips nearly together, so that there is only a slit between them. In Ewe the name of the language itself is [èβè], whereas the word for "two" is [èvè]. Try to pronounce these contrasting words yourself. Note also the contrast between voiceless bilabial and labiodental fricatives in the Ewe words [éɸá], "he polished," and [éfá], "he was cold."

(2) Many languages are like English in having the labiodental fricatives [f, v]. But no language has labiodental stops or nasals except as allophones of the corresponding bilabial sounds. In English a labiodental nasal may occur when /m/ occurs before /f/, as in "emphasis" or "symphony." Say these words in a normal conversational style and see if your lower lip ever contacts your upper lip during the nasal.

Some languages have affricates in which the bilabial stop is released into a labiodental fricative. Practice these sounds by learning to say the German words "Pfanne" [ˈpfanə] (bowl) and "Pflug" [pfluk] (plough).

(3) In English there are dental fricatives [θ, ð] but no dental stops or nasals except allophonically. Yet some languages, such as French and Italian, have dental stops and nasals in most circumstances. In these languages [t̪, d̪, n̪] are not just coarticulated allophones that occur only before [θ, ð] as in English. There are even some languages (for example, Malayalam, a Dravidian language spoken in Southern India) that contrast dental stops and nasals with alveolar stops and nasals, as shown in Table 7.1.

Table 7.1

Contrasts involving bilabial, dental, alveolar, retroflex, palatal, and velar places of articulation in Malayalam, illustrating the necessity for six points of articulation. Dental articulations are indicated by a subscript of the form [‿]. Retroflex articulations are indicated by a subscript dot [.].

Bilabial	Dental	Alveolar	Retroflex	Palatal	Velar
	muṯṯu pearl	muttu density	muṭṭu knee		
	kuṯṯɪ stabbed	kuttɪ peg	kuṭṭɪ child		
kʌmmi shortage	pʌṉṉi pig	kʌnni Virgo	kʌṇṇi link in chain	kʌɲɲi boiled rice and water	kʌŋŋi crushed
	eṉṉʌ named	enne me	eṇṇʌ oil	teːɲɲʌ worn out	teːŋŋʌ coconut

(4) Alveolar stops, nasals, and fricatives all occur in English and in many other languages. They need no further comment here.

(5) Retroflex stops, nasals, and fricatives do not occur in most forms of English. The outstanding exception is the English spoken in India. Retroflex sounds are made by curling the tip of the tongue up and back so that the underside touches or approaches the back part of the alveolar ridge. They may be indicated by adding a subscript [.] beneath the corresponding alveolar symbol, forming the symbols [ṭ, ḍ, ṇ]. The symbols that have been traditionally used by IPA for retroflex sounds include [ʈ, ɖ, ɳ]. Remember that, just as dental is a separate place of articulation that can be symbolized by adding [‿] to the alveolar symbol, so also retroflex is considered to be a separate *place* of articulation. This is a somewhat confusing notion in that the term retroflex specifies a particular gesture of the tongue, and one might imagine that it describes how a sound is made (its manner of articulation) rather than where it is made (its place of articulation). But in fact retroflex is a place of articulation like dental and alveolar. At each of these places of articulation it is possible to produce stops, nasals, fricatives, and sounds made with other manners of articulation. As you can see from the data in Table 7.1, languages such as Malayalam actually contrast both stops and nasals at each of the three places of articulation—dental, alveolar, and retroflex. In addition,

Malayalam has bilabial, palatal, and velar sounds, so that it has contrasts between nasals at six places of articulation, all of which are exemplified in Table 7.1.

Because the undersurface of the tip of the tongue is touching the back of the alveolar ridge, the blade (the upper surface of the tip) of the tongue is usually a considerable distance from the roof of the mouth. As a result the tongue is somewhat hollowed, as shown in the diagram of a retroflex fricative [ʂ] in Figure 7.2. Try making this sound yourself. Start with [s] in which the

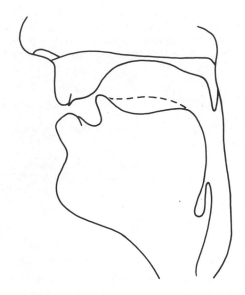

Figure 7.2 *The articulation of the retroflex fricative* [ʂ]. *The dashed lines indicate the position of the sides of the tongue.*

tip of the tongue is raised towards the front part of the alveolar ridge. Now, while maintaining the fricative noise, slowly slide the tongue back, and curl up the tip. The result should sound something like [ʃ], although the articulatory position is different. (See (6) below for discussion of the articulatory position of [ʃ].)

When you have learned to say [ʂ], try adding voice so that you produce [ʐ]. Alternate the voiced and voiceless sounds [ʂʂʂʐʐʐʂʂʂʐʐʐ]. Next, still with the tip of the tongue curled up and back in this position, make the stops [ʈa, ɖa]. Notice how the stops affect the quality of the following vowel, giving it a sort of *r*-coloring at the beginning. Now produce the corresponding nasal [ɳ]. Learn to say all these sounds before and after different vowels. Finally, try to say the Malayalam words in the first three lines of Table 7.1. Retroflex stops and nasals occur in many of the major languages of India and retroflex fricatives are not at all uncommon.

(6) The palato-alveolar sounds [ʃ, ʒ] differ from retroflex sounds in the part of the tongue involved. In palato-alveolar sounds the upper surface of the tip of the tongue is near the roof of the mouth. In addition, the front of the tongue is slightly domed, as opposed to being hollowed. At this point you should compare Figure 1.8, which shows the position of the vocal organs in the palato-alveolar fricative [ʃ] as in "shy," with Figure 7.2. Note that in both [ʂ] and [ʃ] the maximum constriction of the vocal tract occurs near the back of the alveolar ridge. But these two sounds are said to have different places of articulation, because the terms specifying place of articulation designate both what part of the roof of the mouth is involved and what part of the tongue is involved. In retroflex sounds the underside of the tip of the tongue forms the articulation, but in palato-alveolar sounds the articulation is made by the upper surface of the tip of the tongue.

In English the only palato-alveolar sounds are the fricatives and affricates [ʃ, ʒ, tʃ, dʒ]. In other languages there are stops and nasals made in either the same or in a very similar position. They are often, arbitrarily, considered to be palatal sounds.

(7) Palatal sounds can be defined as being made with the front of the tongue approaching or touching the hard palate. But there is no clear cut distinction between these sounds and palato-alveolar sounds. The only true palatal in English is /j/, which is usually an approximant but may be allophonically a voiceless fricative in words such as "hue." The symbol for a voiceless palatal fricative is [ç], so this word may be transcribed phonemically as /hju/ and phonetically as [çu]. Voiceless palatal fricatives occur in German in words such as "ich" [ɪç], meaning "I," and "nicht" [nɪçt], meaning "not."

Say [ç] as in "hue" and then try to prolong this sound. Add voice so that you make a fricative something like the [j] as in "you," but with the front of the tongue nearer the hard palate. The symbol [j] is used for both a palatal fricative and a palatal approximant. While saying [ççjjjçççjjj], make sure that the tip of the tongue is down behind the lower front teeth. Now change the fricative [ç] into a stop by raising the front of the tongue still more, while keeping the tip of the tongue down. The symbols for voiceless and voiced palatal stops are [c,ɟ]. Say sequences such as [aca] and [aɟa], making sure that the front of your tongue touches the hard palate. Then try making similar sequences with a palatal nasal (for which the symbol is [ɲ], reminding one of [n] and [j] combined).

Palatal nasals occur in several languages, including French, Italian, Spanish, and many non-Indo-European languages. Try saying French words such as "agneau" [aɲo] (lamb) and Spanish words such as "Señor" [seˈɲor] (Mr.).

Palatal stops are only slightly less common. They occur, for example, in Modern Greek and in the Akan languages of Ghana. Because of the shape of the roof of the mouth, the contact between the front of the tongue and the hard palate often extends over a fairly large area. As a result, the formation and release of a palatal stop is often not as rapid as in the case of other stops, and they tend to become affricates.

(8) Velar stops and nasals [k, g, ŋ] occur in English. But unlike other languages such as German, we no longer have velar fricatives. They are not, however, hard to make. Starting from a syllable such as [ak], build up pressure behind the velar closure, and then lower the tongue slightly. The result will be a voiceless velar fricative, which we write as [x]. The symbol for the corresponding voiced sound is [ɣ]. As with other fricatives, learn to say [xxxɣɣɣxxx]. Then produce sequences such as [axa, exe, oɣo, ɛɣɛ].

Examples of words in other languages containing velar fricatives are: German "achtung" [ˈʔaxtɒŋ] (warning), "Bach" [bax] (Bach; proper name); and Spanish "jamás" [xaˈmas] (never), "ojo" [ˈoxo] (eye), "pago" [ˈpaɣo] (I pay), "diga" [ˈdiɣa] (speak!). The Spanish [ɣ] is often not very fricative, and more like an approximant.

(9) Uvular sounds are made by raising the back of the tongue towards the uvula. They do not occur at all in most forms of English. But in French a voiced uvular fricative—[ʁ]—is the common form of *r* in words such as "rouge" [ʁuʒ] (red) and "rose" [ʁoz] (rose). The voiceless uvular fricative, [χ], also occurs in French as an allophone of /ʁ/ after voiceless stops, as in "lettre" [lɛtχ] (letter). French differs from English in that it often has perseverative assimilations in which, for example, the voicelessness of one sound continues on through the following sound.

Uvular stops, written [q, ɢ], and nasals, written [N], occur in Eskimo and other American Indian languages. Table 7.2 illustrates contrasts between uvular, velar, and palatal stops in Quechua, an American Indian language widely spoken in Bolivia, Chile, and Peru. Note that Quechua has voiceless unaspirated plosives, aspirated plosives, and ejectives.

Table 7.2

Contrasts involving palatal, velar, and uvular stops in Quechua.

Palatal	Velar	Uvular
caka	kara	qara
bridge	expensive	skin
c'ici	k'icij	q'acu
dirty	pinch	grass

One way of learning to produce uvular sounds is to start from a voiceless velar fricative [x]. While making this sound slide your tongue slightly further back in your mouth so that it is close to the uvula. The result will be the voiceless uvular fricative [χ]. Learn to make this sound before and after vowels, in sequences such as [axa, oxo, uxu]. You will find it easier to use back vowels at first, then go on to sequences such as [exe, ixi]. Next add voice to this sound, saying [χχχʁʁʁχχχʁʁʁ]. Practice saying [ʁ] before and after vowels. Try saying the French words cited in the first paragraph of this section.

Once you have mastered the pronunciation of uvular fricatives, try changing them into uvular stops. Say [aχa], then make a stop at the same place of articulation, saying [aqa]. Now produce a voiced uvular stop [aɢa] and a uvular nasal [aɴa]. Practice all these sounds before and after different vowels.

(10) Pharyngeal sounds are produced by pulling the root of the tongue back towards the back wall of the pharynx. Most people cannot make a stop at this position. Furthermore, it would be literally impossible to make a pharyngeal nasal, for closure at that point would prevent the airstream from coming through the nose. But pharyngeal fricatives, shown by the symbols [ħ, ʕ], can be made, and they do in fact occur in Semitic languages such as Arabic. The Arabic word for "bath" is [ħammaam], for "uncle," [ʕamm]. The voiced pharyngeal fricative [ʕ] usually has a great deal of laryngealization (creaky voice), perhaps because the necessary constriction in the pharynx also causes a constriction in the larynx.

The sounds [ħ, ʕ] are fairly difficult to learn to pronounce. Try pulling the root of your tongue as far back as possible, and producing the voiceless sound [ħ]. Now, if you can, produce this sound before a vowel. Next try to make the voiced sound [ʕ], not worrying if it turns out to have creaky voice. Produce these sounds in the Arabic words cited above.

Before finishing this section on places of articulation, we must note that some sounds involve the simultaneous use of two places of articulation. The English approximant [w] has both an approximation of the lips (making it a bilabial sound) and of the back of the tongue and the soft palate (making it a velar sound). Sounds that involve these two articulations are called **labial velars**, or **labiovelars**.

Yoruba, Ewe, Akan, and many other languages spoken in West Africa have labial velar stops. Some of the languages spoken in this area also have labial velar nasals. As in the case of nasal and voiced clicks, we symbolize two co-occurring articulations with a tie-bar joining two symbols. The Yoruba for "arm" is [ak͡pá] and for "old" is [àg͡bà]. In these words the two closures occur almost simultaneously.

There is another complication in the production of these sounds in Yoruba and in most West African languages that have labial velar stops or nasals. During the labial and velar closures the back of the tongue moves slightly farther back, creating a slight suction effect as in a click. Thus the stops [k͡p, g͡b] and the nasal [ŋ͡m] often have a weak velaric ingressive mechanism, so they can be classified as voiceless or voiced or nasal bilabial clicks. One of the best ways of learning to say these sounds is to start by making a bilabial click (a kissing sound) in between vowels. Say [a](kiss)[a] at first slowly, and then as fast as you can. Then weaken the suction component of the kiss, so that you are making little more than a labial velar articulation between vowels. The result should be a labial velar stop much as in the Yoruba word [ak͡pá], "arm."

This is a convenient place to review all the places of articulation we have discussed so far. Table 7.3 is a consonant chart showing the symbols for all the nasals, stops, and fricatives that have been mentioned, except for the stops with double articulations. Check that you know the values of all these symbols.

Table 7.3

Symbols for nasals, stops, and fricatives. As in all consonant charts, when there are two symbols within a single cell, the one on the left indicates a voiceless sound. Note also the possibility of double articulations as in the labial velars [k͡p, g͡b, ŋ͡m].

	bilabial	labiodental	dental	alveolar	retroflex	palato-alveolar	palatal	velar	uvular	pharyngeal
nasal	m		n̪	n	ɳ		ɲ	ŋ	N	
stop	p b		t̪ d̪	t d	ʈ ɖ		c ɟ	k g	q ɢ	
fricative	Φ β	f v	θ ð	s z	ʂ ʐ	ʃ ʒ	ç j	x ɣ	χ ʁ	ħ ʕ

Manners of Articulation

Stops

We can begin our consideration of the different manners of articulation that occur in the languages of the world by reviewing what has been said already about stop consonants. Table 7.4 illustrates a number of different types of stops, most of which have been discussed earlier in this book. The first seven possibilities were discussed in Chapter 6. Make sure that you understand all these terms, and know what all these stops sound like, even if you cannot make them all yourself.

The only comment on these first seven sounds that it is necessary to add here—where they are all listed together—is that no language distinguishes between (5), an implosive [ɓ], and (6), a laryngealized (creaky voiced) [b̰]. Certain languages have the one sound, and others the other. In a few languages both sounds occur as allophones or as free variants of the same phoneme. They have not been found in contrast with one another.

Stops with nasal release, the eighth possibility listed in Table 7.4, were discussed in relation to English in Chapter 3. Nasal plosion occurs in English at the ends of words, such as "hidden, sudden." In some languages, however, it can occur at the beginning of a word. Try to say the Russian word for "bottom," which is [dno].

Table 7.4

Examples of stop consonants.

Description	Symbol	Example	
1. voiced	b	bənu	(Sindhi "forest")
2. voiceless unaspirated	p	pənu	(Sindhi "leaf")
3. aspirated	pʰ	pʰənu	(Sindhi "snake hood")
4. murmured (breathy)	b̤ɦ	b̤ɦənəṇu	(Sindhi "lamentation")
5. implosive	ɓ	ɓəni	(Sindhi "curse")
6. laryngealized (creaky)	b̰	b̰áábḛ̀	(Hausa "quarrel," *vb*.)
7. ejective	k'	k'ààkà	(Hausa "how")
8. nasal release	dn	dno	(Russian "bottom")
9. prenasalized	nd	ndizi	(Swahili "banana")
10. lateral release	tɬ	tɬàh	(Navaho "oil")
11. ejective lateral release	tɬ'	tɬ'ée?	(Navaho "night")
12. affricate	ts	tsait	(German "time")
13. ejective affricate	ts'	ts'áal	(Navaho "cradle")

The next possibility listed in Table 7.4 is the prenasalized stop [ⁿd], which is in some senses the reverse of a nasally released stop. In a prenasalized stop the oral closure—in this case the alveolar closure—is formed first, while the soft palate is lowered. Then there is a short nasal consonant, after which the soft palate is raised so that there is a stop. This stop is released by removing the oral closure (in this case by lowering the tongue tip) while the soft palate remains raised. Prenasalized stops occur in many African languages. Additional words for practice are given in Table 7.5. When you try to make these sounds, be careful not to make the initial nasal component into a separate syllable. Make it as short as possible.

Table 7.5

Prenasalized stops in Margi, a language spoken in Northern Nigeria.

mpà	"fight"	mbà	"tie"
ntà	"split"	ndàl	"throw"
ntsàntsà	"shouted"	ndzə̀ndzə̀ʔbɔ́	"covered"
ntʃà	"point at"	ndʒà	"open wide"
ɲcàhɔ̀	"break"	ɲɟárí	"leave"

Stops with lateral release (see (10) in Table 7.4) were also discussed in relation to their occurrence in English (for example, in "little, ladle"). In other languages they too can occur initially in a word. Sometimes, as indicated by (11) in Table 7.4, laterally released stops can occur with an ejective airstream mechanism. On these occasions the stop closure for [t] is formed, the glottalic egressive (ejective) airstream mechanism is set in motion, and then the stop is released laterally by lowering the sides of the tongue.

The only affricates that can occur initially in most forms of English are [tʃ, dʒ]. Some dialects (e.g., London Cockney) have a slightly affricated stop of a kind that might be written [tˢ] in words such as "tea"[tˢəi]. Alveolar affricates also occur in German, as shown in (12) in Table 7.4. Remember that German has a bilabial affricate [pf], as in "Pflug" [pfluk] (plough). Affricates can also occur with an ejective airstream mechanism. Example (13) in Table 7.4 is from an American Indian language, Navaho, which in addition to the ejective [ts'], also has the affricate [ts] made with a pulmonic airstream mechanism as in German.

Nasals

We will now consider the other manners of articulation that are used in the languages of the world. There is little more that need be said about nasals. We have already seen that, like stops, they can occur voiced or voiceless (for example, in Burmese). But as voiceless nasals are comparatively rare, they are symbolized simply by adding the voiceless diacritic [₀] under the symbol for the voiced sound. There are no special symbols for voiceless nasals.

Fricatives

There are two ways to produce the rough, turbulent flow that occurs in the airstream during a fricative. It may be just the result of the air passing through a narrow gap, as in the formation of [f]. Or it may be due to the airstream first becoming speeded up by being forced through a narrow gap and then being directed over a sharp edge, such as the teeth, as in the production of [s]. Partly because there are these two possible mechanisms, the total number of different fricatives that have been observed is larger than the number of stops or the number of nasals. In Table 7.3 there are ten pairs of fricative symbols, in comparison with seven pairs of stop symbols and seven nasal symbols.

So far, we have classified fricatives as being voiced or voiceless and as being made at a number of different places of articulation. But we can also subdivide fricatives in accordance with their manner of production. Some authorities have divided fricatives into those such as [s], in which the tongue is grooved so that the airstream comes out through a narrow channel, and those such as [θ], in which the tongue is flat and forms a wide slit through which the air flows. Unfortunately, not enough is known about fricatives to be sure how this distinction should be applied in all cases. It is also clearly irrelevant for fricatives made with the lips and the back of the tongue.

A slightly better way of dividing fricatives is to separate them into groups on a purely auditory basis. Say the English voiceless fricatives [f, θ, s, ʃ]. Which two have the loudest high pitches? You should be able to hear that [s, ʃ] differ from [f, θ] in this way. The same kind of difference occurs between the voiced fricatives [z, ʒ] and [v, ð]. The fricatives [s, z, ʃ, ʒ] are called **sibilant** sounds. They have more acoustic energy—that is, greater loudness—at a higher pitch than the other fricatives.

The sound patterns that occur in languages often arise because of auditory properties of sounds. We can divide fricatives into sibilant and non-sibilant sounds only by reference to auditory properties. We need to divide them into these two groups to show how English plurals are formed. Consider words ending in fricatives, such as "cliff, moth, kiss, dish, church, dove, lathe, maze, rouge, judge." Which of these words add an extra syllable in forming the plural? If you say them over to yourself you will find that they are all monosyllables in the singular. But those that end with one of the sounds [s, ʃ, z, ʒ]—that is, with a sibilant fricative or an affricate containing a sibilant fricative—become two syllables in the plural. It seems as though English does not favor two sibilant sounds together. It breaks them up by inserting a vowel before adding a sibilant suffix to words ending in sibilants.

Trills, Taps, and Flaps

In some forms of English /r/ is pronounced as a tongue-tip trill. In making a **trill**, one articulator is held loosely near another so that the flow of the air between them sets them in motion, alternately sucking them together and blowing them apart. There are usually about three vibrating movements in a typical trill.

Even in the case of a very short trill where there is only a single contact with the roof of the mouth, the movement is different from that in a tap. A **tap** is caused by a single contraction of the muscles so that one articulator is thrown against another. It is simply a very rapid articulation of a stop closure. Taps occur in many forms of American English as the regular pronunciation of /t, d, n/ in words such as "latter, ladder, tanner." In Scottish English /r/ is often pronounced as a tap. The American pronunciation of "petal" with a voiced alveolar tap in the middle will sound to a Scotsman from Edinburgh like his regular pronunciation of "pearl."

The distinction between taps and flaps is not very important in English. A **flap** is an articulation in which one articulator strikes another in passing while on its way back to its rest position. In some forms of American English /t, d, n/ are flaps when they occur after /r/ in words such as "dirty, birdie, Ernie." These sounds may be made by curling the tip of the tongue up for /r/, then allowing it to flap against the back part of the alveolar ridge as it returns to its position behind the lower front teeth. As the place of articulation involves the underside of the tongue and the back of the alveolar ridge, these sounds are classified as retroflex flaps.

The distinction between trills, taps, and flaps is much more important in other languages. But before this point can be illustrated, we must review the symbols that can be used for different types of "r" sounds. In a broad transcription they can all be transcribed as /r/. But in a narrower transcription this symbol may be restricted to voiced alveolar trills. An alveolar tap may be symbolized by the special symbol [ɾ], and the flap, which is usually post-alveolar (retroflex), by [ɽ]. The approximant that occurs in many people's pronunciation of /r/ may by symbolized by [ɹ], an upside-down r. If it is important to show that this sound is particularly retroflex, the diacritic for retroflexion [.] may be added so that the symbol becomes [ɻ]. All these symbols are shown in Table 7.6.

Table 7.6

Specific symbols for types of *r*. Note the use of [∗] as a special symbol that can be defined and used when there is no prescribed symbol.

r	voiced alveolar trill	[pero]	(Spanish "dog")
ɾ	voiced alveolar tap	[peɾo]	(Spanish "but")
ɽ	voiced retroflex flap	[báɽà]	(Hausa "servant")
ɹ	voiced alveolar approximant	[ɹɛd]	(British-English "red")
ɻ	voiced retroflex approximant	[ɻɛd]	(American-English "red")
R	voiced uvular trill	[Ruʒ]	(Provençal-French "red")
ʁ	voiced uvular fricative or approximant	[ʁuʒ]	(Parisian-French "red")
∗	voiced labiodental flap	[bɔ́∗ú]	(Margi "flying away")

As illustrated in Table 7.6, Spanish distinguishes between a trill and a tap in words such as "perro" [pero] (dog) and "pero" [peɾo] (but). Similar distinctions also occur in some forms of Tamil, a language of South India. This language, like Hausa (Nigeria), may also distinguish between a tap and a flap.

Learning to make a trill involves placing the tongue, very loosely, in exactly the right position so that it will be set in vibration by a current of air. The easiest position seems to be with the tongue just behind the upper front teeth and about one mm away from the alveolar ridge. The jaw should be fairly closed, leaving a space of five mm between the front teeth. Check this by inserting the top of a pencil between your teeth, and then removing it before making the sound. The problem experienced by most people who fail to make trills is that the blade of the tongue is too stiff.

Most people can learn to produce a tap in words such as "Betty" (which would then be transcribed as [ˈbɛɾi]). You should also be able to learn to produce a flap in a sequence such as [ɑɽɑ]. While saying [ɑ] curl the tip of your tongue up and back. Then bring it rapidly back to its resting position, making sure that it strikes against the alveolar ridge on the way.

When you have mastered all these sounds, try saying them in different contexts. You might also learn to say voiced and voiceless trills, taps, and flaps. Try varying the place of articulation, producing both dental and post-alveolar trills, taps, and flaps. At least one language—Malayalam, spoken in South India—contrasts alveolar and dental trills. The word for "room" in this language is [ʌrʌ], whereas the word for "half" is [ʌɾ̪ʌ].

The tongue tip is not the only articulator that can be trilled. Uvular trills occur in some dialects of French, although, as we have noted already, most forms of French have a uvular fricative in words such as "rose" [ʁoz]. The symbol for a uvular trill is [R]. There is no symbol to distinguish between uvular fricatives and approximants. Both sounds are symbolized by [ʁ].

Trills involving the lips occur in a few languages. I have also heard a labiodental flap—in Margi, of Northern Nigeria—in which the lower lip is drawn back inside the upper teeth, and then allowed to strike against them in passing back to its normal position. There are no IPA symbols for any of these sounds. As in all such cases, it is possible to use an asterisk and define it, as I have done in Table 7.6.

Laterals

The only English lateral phoneme is /l/, with allophones [l] as in "led" [lɛd] and [ɫ] as in "bell" [bɛɫ]. As the air flows freely without audible friction, this sound may be specified more precisely as a voiced alveolar lateral approximant. It may be compared with the sound [ɹ] in "red" [ɹɛd], which is for many people a voiced alveolar central approximant. Laterals are usually presumed to be voiced approximants, unless a specific statement to the contrary is made.

Try subtracting and adding voice while saying an English [l] as in "led." You will probably find that the voiceless lateral you produce is a fricative, not an approximant. When the vocal cords are apart the airstream flows more rapidly, so that it produces a fricative noise in passing between the tongue and the side teeth. The symbol for this sound is [ɬ], so in alternating the voiced and voiceless sounds you will be saying [lllɬɬɬlllɬɬɬ]. It is possible to make a nonfricative lateral, but you will find that to do this you will have to move the side of the tongue further away from the teeth. The alternation between a voiced and a voiceless lateral approximant may be symbolized [lllļļļlllļļļ].

It is also possible to make a voiced lateral that is a fricative. Try doing this by starting from an ordinary [l] as in "led," and then moving the sides of your tongue slightly closer to your teeth. You may find it easier to produce this sound by starting from the voiceless alveolar lateral fricative described in the previous paragraph; then add voicing.

To summarize, there are four lateral sounds under discussion: voiced alveolar lateral approximant, [l]; voiced alveolar lateral fricative, [ɮ]; voiceless alveolar lateral approximant, [l̥]; and voiceless alveolar lateral fricative, [ɬ]. No language uses the difference between the last two sounds contrastively. But some languages make a phonemic distinction between three of the four possibilities. Zulu, for example, has words such as [lòndá] "preserve"; [ɮùɮá] "roam loose"; and [ɬòɬá] "prod." Voiceless lateral fricatives can also be exemplified by Welsh words such as [ɬan] "church" and [ˈkəɬɛɬ] "knife."

The distinction between a central and a lateral articulation can be applied to other manners of articulation in addition to approximants and fricatives. Trills are always centrally articulated, but flaps and taps can be made with either a central or a lateral articulation. If, when making a tap [ɾ] or a flap [ɽ], you allow the airstream to flow over the sides of the tongue, you will produce a sound which is intermediate in quality between those sounds and [l]. This will be a voiced alveolar lateral tap or flap. The symbol for either of these possibilities is [ɺ]. A sound of this kind sometimes occurs in languages such as Japanese, that do not distinguish between /r/ and /l/. But some African languages, for example, Chaga, spoken in East Africa, make a phonemic distinction among all three of these sounds.

The central-lateral distinction can in some senses be said to apply to stops as well. English stops with lateral plosion, as in "little, ladle," can, of course, be considered to be sequences of stop plus lateral. But the Navaho sound [tl'], in which the ejective airstream mechanism applies to both the stop and the lateral, is appropriately called a lateral ejective. Similarly, we clearly want to distinguish between the central and lateral clicks [ʘ] and [ʖ].

Having seen that the central-lateral distinction can apply to a number of different manners of articulation, we must now consider whether it applies to several different places of articulation. Here the limitations are obvious. Laterals can be made only with the tip, blade, or front of the tongue. They must be either dental (as in French), alveolar (as in English), retroflex (as in Malayalam and other Indian languages), or palatal sounds (as in Italian). The symbols for voiced retroflex and palatal laterals are [ɭ] and [ʎ] respectively. Try saying Italian words such as "famiglia" [faˈmiʎʎa] (family) and "figlio" [ˈfiʎʎo] (son). In both of these words the lateral sound is doubled in that it acts as the final consonant for one syllable as well as the first consonant of the next syllable. Note that some forms of Spanish distinguish between [ʎ] and the similar sounding sequence [lj] in words such as "pollo" [ˈpoʎo] (chicken) and "polio" [ˈpoljo] (polio). See if you can make this distinction. If you are feeling ambitious you might also try making the palatal lateral ejective in the Zulu word [cʎ'ècʎ'á], which means "tattoo."

Summary of Manners of Articulation

Table 7.7 presents a summary of the manners of articulation we have been discussing. Note that the terms central and lateral have been placed separately, to indicate that they can be used in conjunction with many of the terms in the upper part of the table. This table also lists many of the symbols that have been mentioned in the latter part of this chapter. You should be sure that you can pronounce each of them in a variety of contexts.

The only consonants that we have not considered in detail in this chapter are approximants. Alveolar approximants—both central [ɹ] and lateral [l]—have been discussed. But sounds such as [w, j] as in "wet, yet" have not. Approximants of the latter kind are sometimes called semivowels or glides. It will be more appropriate to discuss them after we have considered the nature of vowels more fully. But in order to describe vowels, we must first leave the field of articulatory phonetics and consider some of the basic principles of acoustic phonetics.

Table 7.7

Manners of Articulation.

Phonetic term	Brief description	Symbols
Nasal (stop)	Soft palate lowered so that air flows out through the nose; complete closure of two articulators.	m, n, ŋ, etc.
(Oral) stop	Soft palate raised, forming a velic closure; complete closure of two articulators.	p, b, t, etc.
Fricative	Narrowing of two articulators so as to produce a turbulent airstream.	f, v, θ, etc.
Approximant	Approximation of two articulators without producing a turbulent airstream.	w, j, l, ɹ, etc.
Trill	An articulator set in vibration by the airstream.	r, ʀ
Tap	One articulator thrown against another.	ɾ
Flap	One articulator striking another in passing.	ɽ, ɺ
Lateral	With a central obstruction, so that air passes out at the side.	l, ɫ, ɬ, ɭ,ʎ,ʟ
Central	Articulated so that air passes out over the center.	s, ɹ, ɕ, etc.

EXERCISES

Figure 7.3 shows most of the terms necessary for classifying consonants. Redundant terms have been omitted. Thus nasals are presumed to be stops; all other sounds are oral; and all sounds are central unless specifically stated to be lateral. One of the uses of the figure is that it enables you to study the ways in which terms can be combined.

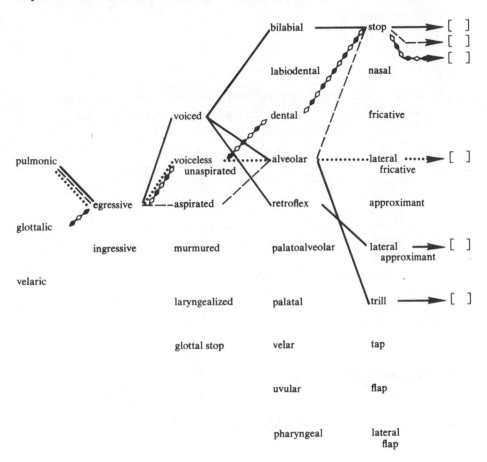

Figure 7.3 *Terms used in classifying consonants.*

A Follow the different lines from the left of the figure to the right. Fill in the symbols for the designated sounds.

B Draw lines linking the sets of terms required to designate three more sounds. Put the symbols for the appropriate sounds on the right.

C Draw three sets of dashed lines (– – –) indicating combinations of terms that do *not* occur.

D If we overlook secondary articulations such as rounding, most consonants can be specified by taking one term from each of these five columns. But, in addition to the affricates [tʃ, dʒ], two of the English consonants listed in the chapter on transcription cannot be specified in this way. Which consonants are these?

      [   ]   [   ]

State whether this deficiency can be remedied by adding terms to one or more columns.

_____

_____

E Still without considering secondary articulations and affricates, what sounds mentioned in this chapter cannot be specified by taking one term from each of the five columns?

_____

_____

F By now you should be fairly proficient at transcribing your own speech. As a last exercise of this sort, make a narrow systematic phonetic transcription of your pronunciation of the following passage.

     The phonetic roots of Chomsky and

   [_____

Halle's work derive from the

   [_____

distinctive-feature theories

   [_____

originated by the linguists in Prague,

   [_____

headed by N. S. Trubetzkoy and Roman

   [_____]tɹuˈbɛtskɔɪ [_____

Jakobson. The culmination of Trubetzkoy's

ˈjɑkəbsən [_____

work was his *Principles of Phonology*

   [_____

(in German), which was published in

[————————————————————
1939, the year after he died. Jakobson

1939[————————————————————
emigrated to the United States in

[————————————————————
1941 ; his most complete statement

1941[————————————————————
of the theory of distinctive features,

[————————————————————
which was written in collaboration

[————————————————————
with Gunnar Fant and Morris Halle,

[————— ˈgɒnəɹ ˈfænt ————————
appeared in 1951. Another view of the

[—————————]1951[—————————
phonetic framework necessary for

[————————————————————
describing the languages of the world

[————————————————————
appears in Chomsky and Halle's *The*

[————————————————————
Sound Pattern of English, first

[————————————————————
published in 1968.

[—————————————]1968.

PERFORMANCE EXERCISES

This chapter, like the last, introduced many non-English sounds. During this part of the course it is important to do as much practical work as time will allow. But do not try to go too fast. Make sure that you have thoroughly mastered the performance exercises at the end of Chapter 6 before going on to do the exercises below. Note that there are no performance exercises at the end of Chapter 8, so that you can allow more time for the exercises here and at the end of Chapter 6.

A   Learn to produce voiceless stops before [ɑ] at a number of different places of articulation. Begin by making a clearly interdental stop, [t̪ɑ], with the tongue tip between the teeth. Next make a very retroflex stop, [ʈɑ], with the tongue tip curled back and up towards the hard palate. Now try to make as many stops as you can with tongue positions between these two extremes. Using the diacritics [<] and [>] to mean more forward and more retracted, a series of this kind could be symbolized [t̪ɑ, t̪ɑ, t̪ɑ, tɑ, t̪ɑ, t̪ɑ, t̪ɑ]. Try to feel different articulatory positions such as these.

B   Repeat exercise **A** using a voiced stop:
    [d̪ɑ, d̪ɑ, d̪ɑ, dɑ, d̪ɑ, d̪ɑ, d̪ɑ]

C   Repeat exercise **A** using a nasal:
    [n̪ɑ, n̪ɑ, n̪ɑ, nɑ, n̪ɑ, n̪ɑ, n̪ɑ]

D   Repeat exercise **A** using a voiceless sibilant fricative of the [s] type. Note that it is perfectly possible to make a sibilant interdental fricative [s̪], although, in English, the interdental fricative is normally a non-sibilant [θ]. Say:
    [s̪ɑ, s̪ɑ, s̪ɑ, sɑ, s̪ɑ, s̪ɑ, s̪ɑ]

E   Repeat this exercise using a voiced sibilant fricative of the [z] type. Say:
    [z̪ɑ, z̪ɑ, z̪ɑ, zɑ, z̪ɑ, z̪ɑ, z̪ɑ]

F   Make a series of voiceless fricative articulations with the tongue tip down. Start with a palato-alveolar fricative [ʃ] with the blade of the tongue. (Be careful it is not made with the tip of the tongue up, which may be your normal articulation of this sound.) Next move the point of articulation backward by raising the front of the tongue, so that you produce a palatal fricative [ç]. Then move the articulation farther back, producing first [x] and then [χ]. Finally pull the tongue root back so that you produce a pharyngeal fricative [ħ]. Try to move in a continuous series, going through all the articulations:
    [ʃ, ç, x, χ, ħ]

G   Say these fricatives before vowels:
    [ʃɑ, çɑ, xɑ, χɑ, ħɑ]

H   Repeat exercise **F** with the corresponding voiced sounds, producing the series:
    [ʒ, j, ɣ, ʁ, ʕ]

Note that the symbol [j] can represent a voiced palatal fricative, as in this series, or an approximant, as in transcriptions of English "you" [ju].

I Say these fricatives before vowels:

     [ʒɑ, jɑ, ɣɑ, ʁɑ, ʕɑ]

J After you are fully aware of the positions of the tongue in all these fricatives, try saying some of the corresponding voiceless stops. There is no significant difference between palato-alveolar and palatal stops, and pharyngeal stops do not occur, so just say:

     [cɑ, kɑ, qɑ]

K Repeat exercise **J** with the voiced stops:

     [ɟɑ, gɑ, ɢɑ]

L Repeat exercise **J** with the voiced nasals:

     [ɲɑ, ŋɑ, ɴɑ]

M Consolidate your ability to produce sounds at different places of articulation. Produce a complete series of nasals between vowels:

     [amɑ, aṇɑ, anɑ, aɳɑ, aɲɑ, aŋɑ, aɴɑ]

N Produce a series of voiceless stops between vowels:

     [apɑ, aṭɑ, atɑ, aṭɑ, acɑ, akɑ, aqɑ]

O Produce a series of voiced stops between vowels:

     [abɑ, aḍɑ, adɑ, aḍɑ, aɟɑ, agɑ, aɢɑ]

P Produce a series of voiceless fricatives between vowels:

     [aɸɑ, afɑ, aθɑ, asɑ, aṣɑ, aʃɑ, açɑ, axɑ, aχɑ, aħɑ]

Q Produce a series of voiced fricatives between vowels:

     [aβɑ, avɑ, aðɑ, azɑ, aẓɑ, aʒɑ, ajɑ, aɣɑ, aʁɑ, aʕɑ]

R Repeat all these exercises using other vowels.

S Review the pronunciation of trills, taps, flaps, and similar sounding approximants. Say:

     [arɑ, aɾɑ, aɽɑ, aɹɑ, aɻɑ, aʀɑ, aʁɑ]

T Some of these sounds are more difficult to pronounce between high vowels. Say:

     [iri, iɾi, iɽi, iɹi, iɻi, iʀi, iʁi]

U Make sure that you can produce contrasting lateral sounds. Say:

     [lɑ, ɮɑ, ɬɑ, ḷɑ, ʎɑ, tlɑ, tɬ'ɑ, dlɑ]

V Repeat exercise **U** with other vowels.

W Incorporate all these sounds into simple series of nonsense words such as:

ʁeˈsaʔi	taˈŋoʒe	ˈpʼexonu
ˈɭupeʐo	ˈbeɾeɬa	doʔeˈɗo
fiɣoˈca	βinoˈɟe	ṣeˈʃetʼe
koˈriɖo	ʀeˈʎaxɑ	ˈɢeɦeɹu
ˈɲeqeɸu	ɮaɳeχo	moˈɓale

Remember that you should look as well as listen to anyone saying ear-training words.

Acoustic Phonetics 8

So far we have been describing speech sounds mainly by stating how they are made, but it is also possible to describe them in terms of what we can hear. The way in which we hear a sound depends on its acoustic structure. In an introductory discussion of phonetics there is no need to go into too much detail concerning the acoustic nature of speech sounds. (I discuss this topic at greater length in my book *Elements of Acoustic Phonetics*.) But it is important to understand the basic principles involved. We want to be able to describe the acoustics of speech for many reasons—for example, in order to explain why certain sounds are confused with one another, or to specify sounds (such as vowels) that are difficult to describe in terms of articulatory movements. Furthermore, the only record that we can usually get of a speech event is a tape recording. It is normally impossible to obtain photographs or x-rays showing what the speaker is doing. Accordingly, if we want permanent data that we can study, it will often have to be a result of analyzing a tape recording.

We can hear that sounds can differ from one another in three ways. They can be the same or different in (1) pitch, (2) loudness, and (3) quality. Thus two vowel sounds may have exactly the same pitch and loudness, but might differ in that one might be [e] and the other [o]. On the other hand, they might have the same vowel quality, but differ in that one was said on a higher pitch than the other or that one of them was spoken more loudly. In this chapter we will discuss each of these three aspects of speech sounds and consider the techniques of experimental phonetics that may be used for recording them.

Sound Waves

Sound consists of small variations in air pressure that occur very rapidly one after another. These variations are caused by actions of the speaker's vocal organs that are (for the most part) superimposed on the outgoing flow of lung air. Thus in the case of voiced sounds, the vibrating vocal cords chop up the stream of lung air so that pulses of relatively high pressure alternate with moments of lower pressure. In fricative sounds the airstream is forced through a narrow gap so that it becomes turbulent, with irregularly occurring peaks of pressure. The same principles apply in the production of other types of sounds.

Variations in air pressure in the form of sound waves move through the air somewhat like the ripples on a pond. When they reach the ear of a listener, they cause the eardrum to vibrate. A graph of a sound wave is very similar to a graph of the movements of the eardrum.

Figure 8.1 shows the variations in air pressure that occur during a small part of my pronunciation of the vowel [ɔ], as in "caught." The vertical axis represents air pressure (relative to the normal surrounding air pressure), and the horizontal axis represents time (relative to an arbitrary starting point). As you can see, the major peaks in air pressure recur about every .01 seconds (that is, every one-hundredth of a second). This is because on this particular occasion my vocal cords were vibrating at a rate of approximately one hundred times a second. The smaller variations in air pressure that occur within each one-hundredth of a second period are due to the way air vibrates when the vocal tract has the particular shape required for the vowel [ɔ].

There are a number of devices that will allow us to observe the waveform of a sound that has been sensed by a microphone. The most common device

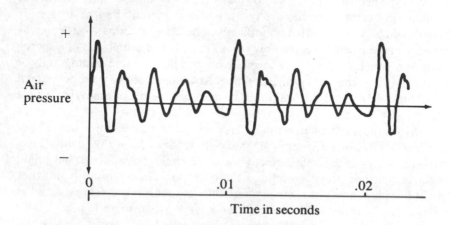

Figure 8.1 *The waveform during a short period (a little over two vocal-cord vibrations) in my pronunciation of [ɔ], as in "caught."*

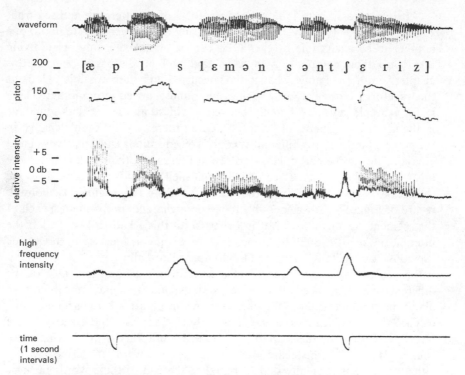

Figure 8.2 Oscillomink records of the phrase "Apples, lemons, and cherries," as spoken by an American from California. The top line is the waveform; the second line the fundamental frequency (indicative of the pitch); the third line is the intensity (indicative of the loudness); the fourth line is the intensity of the higher frequencies (the fricatives); and the bottom line is a time marker.

of this kind is the Cathode Ray Oscilloscope (CRO), which displays a waveform on the face of a tube similar to that of a television screen. Figure 8.1 is based on a photograph of an oscilloscope. This system is very useful for examining small parts of an utterance.

An easier way of recording the waveform throughout a whole utterance is to use an ink-writing oscillograph. The particular instrument in use in many phonetics laboratories is called an Oscillomink. This device will not record all the rapid variations in air pressure, because the "pen" (actually a small nozzle that produces a jet of ink) cannot be made to move fast enough. But it will show the pulses corresponding to each vibration of the vocal cords.

The top line in Figure 8.2 shows an Oscillomink record of the waveform produced when a speaker of American English said the phrase "apples, lemons, and cherries." As you can see, there were about twelve pulses of the vocal cords during the first vowel, before the silence corresponding to the closure for [p]. There were about twice as many pulses in the syllabic [l] following the release of the [p].

It is not possible to look at the waveform of an utterance and say what sounds occurred. The waveforms of many sounds are much too similar to one another to be analyzable by eye. They can be interpreted only by resolving them into their components in ways that will be discussed later in this chapter. But if one knows what sounds occurred it is often possible to look at the waveform and see at which point one sound changed into another. There is, for example, a clear difference between a voiced and a voiceless sound, as in the first two segments of "apples." Often there is a noticeable change in the pattern between two different types of voiced sounds, such as a vowel and a nasal. Thus in the particular utterance in Figure 8.2, the break between the [ɛ] and the [m] in "lemons" can be distinguished, and it is also possible to see the break between the [ə] from the [n] in "and." In the original Oscillomink record of Figure 8.2 it was possible to see enough detail to distinguish each of the segments in "lemons." But in order to do this I had to know what the utterance was. It would be impossible to distinguish between the words "lemons" or "melons" from an Oscillomink record alone.

Since an Oscillomink record of a waveform is a good indicator of the difference between voiced and voiceless sounds, one can make some inferences about the pronunciation of the phrase shown in Figure 8.2. In particular, one can see that the fricatives at the ends of both "apples" and "lemons" are largely voiceless, for there are no vocal cord vibrations visible during these sounds. It was for this reason that these sounds were transcribed as [s], although there is normally said to be [z] at the end of these words in these circumstances.

Pitch and Frequency

As we saw in Chapter 1, the pitch of a sound depends on the rate of vibration of the vocal cords. In a sound with a high pitch there is a higher frequency of vibration than in a sound with a low pitch. Because each opening and closing of the vocal cords causes a peak of air pressure in the sound wave, we can estimate the pitch of a sound by observing the rate of occurrence of the peaks in the waveform. To be more exact, we can measure the frequency of the sound in this way. **Frequency** is a technical term for an acoustic property of a sound—namely the number of complete repetitions (cycles) of variations in air pressure occurring in a second. The unit of frequency measurement is the Hertz, usually abbreviated as Hz. If the vocal cords make 220 complete opening and closing movements in a second, we say that the frequency of the sound is 220 Hz. The frequency of the sound shown in Figure 8.1 was 100 Hz.

The **pitch** of a sound is that auditory property that enables a listener to place it on a scale going from low to high, without considering its acoustic properties. In practice, when a speech sound goes up in frequency, it also goes up in pitch (though equal steps of increasing frequency do not produce the effect of equal steps of increasing pitch). For the most part, at an introductory level of the subject, the pitch of a sound may be equated with its frequency.

It is possible to determine the frequency of a sound by counting the peaks of air pressure in a record of its waveform. Thus in the first vowel in "apple" in the utterance shown in Figure 8.2, the twelve peaks occurred in about one-tenth of a second. This syllable therefore had a frequency of about 120 Hz. (12 × 10). At the end of this utterance there were only about eight peaks in a tenth of a second, indicating that the frequency fell to about 80 Hz. You can check your understanding of what is meant by frequency by trying to estimate the frequency of the vocal cord pulses in the first tenth of a second in "lemons." (You should find that it is about 110 Hz.)

Looking at the peaks in the waveform is a very time-consuming way to determine the pitch of an utterance. Fortunately there are devices that will automatically determine the interval between successive peaks, so that a mark can be recorded corresponding to the instantaneous frequency of each part of an utterance. These devices, which are known as pitch meters, work reasonably well, but all of those that are easily available at the moment make occasional errors. The second line in Figure 8.2 shows the output of a fairly good pitch meter. You can see that the pitch goes up in the second syllable of each of the first two words, and falls nearly throughout the last word. As we saw in Chapter 5, this is a typical intonation pattern for a list of items in English.

Voiced sounds have a regular waveform of the kind that gives rise to a precise sensation of pitch. In voiceless sounds, the variations in air pressure are caused by the smooth flow of the airstream being interrupted by being forced through a narrow channel or directed over irregular surfaces. In the sound waves that are produced, there are usually more rapid (and therefore higher frequency) variations in air pressure than occur during voiced sounds. For a male voice the frequency of the vocal cord vibrations in speech may be between 80 and 200 Hz. A woman's voice may go up to about 400 Hz. But the predominant frequencies in voiceless sounds are usually above 2000 Hz.

Loudness and Intensity

In general the **loudness** of a sound depends on the size of the variations in air pressure that occur. Just as frequency is the acoustic measurement most directly corresponding to the pitch of a sound, so acoustic intensity is the appropriate measure corresponding to loudness. The **intensity** is proportional to the average size, or amplitude, of the variations in air pressure. It is usually measured in decibels (abbreviated as dB) relative to the amplitude of some other sounds. When one sound has an intensity 5 dB greater than another, then it is approximately twice as loud. A change in intensity of 1 dB is a little more than the smallest noticeable change in loudness.

There are various electronic circuits that can be used for determining the average intensity of an utterance. The third line in Figure 8.2 shows the

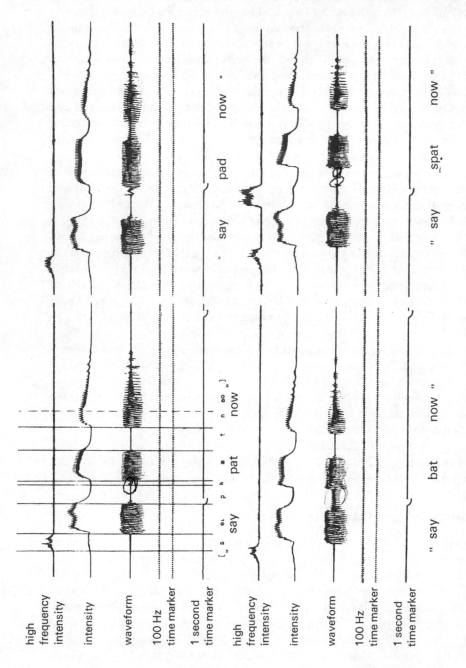

Figure 8.3 Oscillomink records of "Say pat now; say bat now; say pad now; say spat now."

output of one such circuit for the phrase "Apples, lemons, and cherries." In general, vowels have the highest intensity, with the vowel [æ] in "apples" being the greatest of all in this phrase. The lateral and nasal sounds in "lemons" had only slightly less in intensity than the vowels. The [ʃ] in "cherries" had a fair amount of intensity, but the voiceless fricatives at the ends of "apples" and "lemons" had very little intensity. The [p] in "apples" had none during the closure. Of course, if you are able to make intensity records of your own pronunciation of this phrase, you may find that they are slightly different. In any utterance the actual intensity of a segment will depend on many factors, such as its position in the sentence, the degree of stress on each word, and the personal characteristics of the speaker.

Because voiceless sounds have such a low intensity in comparison with voiced sounds, it is often convenient to treat them separately. We have noted that the predominant frequencies in voiceless sounds are usually above 2000 Hz. We can separate these sounds from other speech sounds by using a device known as a high-pass filter. This device blocks or reduces all the sounds with low frequencies, but passes the high frequencies without reduction. We can then determine the average intensity of these sounds. The output of such a system is shown in the fourth line of Figure 8.2. You can see that this line shows the presence of the fricative sounds much more clearly than the line above.

Acoustic Measurements

The frequency (pitch) and overall intensity (loudness) records in Figure 8.2 are calibrated with scales in Hz. and dB, respectively. One of the objectives of any science is to be able to measure the things that are being described, so that they can be expressed in terms of valid, reliable, and significant numbers. A valid number is one that truly measures the thing that you say you are measuring. Thus, technically speaking, a measurement of frequency in Hz. is not a valid measurement of the pitch unless we can show that frequency measurements are related to how people perceive pitch. A reliable measurement is one that does not depend on the procedures being used. Thus a reliable measurement of frequency will not depend on whether it was the result of measuring the waveform or the output of a particular pitch meter. A significant measurement is one that is not due to chance. If we can say that statistically the odds against a given event having occurred by chance are greater than one in a hundred, then we can say that it is very significant.

Should we wish to claim, for example, that the pitch of a certain type of question goes up at the end, we want to be able to do so on the basis of measurements of the frequency that we know are: (1) a valid indication of the pitch, because we know from many published experiments that pitch can be related to frequency; (2) reliable, because the instrumentation has been calibrated so that we know the degree of accuracy with which each frequency has been measured; and (3) significant, because we have made a sufficient number of measurements so that we know that the average increase in these circumstances is significantly greater than a chance increase.

Oscillomink records are useful for studying various kinds of phonetic problems. Records of the waveform and the intensity provide a good way of studying variations in length. Figure 8.3 illustrates records of four sentences of the form "Say ____ now." These sentences allow us to study the relative lengths of the segments in the words "pat, bat, pad, spat." Each word has been said in the same frame "Say ____ now" so as to make sure that the differences are not due to variations in the rate of utterance. If the words "say" and "now" are about the same on each occasion, then we can assume that the speaker was talking at a constant rate. Furthermore, if the words had been said simply as a list of items, then almost certainly the last one would have been longer and with a falling intonation pattern (as in the phrase "Apples, lemons, and cherries" in Figure 8.2). Even when reading a list of sentences such as those in Figure 8.3, it is difficult not to make the last one longer. If you are getting someone else to read a list of words or sentences that you are going to measure, it is often a good idea to add one or two extra items at the end which you simply disregard when you make the relevant measurements.

The first utterance in Figure 8.3 has been segmented so that you can measure the duration of each item. Of course, I have made no attempt to split either of the diphthongs [eɪ] or [aɔ] into two elements. It would be meaningless to do so, since they are both single vowels with continuously changing qualities. The fact that each of them is written with two separate symbols does not mean that each contains two distinct elements.

You should now try to segment the other utterances in Figure 8.3 in a similar way. Observe that the [b] in "bat" is voiced throughout. Is it longer or shorter than the [p] closure in "pat"? Which of these two words has the longer vowel (counting the vowel as the voiced portion between the consonants)? How much longer is the vowel in "pad" than in "pat"? Is the [t] in "pat" longer or shorter than the [d] in "pad"? Is the [p] in "spat" aspirated or does the voicing start immediately after the release of the consonant? Is the vowel in "spat" longer than the vowel in "pat"?

Now consider the two utterances in Figure 8.4. Both of them contain the sentence "Jenny gave Peter instructions to follow." This sentence can be said in two different ways. It could mean "Jenny gave Peter a set of instructions that he had to follow in order to carry out a certain task." Or it could mean "Jenny gave Peter instructions that he was to follow after her." Try to read the sentence in these two different ways, and notice how the intonation patterns differ. In the one meaning, the major pitch fall is likely to be on the second syllable of "instructions." In the other, the fall will be on "follow."

Now try to segment the two utterances in Figure 8.4 and decide which is which. Of course it is virtually impossible to make a phonetic transcription and show exactly where each segment belongs. There are several places where

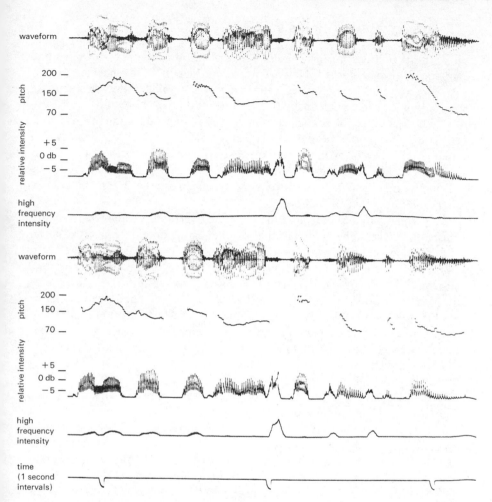

Figure 8.4 Oscillomink records of "Jenny gave Peter instructions to follow" said in two different ways.

it is very difficult to say how the segments should be divided. For example, there is no way of segmenting the end of "Peter" and the beginning of "instructions." But you can see some things very clearly. Look for the voiced stop at the beginning of "gave," the voiceless aspirated stop at the beginning of "Peter," the [st] cluster in "instructions" and the [ʃ] at the beginning of the last syllable in this word, the voiceless stop of "to," and the voiceless fricative in "follow." The sentence in the lower part of the picture has the major fall on "instructions." Can you say whether these sentences are likely to have been spoken by a British or an American speaker? Remember that British speakers usually have a voiceless stop in the middle of "Peter," whereas most Americans have a voiced tap in these circumstances.

Spectrographic Analysis

In the first part of this chapter I described how differences in pitch and loudness can be recorded. Now we must consider the differences in quality. A set of vowel sounds provides a suitable starting point, since vowels can all be said on the same pitch and with the same loudness.

The quality of a sound such as a vowel depends upon its overtone structure. Putting this another way, we can say that a vowel sound contains a number of different pitches simultaneously. There is the pitch at which it is actually spoken, and there are the various overtone pitches that give it its distinctive quality. We distinguish one vowel from another by the differences in the overtones that are audible.

Normally, one cannot hear the separate overtones of a vowel as distinguishable pitches. The only sensation of pitch is the note on which the vowel is said, which depends on the rate of vibration (the frequency) of the vocal cords. But there are circumstances in which the characteristic overtone structure of each vowel can be heard. Try saying the vowels [i, ɪ, ɛ, æ, ɑ, ɔ, ʊ, u] as in the words "heed, hid, head, had, hod, hawed, hood, who'd." Now whisper these vowels. In a whispered sound the vocal cords are not vibrating, and there is no regular pitch of the voice. Nevertheless, when you whisper these vowels you can hear that they form a series of sounds on a continuously descending pitch. What you are hearing is one of the overtones that characterize the vowels. This particular overtone is highest for [i] and lowest for [u], with the other words in the series being in between. Now try whistling a very high note, and then the lowest note that you can. You will find that for the high note you have to have your tongue in the position for [i]—but of course with the lips rounded, as in the vowel in the French word "tu"—and for the low note your tongue and lips are in the [u] position. Again, intermediate notes would have the tongue positions of the other vowels in the series.

Another way of removing or minimizing the auditory effect of the vocal cord frequency is to say the vowels in a very low, creaky voice. It is easiest to produce this kind of voice with a vowel such as [æ] or [ɑ]. Some people can produce a creaky voice sound in which the rate of vibration of the vocal cords is so low that you can hear the individual pulsations.

Try saying just the four vowels [i, ɪ, ɛ, æ] as in the words "heed, hid, head, had" in a creaky voice. You should be able to hear a change in pitch, although, in one sense, the pitch of all of them is just that of the low creaky voice. In this series of vowels there is a clearly audible overtone that steadily increases in pitch by approximately equal steps with each vowel. Now say the four vowels [ɑ, ɔ, ʊ, u] as in "hod, hawed, hood, who'd" in a creaky voice. These four vowels have an overtone with a steadily decreasing pitch.

There is another way in which it is possible to hear the pitch of this overtone. Make a vowel such as [æ], and then make a glottal stop while retaining the same tongue position. Now flick a finger against your throat just above the larynx. You should hear a dull hollow note corresponding to the pitch of the overtone. Try making another vowel position and hear how the pitch changes. If you tilt your head slightly backwards so that the skin of the neck is stretched, you may be able to hear this sound somewhat better. But be careful to maintain a vowel position and not to raise the back of the tongue against the soft palate. If you check a complete set of vowel positions [i, ι, e, ε, æ, ɑ, ɔ, ω, u] with this technique, you should hear the pitch go up for the first four vowels and down for the second four vowels, just as it does in creaky voice.

Summarizing what I have said about acoustic quality so far, vowels are distinguished by two characteristic pitches. One of them (actually the higher of the two) goes downwards throughout the series [i, ι, e, ε, æ, ɑ, ɔ, o, u]. The other goes up for the first four vowels, and then down for the next four. These characteristic overtones are called the **formants** of the vowels, the lowest of the two being called the first formant, and the higher the second formant. Actually there is also another characteristic overtone, the third formant, which is also present, but there is no simple way of demonstrating its pitch.

It is possible to analyze sounds so that we can measure the actual frequencies of the formants. We can then represent them graphically as in Figure 8.5. This figure gives the average of a number of authorities' values of the frequencies of the first three formants in eight American English vowels. Try to see how your own vowels compare with these. Do you have a much larger jump in the pitch of the second formant (which you hear when whispering) between [ε] and [æ] as compared with [ι] and [ε]? Do you distinguish between "hod" and "hawed" in terms of their formant frequencies?

The formants that characterize different vowels are the result of the different ways in which the air in the vocal tract vibrates. Every time the vocal cords open and close, there is a pulse of air from the lungs. These pulses act like sharp taps on the air in the vocal tract. This body of air is set into vibration in a way that is determined by the size and shape of the tract. In a vowel sound, the air in the vocal tract vibrates at a number of different frequencies simultaneously. These frequencies are the resonant frequencies of that particular vocal-tract shape. Irrespective of the rate of vibration of the vocal cords, the air in the vocal tract will resonate at these frequencies as long as the position of the vocal organs remains the same. A vowel has its own characteristic auditory quality, which is the result of the specific variations in air pressure due to its vocal-tract shape being superimposed on the fundamental frequency produced by the vocal cords.

There is nothing particularly new about this way of analyzing vowel sounds. The general theory of formants was stated by Helmholtz over one hundred years ago. Even earlier, in 1829, the English physicist Robert Willis had said, "A given vowel is merely the rapid repetition of its peculiar note." We would nowadays say that it is the rapid repetition (corresponding to the vibrations of the vocal cords) of its peculiar notes (corresponding to its formants). Willis was one of the first people to make an instrumental analysis of the acoustic structure of speech. But the notion of a single formant

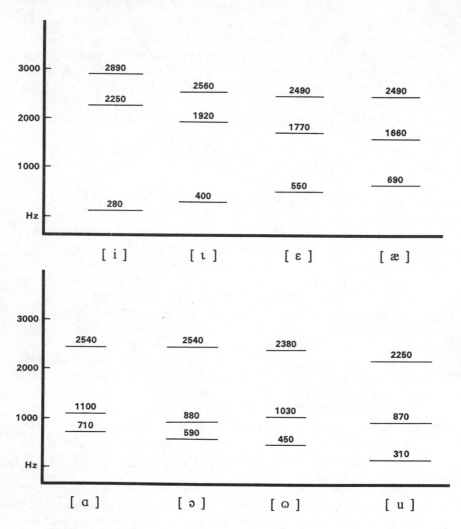

Figure 8.5 *The frequencies of the first three formants in eight American English vowels.*

(actually the second formant) had been observed several centuries earlier. In about 1665 Isaac Newton wrote in his notebook: "The filling of a very deepe flaggon with a constant streame of beere or water sounds ye vowells in this order w, u, ω, o, a, e, i, y." He was about twelve years old at the time.

Although the concepts of acoustic phonetics are not new, it is only since the late 1940's that it has been possible to do extensive work in this field. This is because of the invention of the **sound spectrograph**, a device that translates a sound into a visual representation of its component frequencies. Figure 8.6 shows a spectrogram of my pronunciation (British English) of the words "heed, hid, head, had, hod, hawed, hood, who'd." A time scale (with an arbitrary starting point) is shown along the bottom of the picture, and the

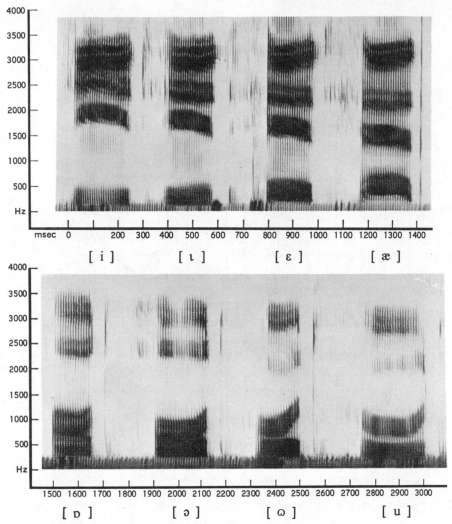

Figure 8.6 *A spectrogram of the words "heed, hid, head, had, hod, hawed, hood, who'd" as spoken in a British (RP) accent.*

vertical scale shows the frequencies in Hz. The relative intensity of each component frequency is shown by the darkness of the mark. Consequently the formants show up as dark horizontal bars.

There is a great deal of similarity between Figures 8.5 and 8.6. Figure 8.5 is like a schematic spectrogram of the isolated vowels. Figure 8.6 differs in that it shows the effects of the consonants (which we will discuss later), the slightly diphthongal character of some of the vowels, and some extra horizontal bars. Most of these bars correspond to additional formants that are not linguistically significant. They remain at a constant frequency, irrespective of the vowel being pronounced. Note in particular the fourth formant at about 3000 Hz. The exact position of the higher formants varies

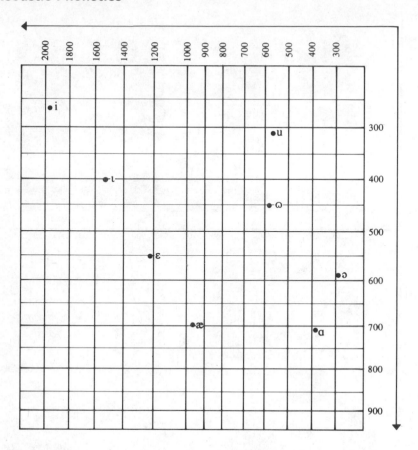

Figure 8.7 *A formant chart showing the frequency of the first formant on the ordinate (the vertical axis) plotted against the distance between the frequencies of the first and second formants on the abscissa (the horizontal axis) for eight American English vowels.*

a great deal from speaker to speaker. They are not uniquely determined for each speaker, but they certainly are indicative of a person's voice quality.

Whenever the vocal cords are vibrating, there are regularly spaced vertical lines on the spectrogram. During a vowel the vertical lines are visible throughout a large part of the spectrogram. In a voiced stop closure, as in the [d] at the end of each of these words, all the acoustic energy has to be transmitted through the walls of the vocal tract. Consequently the vibrations usually produce only small, regularly spaced lines near the base line. But they are still just visible, forming what is sometimes called a voice bar. Each vertical line in the voice bar or in the vowels is the result of the momentary increase of acoustic energy due to a single movement of the vocal cords. We have seen that it is possible to observe the pulses in a record of the waveform, and from this to calculate the pitch. It is equally possible to measure the pitch from observations of the vertical striations on spectrograms. When they are close together the pitch must be higher than when they are farther apart. The vertical striations in Figure 8.6 are slightly closer together in [i] than they are in [ɒ]. Therefore the first vowel must have been on a slightly higher pitch. As we will see, it is possible to make another kind of spectrographic record that gives a better picture of the variations in pitch.

In addition to the higher formants that can be seen in Figure 8.6, there are also some fainter bars at lower frequencies that should be disregarded. For example, in [i] there is something that looks like a faint formant centered at about 1500 Hz., and in [ɒ] there is a similar bar centered at 1700 Hz. These pseudoformants are sometimes due to a slight degree of nasalization. But often they are simply individual peculiarities. Their presence makes reading spectrograms more an art than a pure science.

The traditional articulatory descriptions of vowels are related to the formant frequencies. We can see that the first formant frequency increases as a speaker moves from the high vowel in "heed" to the low vowel in "had," and that it decreases as the speaker goes from the low vowel in "hod" to a high vowel in "who'd." The first formant, therefore, is inversely related to vowel height. We can also see that the second formant frequency decreases as a speaker goes from the front vowel in "heed" to the back vowel in "who'd." But the correlation between the second formant frequency and the degree of backness of a vowel is not as good as that between the first formant frequency and the vowel height. The second formant frequency decreases continually through the series of vowels [ɑ, ɔ, ʊ, u] even though the third and fourth of these vowels are not fully back. There is a better correlation between the degree of backness and the distance between the first two formants, which are far apart in front vowels and close together in back vowels. Furthermore, the distance between the two formants decreases in the front vowels, a fact that fits the traditional articulatory descriptions that show these vowels on a slanting line with [i] being more front than [æ].

The degree of lip rounding also affects the frequencies of the formants. In general, as sounds become more rounded, the frequencies of the higher formants decreases. But the situation is complicated in that the effect is greater in the third formant for front vowels, and in the second formant for back vowels.

We can see some of these relationships when we plot the formant frequencies given in Figure 8.5 along axes as shown in Figure 8.7. Because the formant frequencies are inversely related to the traditional articulatory parameters, the axes have been placed so that zero frequency would be at the top right corner of the figure rather than at the bottom left corner, as is more usual in graphical representations. In addition, the frequencies have been arranged in accordance with the so-called Mel scale, in which perceptually equal intervals of pitch are represented as equal distances along the scale. On this kind of plot, [i] and [u] appear at the top left and right of the graph, and [æ] and [ɑ] at the bottom, with all the other vowels in between. Consequently, this arrangement allows us to represent vowels in the way that we have become accustomed to seeing them in traditional articulatory descriptions.

In the preceding paragraphs I have been careful to refer to the correlation between formant frequencies and the *traditional* articulatory descriptions. This is because, as we noted in Chapter 1, traditional articulatory descriptions are not entirely satisfactory. They are often not in accord with the actual articulatory facts. For over a hundred years phoneticians have been describing vowels in terms such as high vs. low and front vs. back. There is no doubt that these terms are appropriate for describing the relationships between different vowel qualities, but to some extent phoneticians may have been using these terms as labels to specify acoustic dimensions rather than as descriptions of actual tongue positions. As G. Oscar Russell, one of the pioneers in x-ray studies of vowels, said, "Phoneticians are thinking in terms of acoustic fact, and using physiological fantasy to express the idea." Phoneticians have not been fantasizing in their descriptions of the lip positions of vowels, but there is no doubt that vowel "height" is more closely determined by the first formant frequency than by the height of the tongue. And the so-called front-back dimension is obviously more simply expressed by reference to the difference between the first and the second formant frequencies than to any measurement of the actual position of the tongue.

Formant charts are now commonly used to represent vowel qualities. Phoneticians sometimes plot formant one against the distance between formants one and two, as in Figure 8.7. More frequently, however, the charts simply show formant one plotted against formant two. There is only a slight difference in the resulting arrangement of vowels in these different kinds of plots. If you plot formant one against formant two, the vowels will be arranged in the form of a triangle. Because the second formant decreases throughout the back series of vowels, there will be a greater distance between [i] and [u] than between [e] and [o]. For this reason it seems preferable to plot formant one against the difference between formant two and formant one. This kind of plot results in the back vowels being placed more appropriately; thus [ʊ] and [u] can be seen to be less fully back than [ɑ] and [ɔ]. In order to consolidate acoustic notions about vowels, you should now try to represent the vowels in Figure 8.6 in terms of a formant chart. A blank chart is provided in Figure 8.8. Begin by finding a comparatively steady state portion near the beginning of each word. Now mark the centers of the dark bars corresponding to the first and second formants at these points. Measure these frequencies in terms of the scale on the left of the figure. Fill in the table in Figure 8.8 and plot the vowels.

The acoustic structure of consonants is usually more complicated than that of vowels. In many cases a consonant can only be said to be a particular way of beginning or ending a vowel. Thus there is virtually no difference in the sounds during the actual closures of [b, d, g], and absolutely none at all during the closures of [p, t, k], for at these moments there is only silence.

Each of the stop sounds conveys its quality by its effect on the adjacent vowel. We have seen that during a vowel such as [æ] there will be formants

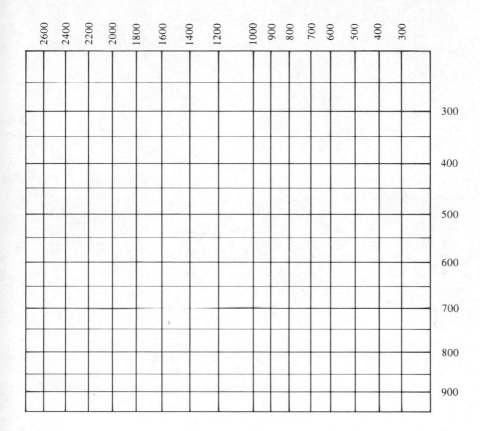

Vowel	i	ι	ε	æ	ɒ	ɔ	ʊ	u
F2								
F1								
F2–F1								

Figure 8.8 *A blank formant chart for showing the relation between vowels. Using the information in Figure 8.6, plot the frequency of the first formant on the ordinate (the vertical axis) and the difference between the frequencies of the first and second formants on the abscissa (the horizontal axis). Remember that the bars of the first and second formants are very close together in the back vowels.*

corresponding to the particular shape of the vocal tract. Similarly, in a syllable such as [bæ] there will be formants corresponding to the particular shape that occurs at the moment that the lips open. As the lips come farther apart and the vocal-tract shape changes, the formants will move correspondingly. Closure of the lips causes a lowering of all the formants. Consequently the syllable [bæ] will begin with the formants in a fairly low position and will be distinguished by their rapidly rising to the positions for [æ]. At the moment of release or formation of each of the other stops there will also be particular shapes of the vocal tract that will be characterized by particular formant frequencies.

The apparent point of origin of the formant for each place of articulation is called the **locus** of that place of articulation. It used to be said that there was a fairly precise locus for each place of articulation, but we now know that this is not true. The actual point of origin of the formants will depend on the adjacent vowels. This is because the position of that part of the tongue that is not involved in the formation of a consonant closure will be largely that of the adjacent vowel. The formant frequencies at the moment of release will be determined by the shape of the vocal tract as a whole, and hence will vary according to the vowel.

Figure 8.9 shows spectrograms of the words "bab, dad, gag" in my pronunciation. You can see that at the beginning of the word "bab" there is a rapid increase in all three formant frequencies. At the end of this word there is a corresponding rapid decrease. In the word "dad" the first formant again begins with an increase in frequency. But both the second and the third formants have a very slight fall in frequency. In "gag" the most noticeable feature is the narrowing of the distance between the second and third formants. At

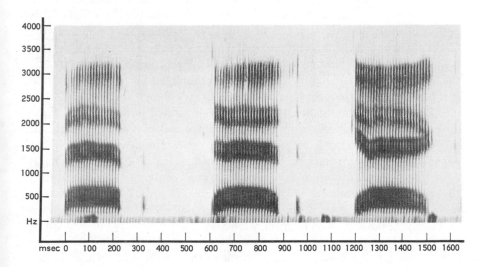

Figure 8.9 *A spectrogram of the words "bab, dad, gag" (British accent).*

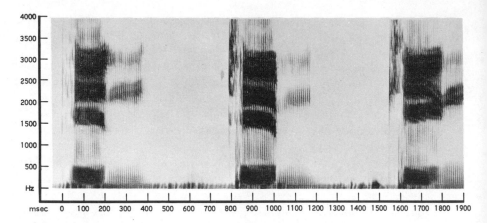

Figure 8.10 *A spectrogram of "pin, Tim, king" (British accent).*

the end of the word it is almost as if they went toward a common point. This coming together of the second and third formants is very characteristic of velar consonants. It is also characteristic of velars that the formant transitions take longer than in the corresponding alveolar or bilabial sounds. Note also the asymmetrical nature of the transitions at the beginning and end of the word "gag." The initial velar stop is not made in exactly the same place as the final velar stop. Try saying the word "gag." Does it feel as if you make the two [g] sounds in exactly the same way?

The voiceless stops corresponding to /b, d, g/ are illustrated in Figure 8.10, in the words "pin, Tim, king." The release of the aspirated stops in each word is marked by a sharp onset of a burst of noise that appears as a comparatively random pattern in the upper frequencies. For the [p] in "pin" this period of aspiration starts at the beginning of the time scale and lasts for about 40 msec. For [t] it is from about time 800 to time 840; and for [k] it is from about time 1550 to time 1600. The major concentration of energy during the noise burst is in a slightly different region for each place of articulation. It is lowest in both frequency and intensity for [p], highest for [t].

The nasal consonants [m, n, ŋ] are also illustrated in Figure 8.10. Each of these sounds has a formant structure similar to that of a vowel, except that the bands are somewhat fainter and are in particular frequency locations that depend on the characteristic resonances of the nasal cavities. In nasal consonants there is usually a very low first formant centered at about 250 Hz.; the additional formants are at 2500 and over 3000 Hz. The difference between each of the nasals is most plainly marked by the different formant transitions that occur at the end of each vowel. There is a clear downward movement of the second and third formants before the bilabial nasal at the end of the second word, and a clear coming together of the second and third formants before the velar nasal at the end of the third word. But as in the case of the alveolar stops in the word "dad" in Figure 8.9, the alveolar nasal at the end of the first word in Figure 8.10 produces a comparatively small movement of the formants. It is typical of nasal consonants that there should be an abrupt change in the pattern at the time of the formation of the articulatory closure (at points 200, 1010, and 1790 on the time scale in Figure 8.10).

An abrupt change in the formant structure is characteristic of lateral sounds as well as nasals. Figure 8.11 shows the words "lash, face, vase." (Note that in my pronunciation the last word is [vɑz], not [veɪs] as in many American pronunciations.) The initial lateral in the first word has formants with center frequencies of approximately 250, 1100, 2400 (very low intensity), and 3200 Hz. The formants with these frequencies change abruptly in intensity at time 80, at the beginning of the vowel. A formant in the neighborhood of 1100 or 1200 Hz. is typical of most laterals for most speakers.

Figure 8.11 also illustrates a number of fricatives. The highest frequencies in speech occur during [s] sounds, the random noise extending well beyond the upper limits of this spectrogram. The noise in [ʃ] is centered at a slightly lower frequency, and extends down to about 2500 Hz. Both [s] and [ʃ] have a comparatively large acoustic intensity, and hence produce darker patterns than [f] (or [θ], which is not illustrated in these words). The marks corresponding to the fricative noise in [f] are scattered in the middle and lower part of the frequency scale.

The voiced fricatives have patterns similar to their voiceless counterparts, but with the addition of the vertical striations indicative of voicing. The initial [v] in "vase" is fainter than the [f] in "face," and only a few vertical striations can be seen. The final [z] in "vase" is also less intense than the [s] in "face." Often, as in these words, the vertical striations indicative of voicing are not evident throughout the sound.

I hope that the vagueness of many of the remarks in the preceding paragraphs has led you to realize that the interpretation of sound spectrograms is often not all straightforward. The acoustic correlates of some articulatory

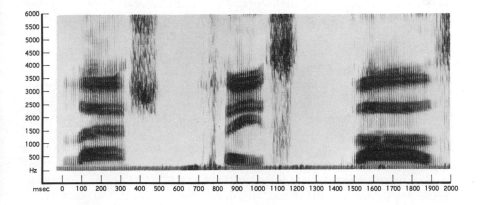

Figure 8.11   *A spectrogram of "lash, face, vase" (British accent).*

Table 8.1

Acoustic correlates of consonantal features.

Note: These descriptions should be regarded only as rough guides. The actual acoustic correlates depend to a great extent on the particular combination of articulatory features in a sound.

Voiced	Vertical striations corresponding to the vibrations of the vocal cords.
Bilabial	Locus of both second and third formants comparatively low.
Alveolar	Locus of second formant about 1700–1800 Hz.
Velar	Usually high locus of the second formant. Common origin of second and third formant transitions.
Retroflex	General lowering of the third and fourth formants.
Stop	Gap in pattern, followed by burst of noise for voiceless stops or sharp beginning of formant structure for voiced stops.
Fricative	Random noise pattern, especially in higher frequency regions, but dependent on the place of articulation.
Nasal	Formant structure similar to that of vowels but with nasal formants at about 250, 2500, and 3250 Hz.
Lateral	Formant structure similar to that of vowels but with formants in the neighborhood of 250, 1200, and 2400 Hz. The higher formants are considerably reduced in intensity.
Approximant	Formant structure similar to that in vowels, usually changing.

features are summarized in Table 8.1. But in a book such as this it is impossible to give a completely detailed account of the acoustics of speech. The descriptions that have been given should be regarded as rough guides rather than accounts of invariable structures that can always be seen in spectrograms.

All the words illustrated in Figures 8.9 through 8.11 were spoken in isolation in a fairly distinct way. In connected speech, as in the remainder of the spectrograms illustrating this chapter, many of the sounds are even more difficult to distinguish. Before reading the next paragraph, try segmenting Figure 8.12, given the information that the utterance was, "She came back and started again." It is a good idea to begin by marking the location of the fricatives—the [s] in "started" is particularly easy to distinguish—then go on and write the correct symbol under each of the other sounds, beginning with those which seem most obvious.

Looking at the segments one at a time, we can see that the initial [ʃ] sound is similar to that in "lash" in Figure 8.11, except that the fricative noise goes down to a slightly lower frequency. The [i] in "she" is slightly diphthongized, as can be seen by the movement of both the first and second formants. At the end of this vowel the second and third formants come together for the velar stop in "came." This stop is followed by a burst of aspiration before the onset of the vowel. My vowel in "came" is not particularly diphthongal, in comparison with that of many speakers, so the formants have a relatively constant frequency. At the end of this vowel the downward transitions of the formants before the bilabial nasal are just barely visible. The upward transitions after the bilabial stop at the beginning of "back" are

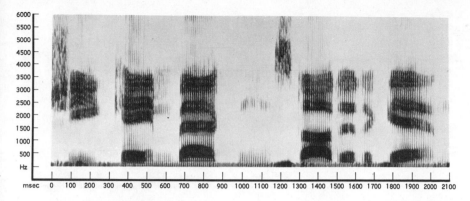

Figure 8.12 *A spectrogram of "She came back and started again" (British accent).*

much more evident. There is also no difficulty in seeing the coming together of the second and third formants before the velar stop at the end of the vowel in this word. This stop is held for a comparatively long time, and there is no sign of aspiration at its release (near time 1000). Nor is there any indication of a change in quality in the word "and." This word evidently did not consist of a vowel segment followed by a nasal segment. Instead the velar stop must have been released nasally, so that the whole word was pronounced as [ŋ].

The [s] in "started" is followed by a short [t], which is only slightly aspirated (as is normal for [t] whenever it occurs after [s] in English). In my pronunciation the first vowel in "started" does not contain any *r*-coloring, so there is no lowering of the third formant. But the very quick stop in the middle of this word is voiced, as can be seen by the voicing striations at time 1500. In a phonetic transcription it should be written [d] rather than [t]. My vowel in nearly all past tense "-ed" forms is fairly high, as you can see from the low value of the first formant. This is why I have written [ɪ] rather than [ə]. The same is true for the first vowel in "again" (and other unstressed vowels before velar consonants). Note also the lengthening of the final syllable in "again," and the lowering of the pitch to creaky voice (shown by the increased distance between the vertical striations) as the sentence ends. Now look at Table 8.2. This shows the centers of each segment. Compare them with the way in which you placed each segment.

Table 8.2

The centers of the segments in Figure 8.12.

Segment	ʃ	i	k	ʰ	eɪ	m	b	æ	k	ŋ
Time scale	40	160	280	350	450	580	650	760	920	1007
Segment	s	t	ɑ	d	ɪ	d	ɪ	g	ɛ	n
Time scale	1220	1280	1400	1500	1570	1630	1680	1750	1900	1980

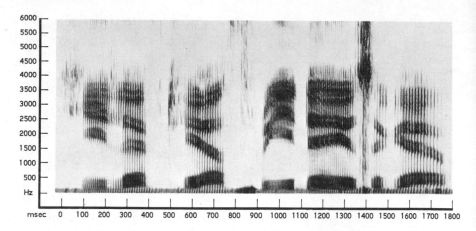

Figure 8.13 *A spectrogram of "He left here three days ago" (British accent).*

Now try to segment Figure 8.13, a spectrogram of the utterance "He left here three days ago." Accompanying Figure 8.13 is Table 8.3, which shows the centers of the segments in the above sentence, but do not consult this table or read on until you have tried to label the spectrogram yourself.

The first point to note is the amount of friction in the initial [h]. This sound might well have been transcribed as a voiceless palatal fricative (ç]. This amount of friction probably occurs only when the word "he" is strongly stressed.

In this particular utterance the initial [l] in "left" has a second formant slightly higher than usual (at about 1550 Hz.) so that it is rather close to that of the following vowel. But the characteristic abrupt change in intensity between the lateral and the vowel in "left" is still evident. Only very faint marks of the [f] are visible; and the [t] closure at the end of the word is very short. (Like many speakers, I tend to omit stops after fricatives in final clusters; if the next word had been "me" or any word beginning with a stop, nasal, or fricative, the [t] would have been completely left out. Check how you pronounce combinations such as "left boy, left man, left side.")

Because of the preceding [t], the [h] in "here" has a great deal of aspiration. In my pronunciation this word contains a diphthong going from

Table 8.3

The centers of the segments in the utterance in Figure 8.13.

Segment	h	i	l	ɛ	f	t	h	iə	θ
Time scale	50	160	250	340	430	480	540	670	850
Segment	r	i	d	eɪ	z	ɩ	g	əʊ	
Time scale	950	1010	1120	1260	1410	1470	1540	1680	

approximately [i] to [ə], as you can see from the movements of the formants.

The [θ] in "three" has not been illustrated in any of the previous spectrograms. It has comparatively little intensity, and has only a faint fricative noise mainly in the upper part of the spectrum. An [r] as in "three" has also not been illustrated previously. It is distinguished mainly by the lowering of the higher formants, including even the fourth formant.

Most of the remaining sounds in this utterance need only a few words of comment. The same kinds of formant transitions occur as in the previous spectrograms. Perhaps the most interesting point is the information on the quality of the last vowel in "ago." The wide separation of the first and second formants shows that in my pronunciation (as often in British English) this diphthong begins with a central vowel, which I represented as [ə] in Table 8.3. Even at the end of the diphthongal movement, the vowel is still not fully back. There are also some points to be observed about the pitch. As in the case of the previous utterance, this phrase ends in creaky voice. But in this case there is a very high pitch in the middle of the phrase, as you can see by the voicing striations that are very close together in the vowel in "three."

Now you should try segmenting a more difficult utterance. Figure 8.14 shows a spectrogram of me saying, "I should have thought spectrograms were unreadable." This phrase was spoken in a normal, but rapid, conversational style. Begin by trying to find the [s] in "spectrograms." Now go backward and identify the vowel in "thought." Is there any voicing in any of the segments between this vowel and the vowel [aɪ] in the first word? Make sure that the symbols you write below the spectrogram correctly indicate how the phrase was actually pronounced, rather than how you might say it. Similarly, when going on from the [s] note that some of the sounds you might have expected to be voiced are actually voiceless. There are also some simple aspects of the intonation to be noted about this phrase. Which syllable was said on the highest pitch, and which on the lowest?

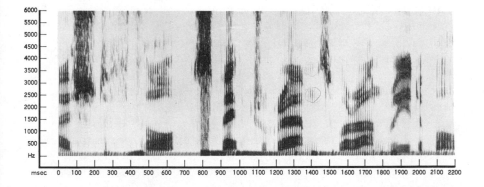

Figure 8.14 *A spectrogram of "I should have thought spectrograms were unreadable." Spoken in a normal, but rapid, conversational style.*

Table 8.4

The centers of the segments in the spectrogram in Figure 8.14.

Segment	aɪ	ʃ	t	f	θ	ə	t	s	p	ʰ	ɛ
Time scale	30	140	220	300	440	560	700	810	870	900	950
Segment		k	t	ɹ̥	ə	g	r	æ	m	z̧	w
Time scale		1000	1040	1110	1140	1180	1240	1280	1380	1500	1580
Segment		ə	r	ʌ	n	r	i	d	ə	b	ɯ
Time scale		1590	1620	1680	1790	1870	1920	1980	2020	2070	2180

Table 8.4 shows the centers of the segments in this phrase, as well as I can determine them. Check your transcription against that shown in the table. There is no problem with the first word (except that the diphthong is not a very large one, due to the high rate of speech). But from there till the vowel in "thought," which begins at about time 500, there is no voicing. The vowels in "should" and "have" have been left out, and all the consonants have become voiceless. The [f], which is all there is of the word "have," is as long as many syllables in this phrase.

Note that there is a very short burst of aspiration after the [p] in "spectrograms." Surprisingly, considering the rate of utterance, the release of the [k] in this word is just visible (at time 1020). The [t] appears to be highly aspirated, so that the following [r] is almost completely voiceless (and hence more properly written [ɹ̥] or [ʌ̥]). Note the lowering of the third and fourth formants at time 1240, due to the [r] after the release of the velar stop. The fricative at the end of this word appears to be voiceless. I have written it [z̧] rather than [s] because of its lack of intensity.

The third and fourth formants drop down at the end of "were" (time 1620), showing that on this occasion I did pronounce the [r] in this word. This is normal for most speakers of British English when the next word begins with a vowel.

The syllable "read" has the highest pitch in this utterance, and it is immediately followed by two syllables in a very low creaky voice. The first vowel in "-able" contains only two glottal pulses. The final syllable is a back unrounded vowel, which I (and many others) commonly use instead of a syllabic alveolar lateral consonant.

If you want a more difficult exercise in interpreting sound spectrograms, look at Figure 8.15. The text of this utterance has not been given, but it is perfectly possible for you to find out what was said. The utterance was a normal English sentence, containing no proper nouns. It was spoken by the same speaker (myself) and in the same style as all the other spectrograms in this chapter. The rate of speech was more like that of the utterances in Figures 8.12 and 8.13, rather than that of the more rapid utterance in Figure 8.14. There are no sounds that have not occurred in one of the spectrograms in Figures 8.9 through 8.14. However, many of the sounds occur in new combinations, which means that they have slightly different patterns. But if you start with the more obvious sounds, and use your knowledge of possible English words, you should be able to succeed.

The spectrograms that have been used to illustrate this chapter so far are called wide-band spectrograms. They are very accurate in the time dimension. They show each vibration of the vocal cords as a separate vertical line and indicate the precise moment of a stop burst with a vertical spike. But they are less accurate in the frequency dimension. There are usually several component frequencies present in a single formant, all of them being lumped together in one wide band on the spectrogram.

It is a fact of physics that one can know either fairly precisely when a sound occurred or, to a comparable degree of accuracy, what its frequency is. This should be intuitively clear when you recall that knowing the frequency of a sound involves observing the variations in air pressure over a period of time. This period of time has to be long enough to insure observations of a number of repetitions of the variations of air pressure.

Spectrograms that are more accurate in the frequency dimension (at the expense of accuracy in the time dimension) are called narrow-band spectrograms. Figure 8.16 shows both wide and narrow band spectrograms of the question "Is Pat sad, or mad?" In the wide-band spectrogram there are sharp spikes at the release of each stop. These spikes are smeared in the time dimension in the narrow-band spectrogram. But the frequencies that compose each formant are visible.

When the vocal cords vibrate they produce harmonics of their fundamental frequency of vibration. Thus when they are vibrating at 100 Hz. they produce harmonics at whole-number multiples of this frequency, namely, 200, 300, 400 Hz., etc. In a given vowel, the particular harmonics that are evident are those that correspond to the resonances of the vocal-tract shape occurring

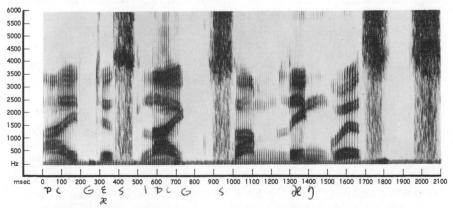

Figure 8.15 *A spectrogram of an ordinary English sentence containing no names (British accent).*

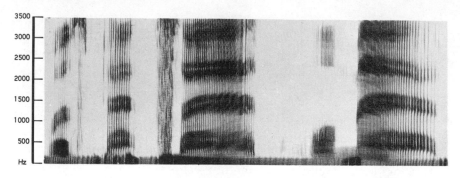

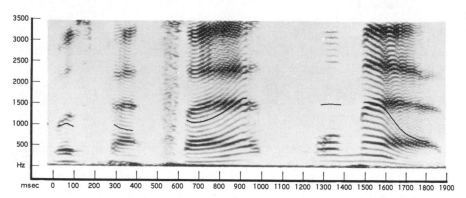

Figure 8.16 *Wide-band spectrogram (upper part of the figure) and narrow-band (lower part) of the question "Is Pat sad, or mad?" A line has been drawn through the tenth harmonic in the narrow-band spectrogram.*

in that vowel. In the beginning of the vowel in "sad," the vocal cords are vibrating at about 100 Hz., and the first formant is at 500 Hz. This indicates that the frequency component that is five times the fundamental frequency (the fifth harmonic) is the most emphasized. At this point, the fourth and sixth harmonics are also within the formant band. But near the end of this vowel, when the vocal cords are vibrating nearer 150 Hz., the first formant is still at about 500 Hz., but is now composed of the third and fourth harmonics —450 Hz. and 600 Hz.

As we have already noted, the quality of a vowel sound depends on the frequencies of the formants. But the pitch depends on the rate of vibration of the vocal cords. In order to make this point clear, examine the second formant in "sad." Note in the wide-band spectrogram that it has a comparatively steady frequency—about 1400 Hz. Count up from the base line in the narrow-band spectrogram and find the harmonic that is darkest near the beginning of the word. Now find the harmonic that is darkest near the end. You should find that the center of this formant is formed by the thirteenth harmonic near the beginning of the word, and the ninth harmonic near the end. Similarly, note that the first and second formants in the vowel in "mad" are also at about 500 and 1400. At the beginning of this word the fourth and ninth harmonics are nearest these values. At the end it is more like the eighth and twentieth.

Narrow-band spectrograms are obviously most useful for determining the intonation—or tone—of an utterance. One can do this by looking at the fundamental frequency itself, but when this goes from, say, 100 to 120 Hz., the frequency of the tenth harmonic will go from 1000 to 1200 Hz., which is much easier to see. In Figure 8.16 a line has been drawn through the tenth harmonic to illustrate this fact. (In places such as the vowel [ə], at time 1300, where the tenth harmonic is not visible, its position had to be estimated on the basis that its frequency must be double that of the fifth harmonic.) The actual pitch—or, to be more exact, the fundamental frequency—at any moment will be one-tenth that of the tenth harmonic.

We may now summarize the kinds of information that can and cannot be obtained from spectrograms. The most reliable measurements will be those of the length of the segments, for which purpose spectrograms are even better than waveforms. Differences among vowels, nasals, and laterals can be seen on spectrograms, whereas it may be impossible to see these differences in the waveforms.

Spectrograms are usually fairly reliable indicators of relative vowel quality. The frequency of the first formant certainly shows the relative vowel height quite accurately. The distance between the first and second formants reflects the degree of backness quite well, but there may be confusions due to variations in the degree of lip rounding.

It is also possible to tell many things about the manner of articulation from spectrograms. For example, one can usually see whether a stop has been weakened to a fricative, or even to an approximant. Affrication of a stop can be seen on most occasions. Trills can be separated from taps, and voiced from voiceless sounds. One can also observe the relative rates of movement of different articulations.

Spectrograms cannot be used to measure degrees of nasalization, nor are they much help in differentiating between adjacent places of articulation. For studying these aspects of speech, techniques such as x-ray cinematography are far more useful.

The last subject that must be dealt with in this chapter is that of differences among individual speakers. This is important for two reasons. First, anyone working in phonetics should be able to form an opinion as to the extent of idiosyncratic qualities in an individual's voice. Second, one must know how to discount purely individual features in an acoustic record if one is to measure features that are linguistically significant.

Spectrograms of a person's voice are sometimes called "voice-prints," and they are said to be as individual as his fingerprints. This is a greatly exaggerated claim. But if it were true it would be very useful. Banks would be able to verify a depositor's identity over the telephone, and the police would

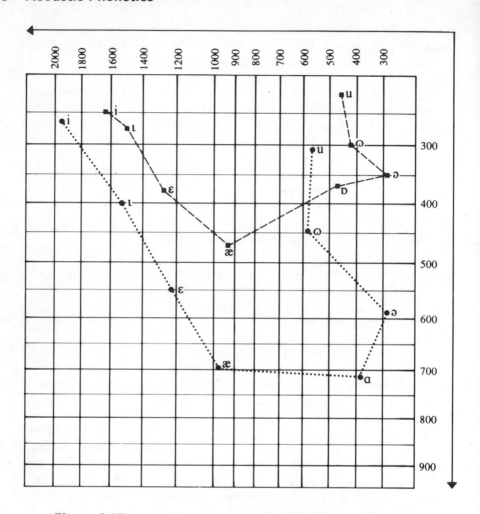

Figure 8.17 *A formant chart showing the relationship between my vowels (dashed line) and the average American English vowels (dotted line). The frequency of the first formant is plotted on the ordinate (the vertical axis), and the difference between the frequencies of the second and first formant is plotted on the abscissa (the horizontal axis).*

be able to positively identify criminals whose conversations had been recorded. Some individual characteristics are recorded in spectrograms. As was already noted, the position of the fourth and higher formants in most vowels is indicative of a speaker's voice quality rather than the linguistic aspects of the sounds. Similarly, the exact locations of the higher formants in nasals depend to a great extent on individual physiological characteristics of the speaker.

There are also a number of features observable on spectrograms that indicate a speaker's speech habits and are not language dependent. For example, there is a great deal of individuality in the length and type of aspiration that occurs after initial voiceless stops. The rate of transition of the formants after voiced stops also varies from one individual to another.

Nobody knows how many individuals share similar characteristics. There are occasions when one can say that the voice on a particular recording is *probably not* the same as the voice on some other recording, and times when one can say that the voice on a recording *could* be the same as the voice on another. Speaker identification using spectrographic evidence has been used in a number of criminal cases. My best guess at the moment, based on studies reported in the literature, my own examination of thousands of spectrograms, and appearances in a large number of court cases, is that an expert may be wrong about one time in twenty in his positive identification of an unknown voice on a recording. In my view, it is completely irresponsible to say, as I have heard witnesses testify in court, "The voice on the recording is that of the accused and could be that of no other speaker."

The other aspect of individual variation is more important from a general phonetic point of view. In summarizing the uses of the sound spectrograph I was careful to say that spectrograms showed *relative* vowel quality. It is clearly true that one can use spectrograms such as that in Figure 8.13 to tell that I have a higher vowel in "three" than I have in the beginning of the diphthong in "here." One can also use formant plots such as that in Figure 8.7 to show that the average American English vowel in "who'd" is further forward than that in "hawed." But it is not so easy to say if the vowel in a given word as pronounced by one speaker is higher or lower than that of another speaker.

When you used Figure 8.8 to plot the formant frequencies of the vowels in Figure 8.6, you may have noticed that each vowel is shifted up and to the right in comparison with the plot of the American English vowels in Figure 8.7. You can see this more clearly when the two sets of vowels are plotted on the same chart, as in Figure 8.17. (This figure will, incidentally, enable you to check your own plot in Figure 8.8.) My formant frequencies are all lower than those of the average American English speaker, but this is not because of a difference between British and American English. It is just that I, as an individual, have larger resonating cavities, and hence lower formant frequencies than the average male speaker.

In general, when two different speakers pronounce sets of vowels with the same phonetic quality, the relative positions of these vowels on a formant chart will be the same, but the absolute values of the formant frequencies will differ from speaker to speaker. Unfortunately, no one has yet determined exactly how to average out the individual characteristics so that a formant plot will show only the phonetic qualities of the vowels. The simplest way to deal with this problem is probably to regard the average frequency of the fourth formant as an indicator of the individual's head size, and then express the values of the other formants as percentages of the mean fourth formant frequency. But this possibility is not open when, as here, the fourth formant

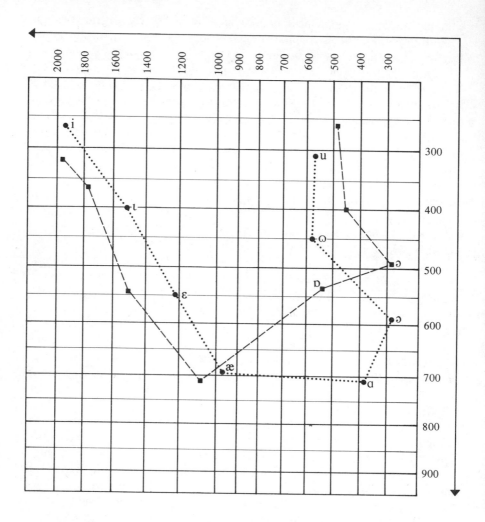

Figure 8.18   *A formant showing the same data as in Figure 8.17, but with my vowels normalized. The frequency of the first formant is plotted on the ordinate (the vertical axis), and the difference between the frequencies of the second and first formant is plotted on the abscissa (the horizontal axis).*

frequencies have not been reported for both sets of vowels. An alternative method is to assume that each set of vowels is representative of the complete range of a speaker's vowel qualities. Then we can express the formant frequency of each vowel in terms of the total range of that formant in that speaker's voice. This method will minimize differences between extreme vowels, falsely assuming that all speakers of all languages pronounce [i, ɑ, u] in much the same way as one another. But, as may be seen from Figure 8.18, it does make it superficially easier to compare sets of vowels spoken by different speakers. The major differences that remain in Figure 8.18 probably do reflect the differences between my speech and American English. It seems true that my vowels in "heed" and "hid" are closer together and that my vowel in "hod" is very different from the average American English vowel. Again, however, the vagueness of these remarks merely demonstrates that phoneticians do not really know how to compare acoustic data on the sounds of one individual with those of another. This task is still the major problem in acoustic phonetics. If we could solve it we would be able to design machines that would type out a phonetic transcription of whatever was spoken into them. And we might be able to isolate the individual characteristics of a person's voice, so that a "voice-print" would really be as distinctive as a fingerprint.

Vowels and Vowel-like Articulations 9

In previous chapters we saw that vowels can be characterized mainly in terms of three features: (1) the so-called vowel height, which is inversely proportional to the frequency of the first formant; (2) the so-called degree of backness, which is directly proportional to the difference between the frequencies of the second and first formants; and (3) the degree of lip rounding, an articulatory feature that has complex acoustic correlates. This chapter will discuss these three features in greater detail and will also consider some additional, less prominent, features of vowel quality.

Figure 4.2 in Chapter 4 shows the relative auditory qualities of the English vowels and diphthongs. As I mentioned at that time, the precise locations of the points in this diagram reflected acoustic measurements, and not mere auditory impressions. It can, therefore, be considered to be a formant chart, similar to that shown in Figure 9.1. Some of the acoustic measurements were the formant frequencies reported in the previous chapter. They were supplemented by measurements of the formant frequencies of the other vowels and diphthongs, all taken from published sources. (For bibliographical details, see the section on sources at the end of the book.)

Most phoneticians would agree that Figure 9.1 is a fairly accurate reflection of both the way in which American English vowels have traditionally been described as well as the way in which listeners perceive the relative auditory qualities. During the discussion of this diagram in Chapter 4 you probably made up your own mind on the extent to which it agrees with your

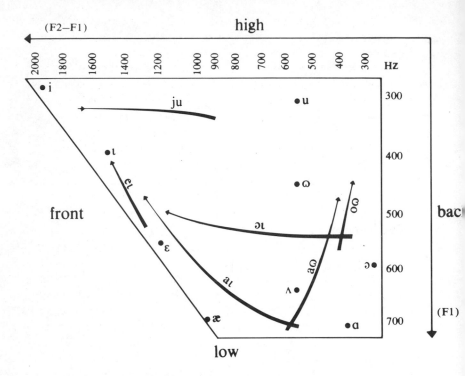

Figure 9.1 *A combined acoustic and auditory representation of some of the vowels of American English. (Compare Figures 4.2 and 8.7.)*

own perception of the relative distance between vowels. But remember that if it seems inaccurate to you, this may be because your accent is not identical with the form of American English represented in the figure.

Cardinal Vowels

When describing the vowels that occurred on a particular occasion, one usually does not have access to measurements of the formant frequencies. The phonetician who wants to describe the vowels of a certain dialect or of a certain speaker usually has to rely on his auditory ability. He plots the vowels on a vowel chart, so that anybody knowing about vowel charts can see where the points are, and can infer the quality of the vowels he is describing.

If a vowel chart is to be truly interpretable, the vowels on it must be plotted with reference to certain fixed points. These points must be known to both the person originally plotting the vowels and to the people who are going to interpret his descriptions. The space within a vowel chart represents a continuum of possible qualities. Before I can convey anything to you by telling you that a certain vowel is half way (or a third of the way) between one vowel and another, I must be certain that we both know the exact quality of the vowels that act as reference points. There are several ways in which known fixed points can be provided.

In the first place, we can rely on the fact that a vowel chart shows the limits of possible vowel quality. Thus a point in the extreme upper left corner of the chart represents a vowel with the highest and most front quality possible. If the tongue were moved higher or more forward, a palatal consonant would be produced. A vowel in the extreme lower right corner represents the lowest and most back quality possible. Further movement of the tongue would produce a pharyngeal consonant. Similarly the points in the other two corners of the diagram represent extreme qualities. We would have some fixed reference point if I could rely on the fact that you and I both know the sound of the highest and most front possible vowel, the lowest and most back possible vowel, and so on.

This use of a vowel chart is quite satisfactory for the description of vowels that are near the corners of the possible vowel area. But it does not provide enough fixed points for the description of other vowels. Recognizing this problem, Daniel Jones proposed a series of eight **cardinal vowels**, evenly spaced around the outside of the possible vowel area and designed to act as fixed reference points for phoneticians. In no case is the quality of a cardinal vowel exactly the same as that of an English vowel. It can happen that a particular language may have a vowel that is virtually identical with a cardinal vowel. Several of the French vowels are at least very similar. But by definition the cardinal vowels are arbitrary reference points.

Two of the cardinal vowels are defined in articulatory terms. Cardinal vowel (1) is produced with the lips spread and the tongue as high and far forward as possible without causing audible friction. It is therefore something like the vowel [i], but with a more extreme quality. The symbol for it is also [i]. When one wishes to show that one is referring specifically to the cardinal vowel, and not to a vowel in a particular language, then the symbol may be underlined [i̲].

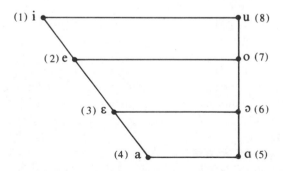

Figure 9.2   *The cardinal vowels.*

The other cardinal vowel that is defined in articulatory terms is cardinal vowel (5). This vowel is made with the lips in a neutral position—neither spread nor rounded—and with the tongue as low and as far back as possible. Accordingly, it is something like some forms of the American English vowel [ɑ] as in "father, hot" or the British English vowel [ɒ] as in "hot." The American [ɑ], however, is not usually made with the tongue as far back as possible, and the British [ɒ] usually has slight lip rounding. The symbol for cardinal vowel (5) is [ɑ]. Again with this and with all the other cardinal vowels, the symbol may be underlined, [ɑ̠], when one is referring specifically to a cardinal vowel.

Try to make cardinal vowels (1) and (5) in accordance with these descriptions. Remember to have your lips fully spread when saying [i̠]. Make sure that your tongue is so close to the roof of the mouth that you would produce a voiced palatal fricative [j] if you raised it any higher. Similarly, when producing [ɑ̠], make sure that the tongue is pulled so far down and back in the mouth that you are almost producing a voiced pharyngeal fricative [ʕ] (not to be confused with a glottal stop, which is [ʔ]).

Cardinal vowels (2), (3), and (4) are defined as front vowels that form a series of auditorily equidistant steps between numbers (1) and (5). As we saw in the last chapter, the acoustic definition of front vowels is that the distance between formant one and formant two is as great as possible. We can also specify in acoustic terms what is meant by auditorily equidistant steps. It implies that when these five vowels are plotted on a formant chart of the kind we have been discussing, they will be represented by points that are equal distances apart.

Cardinal vowels (6), (7), and (8) are defined as vowels that continue on from number (5), with the same size steps as in the first part of the series, but that are in the case of these vowels as back as possible (that is, with as small a distance as possible between formants one and two). In order to continue with these same size steps, the back vowels have to become not only increasingly higher but also increasingly more rounded. As a result, cardinal vowel (8) is in fact the highest, most back, most rounded possible vowel—even though it is not defined in this way.

The symbols for cardinal vowels (2), (3), and (4) are [e, ɛ, a], respectively. The symbols for cardinal vowels (6), (7), and (8) are [ɔ, o, u]. Most of these vowels have qualities something like those of the English vowels we have been symbolizing in a similar way. In accordance with the principles of the IPA, the symbols chosen for most of the English vowels are those of the nearest cardinal vowels. The major exception is the vowel in "fat," which, following the tradition of many English-speaking phoneticians, has been symbolized by [æ] rather than [a].

The cardinal vowel system has been extensively used by phoneticians in the description of a wide variety of languages. There are, however, a number of difficulties in this respect. First, as Daniel Jones said in *An Outline of English Phonetics* (London: Heffer, 1957): "The values of the cardinal vowels cannot be learned from written descriptions; they should be learned by oral instruction from a teacher who knows them." It was for this reason that I did not suggest that you try to produce a complete series of cardinal vowels immediately after reading the descriptions given above. If you have access to a recording of the cardinal vowels and if there is someone who can listen critically to your imitations of them, then it is possible to learn to produce them with a fair degree of accuracy. But the precise use of the cardinal vowel system as advocated by Daniel Jones can probably be achieved only by a group of phoneticians who have been in personal contact with Daniel Jones or someone taught by him.

A second problem with the cardinal vowel system is that no one has been able to show how acoustic analyses of the cardinal vowels recorded by Daniel Jones himself can be reconciled with his definitions of auditory *equidistance* between the vowels. There seems to be no way of plotting a complete set of cardinal vowels on a formant chart without making cardinal vowels (5), (6), (7), and (8) much closer together than (1), (2), (3), (4), and (5). It seems as if the auditory distances between these reference points do in fact correspond more closely to the distances between the points in the chart in Figure 9.2. The line on the left-hand side of the figure slants because the degree of frontness (the distance between formant two and formant one) decreases in going from [i] to [ɑ]. Because of the slope of this line, the auditory distance between each of the front cardinal vowels is greater than that between each of the back vowels.

Another problem with the cardinal vowel system is that there has been a great deal of confusion over whether vowels are being described in terms of tongue height or in terms of acoustic properties. Many phoneticians—and most textbooks on phonetics—talk about diagrams such as Figure 9.2 as if they specified the highest point of the tongue. The distance between the points representing the back vowels is therefore said to be less because the movements of the tongue are said to be less. The differences in auditory quality are presumed to be the same in both front and back vowels, despite the smaller movements of the tongue in back vowels, because back vowels also have increasing lip rounding. But, unfortunately, diagrams such as Figures 9.1 and 9.2 do not specify the position of the highest point of the tongue. Figure 9.3, however, shows the relative positions of the highest point of the tongue in a set of cardinal vowels, and these positions form an outline very different from that in Figure 9.2. The same point can be made by referring to Figures 1.9 and 1.10, which show the articulatory positions of some of the vowels in Figure 9.1. The position of the highest point of the tongue is not a valid indicator of vowel quality. I have tried to avoid describing vowels in terms of tongue height, using instead the term vowel height—meaning an auditory quality that can be specified in acoustic terms rather than in articulatory terms.

Despite all these problems the cardinal vowel system works fairly successfully. It has allowed the vowels of a large number of languages and dialects

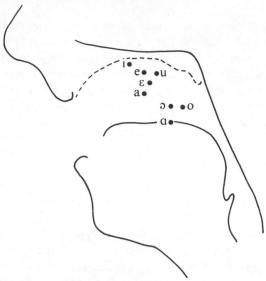

Figure 9.3 *The highest points of the tongue as shown in a published set of x-rays of cardinal vowels (see Sources). The outline of the upper surface of the vocal tract is not clear on the x-rays and is, therefore, estimated.*

to be described with far greater precision than has any other method. The descriptions may have been said in the past to be descriptions of tongue height, but in fact phoneticians had all along been making very accurate judgments of the frequency of the first formant and the distance between the frequencies of the second and first formants.

Secondary Cardinal Vowels

The cardinal vowels have increasing degrees of lip rounding, [i] having spread lips, [a] a neutral lip position, and [u] being fully rounded. For all pairs of vowels that have lip positions similar to those of the nearest cardinal vowels, distances on a vowel chart are accurately reflected by measurements of the formant frequencies. But this is not so for vowels with degrees of rounding that are unlike those of the nearest cardinal vowels. Front vowels that are rounded or back vowels that are unrounded will be misplaced on a chart if we rely simply on acoustic criteria. The degree of rounding is an independent dimension that must be stated separately from the degree of height (the inverse of the first formant) and the degree of backness (the distance between formant two and formant one).

As an aid in the description of vowels with different degrees of lip rounding, there is a series of secondary cardinal vowels numbered (9) through (16). These vowels differ from the eight primary cardinal vowels in having an opposite amount of lip rounding. Cardinal vowel (9) is defined as a vowel with the same tongue position as cardinal vowel number (1), but with closely rounded lips. Cardinal vowels (10) through (16) have the same tongue positions as cardinal vowels (2) through (8), but continually decreasing—instead of increasing—lip rounding. Cardinal vowel (16), therefore, is an unrounded version of cardinal vowel (8).

Figure 9.4 shows the symbols for most of these vowels, together with some additional symbols for central vowels. No special symbols have been given for the low vowels, since these vowels are not much affected by adding

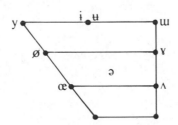

Figure 9.4 *Some secondary cardinal vowels and some central vowels.*

small amounts of lip rounding. The symbols [ɨ] and [ʉ] are used for unrounded and rounded vowels midway between cardinal vowels (1) and (8). The symbol [ə] is not defined in terms of cardinal vowels but is used, as we have seen, for a range of mid-central vowels. In addition, note that the symbol [ʌ], which is the symbol for an unrounded cardinal vowel (6), is often used for a low central vowel.

Even if you cannot make a complete set of the primary cardinal vowels, you should try to make some of the secondary cardinal vowels. Practice rounding and unrounding your lips while saying cardinal vowel (1), so that you say [iyiyiy]. Make sure that you maintain an absolutely constant tongue position and move only your lips. Next, repeat this exercise with cardinal vowel (2) or some similar vowel of the [e] type. Remember that the rounding for [ø] is not as close as that for [y]. Last, try unrounding cardinal vowel (8), producing [uɯuɯuɯ]. The usual difficulty here is in maintaining a sufficiently back tongue position, as most dialects of English do not have a very back variety of [u].

Vowels in Other Languages

For those who do not know the cardinal vowels, an alternative method of describing vowels is to use as reference points the vowels of a particular dialect of a language that is known to both the person making the description and the person reading the description. This is what I have been trying to do in reference to the vowels of Midwestern American English as shown in Figure 9.1. If you and I both know what these vowels sound like, then the points on Figure 9.1 provide good reference points. When I remark, for example, that in some forms of Scottish English the vowel in "sacks" is only a little lower than the Midwestern [ɛ] vowel, then you should be able to pronounce this word in this particular way.

Any language will serve to provide known reference points. For example, when teaching English as a second language one might use the vowels of the first language of the students as reference points for comparison with the dialect of English that one is trying to teach. If a chart of the vowels of this language is not available, then the instructor's first step should be to make one. This will involve comparing the vowels of this language with the vowels of some language known to the instructor for which there is a chart available.

Fortunately, there are published descriptions of the auditory quality of the vowels in a large number of languages. For some of these languages sets of acoustic measurements are also available. In the following paragraphs we will consider the vowels of three languages for which the auditory impressions of phoneticians have been to some extent confirmed by acoustic measurements. Vowel charts for all three languages are shown in Figure 9.5. The sources for the data are listed at the end of the book.

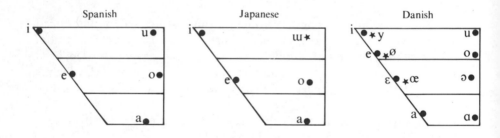

Figure 9.5 *The vowels of Spanish, Japanese, and Danish. Front rounded vowels and back unrounded vowels are indicated by asterisks.*

Spanish has a very simple system, contrasting only five vowels. Note that the symbols used in broad transcriptions of Spanish are [i, e, a, o, u]. Obviously these symbols do not have the same values in Spanish as they do in English or in descriptions of cardinal vowels.

Japanese also has a set of five vowels. In a broad phonetic transcription these might also have been transcribed [i, e, a, o, u]. But in a narrower transcription that reflects the phonetic quality of the vowels more accurately, the high back vowel could be transcribed as [ɯ], as has been done in Figure 9.3. The point representing this vowel has been distinguished from the others. It has been marked by an asterisk to show that this vowel does not have the lip rounding associated with the primary cardinal vowel in this area. Note also that [e] in Japanese is slightly lower than it is in Spanish. This is the kind of small difference between vowels that is easily and conveniently expressible in terms of vowel charts.

Asterisks have also been used to represent the quality of some of the Danish vowels shown in the third chart in Figure 9.5. But in this case it is to indicate that those vowels differ from the primary cardinal vowels in the area by having more rather than less lip rounding. Danish has three front rounded vowels, only two of which are in phonemic contrast. The high front rounded vowel [y] contrasts with [ø] in some contexts and with [œ] in other contexts. All the Danish vowels shown in Figure 9.5 can occur in long or short form. The qualities of most of the short vowels are very similar to those of the long vowels, but in the case of [a, ɔ, o], the short versions are slightly lower and more centralized.

The three charts shown in Figure 9.5 are good examples of the way in which vowels may be described. They are in part descriptions of the relative auditory quality, in part articulatory descriptions. For the vowels in which the lip rounding is the same as that of the primary cardinal vowels, they reflect the acoustic data exactly. In these cases they are equivalent to plots of the first formant frequency against the difference between the frequencies of the second and first formants.

Front rounded and back unrounded vowels cannot be represented in terms of a vowel chart that assumes that the degree of lip rounding is like that of the primary cardinal vowels. In describing these other vowels, the degree of lip rounding must also be specified. One way of doing this is to use asterisks rather than ordinary points. The asterisks indicate that the lip rounding is more like that of the secondary cardinal vowels than that of the primary ones. The locations of the asterisks indicate the vowel qualities in much the same way as the points indicate the qualities of the other vowels. It is as if they show what the formant frequencies would have been had the lip rounding been like that of the primary cardinal vowels.

When we consider the actual formant frequencies of front rounded vowels and back unrounded vowels, we can see why these vowels are not quite so common in most languages. Adding lip rounding to front vowels primarily affects formant two. A high front rounded vowel [y] has a considerably lowered formant two, so that in some sense it sounds as if it were between [i] and [u]. Similarly [ø], which is the rounded vowel corresponding to [e], has a lower formant two (and also a slightly lower formant one) than [e]. If its formants were plotted on a formant chart it would appear nearer the center. Conversely, removing lip rounding from the back vowel [u] to produce [ɯ] raises formant two, so that it would also be nearer the center of a formant chart. If the vowels of a language are to be maximally distinct from one another, then the front vowels will have to be unrounded, the back vowels rounded.

One of the forces acting on languages may be called the **principle of perceptual separation**, whereby the sounds of a language are kept acoustically distinct so as to make it easier for the listener to distinguish one from another. As a result of this principle, the degree of lip rounding can be predicted from the degree of backness and, to a lesser extent, the degree of height in by far the majority of languages. Front vowels are usually unrounded, and back vowels are usually rounded, with the degree of rounding increasing with the degree of height. In this way the vowels of a language are kept maximally distinct.

Vowel Harmony

We have seen that in English there are phonological restrictions on the vowels that can occur in certain positions. The vowels /ɪ, ɛ, æ, ʌ, ɒ/, for example, cannot occur in a stressed syllable without a consonant at the end. In some languages there are phonological restrictions of another kind. It sometimes happens that the vowels of a language can be divided into distinct subsets, and the members of different subsets never occur together within one word. This phenomenon is known as **vowel harmony**. There is said to be vowel harmony in a language if the vowels are constrained so that all the vowels in a single word must have some property or properties in common.

Turkish is an example of a well-known language with vowel harmony. The eight vowels of Turkish may be arranged in four sets of four as shown in Figure 9.6. A monosyllabic Turkish word may contain any of the eight vowels.

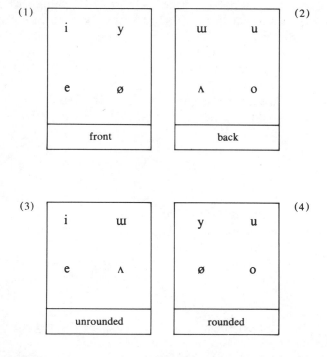

Figure 9.6 *The eight vowels of Turkish arranged so as to show the sets that occur in vowel harmony. Each vowel occurs in set 1 or 2 and also in set 3 or 4.*

But in a word of more than one syllable, the vowels are all either front (set 1) or back (set 2) and either unrounded (set 3) or rounded (set 4). Consequently, if you know that one vowel in a polysyllabic Turkish word is, for example, [i], you also know that all the other vowels in the word must be either the same vowel [i], or one other vowel, in this case [e]. Other languages have forms of vowel harmony in which the two sets of vowels are distinguished by differences in vowel height or, as we will see in the next section, other aspects of vowel quality.

Wide and Narrow Vowels

Differences in vowel quality can usually be described in terms of variations in the degrees of height, backness, and lip rounding. But in some languages there are differences in vowel quality that cannot be described in these terms. For example, in Twi (a West African language spoken mainly in Ghana) the two sets of vowels that operate in the vowel harmony sets differ mainly in the width of the pharynx. In the one set there are **wide** vowels, in which the root of the tongue is drawn forward so that the part of the vocal tract in the pharynx is considerably enlarged. In the other set there are **narrow** vowels, in which there is no advancement of the tongue root. Figure 9.7 shows the positions of the vocal organs in two Twi vowels that differ in this way. Note that in the wide vowel [e] the whole tongue is bunched up lengthwise in comparison with the narrow vowel, here symbolized as [i].

In English there are no pairs of vowels that are distinguished simply by one being wide and the other being narrow. But this aspect of vowel quality does operate to some extent in conjunction with variations in vowel height. The high vowels [i] and [u], as in "heed" and "who'd," are wider than the mid high vowels [ɪ] and [ʊ], as in "hid" and "hood."

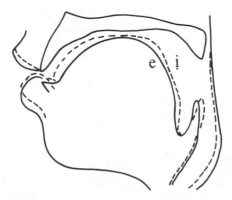

Figure 9.7 *Narrow (broken line) and wide (solid line) vowels in Twi, a language spoken in Ghana.*

The terms tense and lax are sometimes used to describe wide and narrow vowels. As far as the high vowels are concerned, this usage fits in quite well with the way in which we were using these terms to describe English vowels in Chapter 4. But it is less appropriate for describing the difference between other tense–lax pairs of English vowels. It is best to regard vowel width as a phonetic quality, which is definable in physiological terms. The terms tense–lax may then be retained to specify phonologically determined sets of vowels. In this way the set of English vowels that can occur in open syllables may be called the tense vowels, and the set of English vowels that can occur before [ŋ] may be called the lax vowels.

Rhotacized Vowels

As was noted in Chapter 4, many forms of American English have rhotacized vowels in words such as "sir, cur, bird." We noted at the time that rhotacization is an auditory quality—the so-called *r*-coloring that can be produced in more than one way. It is therefore an aspect of vowel quality that, like height and backness, is most appropriately defined in acoustic terms.

In a rhotacized vowel (or portion of a vowel) there is a marked lowering of the frequency of the third formant. The frequencies of the first two formants determine the vowel height and backness. The frequency of the third formant conveys comparatively little information about either of these aspects of vowel quality. If you look back at Figure 8.8 you will see that the third formant falls only slightly throughout the whole series of nonrhotacized vowels. But, as you can see in Figure 9.8, there is a large fall in the frequency of the third formant in words such as "deer" and "bear," in which the ends of the vowels are considerably rhotacized in many forms of American English. Furthermore, throughout a word such as "heard," the third formant may be low (as in Figure 9.8), indicating that the whole vowel has a rhotacized quality.

Nasalization

In all the vowels we have been considering in this chapter so far, the soft palate has been raised so that there is a velic closure and air does not flow out through the nose. But vowels may be **nasalized** if the soft palate is lowered to allow part of the airstream to escape through the nose. The diacritic [˜] may be placed over any vowel to indicate that it is nasalized.

Learn to produce a variety of nasalized vowels. Start by saying the low vowel [æ̃] as in "man" [mæ̃n]. Alternate a series of nasalized and non-nasalized vowels, saying [æ̃ æ æ̃ æ æ̃ æ]. You should be able to feel your soft palate moving up and down when you say these vowels. Try to say a whole series of nasalized vowels [ĩ ẽ ɛ̃ ã ɑ̃ ɔ̃ õ ũ]. Alternate each of these vowels with its nonnasalized counterpart.

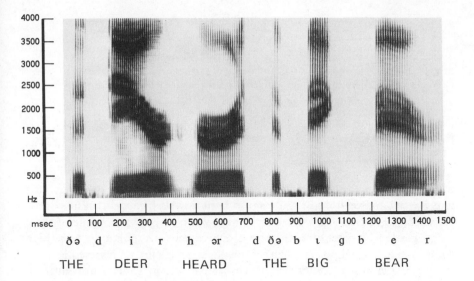

Figure 9.8 *A spectrogram showing the lowering of the frequency of the third formant (and to a lesser extent of the second formant) during rhotacized sounds in a sentence spoken by a Californian.*

Many languages have contrasts between nasalized and nonnasalized (oral) vowels. Thus French contrasts "main" [mɛ̃] (hand) with "mets" [mɛ] (dish), and "ment" [mã] (lies, *vb.*) with "mât" [ma] (mast).

Consonants such as [m, n, ŋ] are, of course, nasals, but they are not *nasalized*, since this term implies that part of the air goes out through the nose and part through the mouth. Contrasts between nasalized and non-nasalized consonants do not occur in any language, but some consonants such as [w, j, r, l] may be nasalized if they occur next to nasalized vowels. In Yoruba the word for "they" is [w̃′ɔ́], with the whole syllable being nasalized.

Summary of Vowel Quality

Table 9.1 summarizes the discussion on vowels. There are two features of vowel quality—height and backness—that are used to contrast one vowel with another in nearly every language, and there are four other features that are used less frequently. Of the six features, three reflect auditory properties of vowels, and three reflect physiological properties.

Semivowels

A semivowel is a kind of approximant consisting of a nonsyllabic vowel occurring at the beginning or end of a syllable. When at the beginning of a syllable, it usually consists of a rapid glide from a high vowel position to that

Table 9.1

The features of vowel quality.

Quality	Properties	Observable correlates
height	auditory	frequency of formant one
backness	auditory	difference between frequencies of formant two and formant one
rounding	physiological	lip position
width	physiological	width of the pharynx
rhotacization	auditory	frequency of formant three
nasalization	physiological	position of the soft palate

of the following vowel. The semivowels in English are [j] and [w], which are like nonsyllabic versions of the English high vowels [i] and [u] respectively. In other languages there are the three high vowels [i, u, y]. In some of these languages (e.g., French) there is also a semivowel corresponding to the high front rounded vowel [y]. The symbol for this sound is [ɥ], an inverted letter h. Examples of words contrasting three semivowels in French are given in Table 9.2.

Table 9.2

Contrasts involving palatal, labial-palatal, and labial-velar approximants in French.

Palatal		Labial-palatal		Labial-velar	
mjɛt	(crumb)	mɥɛt	(mute)	mwɛt	(sea gull)
lje	(tied)	lɥi	(him)	lwi	(Louis)
		ɥit	(eight)	wi	(yes)

Because a semivowel is a kind of approximant, it can be considered to have a particular place of articulation, just like any consonant. We have already noted that [j] is a palatal approximant, and [w] is a labial-velar approximant. The semivowel [ɥ] is a labial-palatal approximant. We have not discussed this place of articulation before because approximants are almost the only sounds that are made in this region.

When learning to produce the distinction between the French sounds /w/ and /ɥ/, note that the English /w/ is in between the two French sounds. It is not the same as French /w/. It is, of course, also true that /u/ in English is in between the two French sounds [u] and [y]. As is often the case, when a language does not have to distinguish between two possibilities, it produces a sound that is in between the two. Recall, for example, the quality of English vowels before [ŋ] and before [r], where there are no oppositions between tense and lax vowels.

In order to produce the French sound /w/ as in "oui" [wi] (yes), start from a high rounded vowel that is fully back, like a cardinal [u]. Glide from this vowel very rapidly to the following vowel. The result will be similar but not identical to the English word "we" [wi]. Now try to say the French sound [ɥ] as in "huit" [ɥit] (eight). This time start from the secondary cardinal vowel [y], and glide rapidly to the following vowel.

It is also possible to consider the common form of English [ɹ], as in "red," as a semivowel. In the same way as [w] may be said to be a non-syllabic counterpart of [u], so [ɹ] as in "red" may be said to be a nonsyllabic version of the vowel in "fur." We have been transcribing this vowel as [ər], but in many forms of English it consists of a single segment that might well be transcribed as [ɚ], or even as a syllabic [ɻ]. From a phonetic point of view this is a valid description. But from a phonological point of view it may not be appropriate in describing the sound patterns that occur in English.

Secondary Articulation

It is appropriate to consider secondary articulations in conjunction with vowels because they can usually be described as added vowel-like articulations. The formal definition of a **secondary articulation** is that it is an articulation with a lesser degree of closure occurring at the same time as another (primary) articulation. We will consider four types of secondary articulation.

Palatalization is the addition of a high front tongue position, like that in [i], to another articulation. Russian and other Slavic languages have a series of palatalized consonants that contrast with their nonpalatalized counterparts. Palatalization can be symbolized by [ʲ] after a symbol. Russian words illustrating palatalized sounds are given in Table 9.3.

Table 9.3

Contrasts involving palatalization in Russian.

brat	(brother)	bratʲ	(to take)
krɔf	(roof)	krɔfʲ	(blood)
stal	(he has become)	stalʲ	(steel)
ʒar	(beat)	ʒarʲ	(cook)

The terms palatalization and palatalized may also be used in a slightly different way from the way in which I have been using them so far. Instead of describing a secondary articulation, these terms may be applied in describing a process in which the primary articulation is changed so that it becomes more palatal. Thus sounds are said to be palatalized if the point of articulation moves toward the palatal region in some particular circumstance. For example, the English /k/ in "key" may be said to be palatalized because, instead of the velar contact of the kind that occurs in "car" [kɑ(r)], the place of articulation in "key" is changed so that it is nearer the palatal area. Similarly, palatalization is said to occur when the alveolar fricative [z] in "is" becomes a palato-alveolar fricative in "is she . . . " [ɪʒʃi]. A further extension of the term palatalization occurs in discussions of historical sound change. In Old English the word for "chin" was pronounced with a velar stop [k] at the beginning. The change of this sound into Modern English [tʃ] is said to be one of palatalization, due to the influence of the high front vowel. All these uses of the terms palatalization and palatalized involve descriptions of a process—something becoming something else—rather than a state, such as a secondary articulation.

Velarization, the next secondary articulation to be considered, involves raising the back of the tongue. It can be considered as the addition of an [u]-like tongue position, but without the addition of the lip rounding that also occurs in [u̱]. We have already noted that in many forms of English, syllable final /l/ sounds are velarized and may be written [ɫ].

As an exercise, so that you can appreciate how it is possible to add vowel-like articulations to consonants, try saying [l] with the tip of your tongue on the alveolar ridge, but with the body of your tongue in the position for each of the vowels [i, e, ɛ, a, ɑ, ɔ, o, u]. The first of these sounds is, of course, a palatalized sound very similar to [lʲ]. The last of the series is one form of velarized [ɫ]. Make sure that you can say each of these sounds before and after different vowels. Now compare palatalized and velarized versions of other sounds in syllables such as [nʲ a] and [ṉa]. Remember that [ṉ] is simply [n] with a superimposed unrounded version of [u] (that is, an added [ɯ]).

Pharyngealization is the superimposition of a narrowing of the pharynx. Since cardinal vowel (5)—[ɑ]—has been defined as the lowest, most back possible vowel without producing pharyngeal friction, pharyngealization may be considered as the superimposition of this vowel quality. The IPA diacritic for symbolizing pharyngealization is [~], exactly as for velarization. If it is necessary to distinguish between these two secondary articulations, the appropriate raised vowel symbol can be used. Velarization can be symbolized by adding a raised [ɯ], pharyngealization by a raised [ɑ].

There is very little difference between velarized and pharyngealized sounds, and no language distinguishes between the two possibilities. In Arabic there is a series of consonants that Arabic scholars call emphatic consonants. Some of these sounds are velarized, and some are pharyngealized. All of them can be symbolized with the IPA diacritic [~]. (Arabic scholars unfortunately often use a subscript [.], which we have been using to denote retroflexion. But it is interesting to note that there is some similarity in quality between retroflex stops and velarized or pharyngealized stops. This is due to the fact that in all these sounds the front of the tongue is somewhat hollowed.)

Labialization, the addition of lip rounding, differs from the other secondary articulations in that it can be combined with any of them. Obviously palatalization, velarization, and pharyngealization involve different tongue shapes that cannot occur simultaneously. But nearly all kinds of consonants can have added lip rounding. In a sense, even sounds in which the primary articulators are the lips—for example, [p, b, m]—can be said to be labialized if they are made with added rounding and protrusion of the lips. The official IPA diacritic indicating labialization is [ω] placed under the symbol, but labialization is commonly symbolized by a raised [ʷ].

In some languages (for instance, Twi and other Akan languages spoken in Ghana), labialization co-occurs with palatalization. As palatalization is equivalent to the superimposition of an articulation similar to that in [i], labialization plus palatalization is equivalent to the superimposition of a rounded [i]—that is, [y]. The corresponding semivowel is [ɥ]. Accordingly, these secondary articulations may be symbolized by a raised [ᵚ]. Recall the pronunciation of [ɥ] in French words such as "huit" [ɥit] (eight). Then try to pronounce the name of the language Twi [tᵚi].

Table 9.4 summarizes the secondary articulations we have been dis-

Table 9.4

Secondary articulations and nasalization.

Phonetic term	Brief description	Symbols		
palatalization	raising of the front of the tongue	sʲ	lʲ	dʲ
velarization	raising of the back of the tongue	ɤ	ɫ	ƌ
pharyngealization	retracting of the root of the tongue	ɤ	ɫ	ƌ
labialization	rounding of the lips	sʷ	lʷ	dʷ

cussing. As in some of the previous summary tables, the terms in Table 9.4 are not all mutually exclusive. A sound may or may not have a secondary articulation such as palatalization, velarization, or pharyngealization; additionally, it may or may not be labialized; and also it may or may not be nasalized. To demonstrate this for yourself, try to make a voiced alveolar lateral [l] that is also velarized, labialized, and nasalized.

EXERCISES

A Look at the positions of the tongue in the English vowels shown in Figure 1.9. It has been suggested (see Sources) that vowels can be described in terms of three measurements: (1) the area of the vocal tract at the point of maximum constriction; (2) the distance of this point from the glottis; and (3) a measure of the degree of lip opening. Which of the first two corresponds to what is traditionally called vowel height for the vowels in "heed, hid, head, had"?

Which corresponds to vowel height for the vowels in "father, good, food"?

Can these two measurements be used to distinguish front vowels from back vowels?

B Another way of describing the tongue position in vowels that has been suggested (see Sources) is to say that the tongue is in a neutral position in the vowel in "head" and that: (1) the body of the tongue is higher than in its neutral position in vowels such as those in "heed, hid, good, food," (2) the body of the tongue is more back than in its neutral position in "good, food, father"; (3) the root of the tongue is advanced in "head, food"; and the root of the tongue is pulled back so that the pharynx is more constricted than in the neutral position in "had, father." How far do the data in Figure 1.9 support these suggestions?

C In the seventeenth, eighteenth, and early nineteenth centuries (see Sources) there were said to be three sets of vowels: (1) a set exemplified by the vowels in "see, play, father" (and intermediate possibilities), which were said to be distinguished simply by degree of jaw opening; (2) a set exemplified by the vowels in "fool, home, father" (and intermediate possibilities), which were said to be distinguished simply by degree of lip rounding; and (3) a set exemplified by the vowels now symbolized by [y, ø] as in the French words "tu, peu" (you, small), which were said to be distinguished both by the degree of jaw opening and the degree of lip rounding. These notions were shown in diagrams similar to that in Figure 9.9. How do they compare with contemporary descriptions of vowels? What general type of vowel cannot be described in these terms?

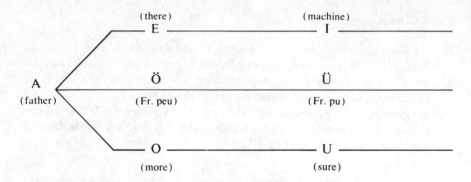

Figure 9.9 *The vowel classification used by Helmholtz (1863), with keywords suggested by Ellis (1885).*

D Try to find a speaker of some language other than English. Elicit a set of minimal pairs exemplifying his vowels. You will probably find it helpful to consult the pronunciation section in a dictionary or grammar of the language. Listen to the vowels and plot them on a vowel chart. (Do not attempt this exercise until you have worked through the Performance Exercises given below.)

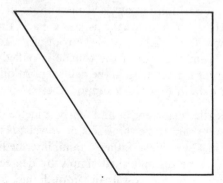

PERFORMANCE EXERCISES

The object of many of the exercises given below is to get you to produce a wide variety of vowels that are not in your own language. When you can produce small differences in vowel quality you will find it easier to hear them.

A   Say the monophthongs [i, e] corresponding to the first part of your vowels in "see, say." Try to make a vowel with a quality in between [i] and [e]. Then make as many vowels as you can in a series between [i] and [e]. Finally, make a similar series going in the opposite direction—from [e] to [i].

B   Repeat this exercise with monophthongs corresponding to the following pairs of vowels in your own speech. Remember to produce each series in both directions.
> [ɪ–ɛ]
> [ɛ–æ]
> [æ–ɑ]
> [ɑ–ɔ], if occurring in your speech
> [ɔ–o], or [ɑ–o]
> [o–u]

C   Try moving continuously from one member of each pair to the other, slurring through all the possibilities you produced in the previous exercises. Do this in each direction.

D   For each pair of vowels, produce a vowel that is, as nearly as you can determine, half way between the two members.

E   Repeat exercises **A**, **C**, and **D** with the following pairs of vowels, which will involve your producing larger adjustments in lip rounding. Remember to produce each series in both directions, and be sure that you try all the different tasks suggested in exercises **A**, **C**, and **D**.
> [i–u]
> [e–o]

F   Now repeat all the same exercises, but with no adjustments in lip rounding, using the following pairs of vowels. Go in both directions, of course.
> [i–ɯ]
> [e–ɤ]
> [y–u]
> [ø–o]

G Practice distinguishing different central vowels. When you have learned to produce a high-central unrounded vowel [ɨ], try to produce mid- and low-central vowels, which may be symbolized [ə] and [ʌ]. Try exercises **A**, **C**, and **D** with the following pairs of vowels:
  [ɨ–ə]
  [ə–ʌ]

H Produce the following nasalized and nonnasalized (oral) vowels. When making the nasalized vowels, be careful to keep the same tongue position, moving only the soft palate.
  [i–ĩ–i]
  [e–ẽ–e]
  [æ–æ̃–æ]
  [ɑ–ɑ̃–ɑ]
  [o–õ–o]
  [u–ũ–u]

I Now compare nasalized vowels with oral vowels that have slightly different tongue positions. Say:
  [i–ĩ–ɩ–ĩ]
  [e–ẽ–ɛ–ẽ]
  [ɛ–ɛ̃–æ–ɛ̃]
  [u–ũ–o–ũ]
  [o–õ–ɔ–õ]

J Make sure that you can produce a variety of different vowels by saying nonsense words such as those shown below, preferably to a partner who can check your pronunciation.

ˈpetuz	syˈtøt	ˈmẽnod
ˈtynob	diˈgɯd	pæˈnyt
ˈbɯgɛd	moˈpɑt	ˈdegũn
ˈnisøp	guˈdob	syˈtõn
ˈbædɨd	kɯˈtyp	ˈkøbɛ̃s

K Learn to produce diphthongs going to and from a variety of vowels. Using the vowel symbols with their values as in English, read the following, first column by column, then row by row.

iɩ	uɩ	ei	ɛi	æi	ɑi	ɔi	oi	ɷi	ui	ʌi
ie	ɩe	eɩ	ɛɩ	æɩ	ɑɩ	ɔɩ	oɩ	ɷɩ	uɩ	ʌɩ
iɛ	ɩɛ	eɛ	ɛe	æe	ɑe	ɔe	oe	ɷe	ue	ʌe
iæ	ɩæ	eæ	ɛæ	æɛ	ɑɛ	ɔɛ	oɛ	ɷɛ	uɛ	ʌɛ
iɑ	ɩɑ	eɑ	ɛɑ	æɑ	ɑæ	ɔæ	oæ	ɷæ	uæ	ʌæ
iɔ	ɩɔ	eɔ	ɛɔ	æɔ	ɑɔ	ɔɑ	oɑ	ɷɑ	uɑ	ʌɑ
io	ɩo	eo	ɛo	æo	ɑo	ɔo	oɔ	ɷɔ	uɔ	ʌɔ
iɷ	ɩɷ	eɷ	ɛɷ	æɷ	ɑɷ	ɔɷ	oɷ	ɷo	uo	ʌo
iu	ɩu	eu	ɛu	æu	ɑu	ɔu	ou	ɷu	uɷ	ʌɷ
iʌ	ɩʌ	eʌ	ɛʌ	æʌ	ɑʌ	ɔʌ	oʌ	ɷʌ	uʌ	ʌu

L Try saying some of these diphthongs in one-, two-, and three-syllable nonsense words such as those shown below. These are good items to use in ear training practice with a partner.

tɩɑp	ˈdoebˈmɔid	sæoˈtɑoneu
tʌep	ˈdeubˈmɑud	sɔɑˈtɛonɩʊ
tɑɔp	ˈdɩʊbˈmʌɔd	soɛˈtæunue
tɛɑp	ˈdoebˈmoid	sɑʌˈtʊinui
toʌp	ˈdʊɛbˈmuɛd	sɔɩˈtɩunæɑ

M Now extend your range by including front rounded and back unrounded vowels as exemplified below.

iy	ey	ɑy	uy	yi	øi	ɯi	yø	øy	ɯy
iø	eø	ɑø	uø	ye	øe	ɯe	yɯ	øɯ	ɯø
iɯ	eɯ	ɑɯ	uɯ	ya	øɑ	ɯɑ	yu	øu	ɯu

N These vowels can also be included in nonsense words such as those shown below for both performance and ear training practice.

dɯeb	ˈtyæbˈmeyd	tɯyˈneɑsʌø
diøb	ˈtuʊbˈmuød	tueˈnøusʊɩ
deub	ˈtɔøbˈmɑud	tɛɯˈnoysæu
doub	ˈtøʌbˈmɯɛd	tyɩˈnøysoɔ
dæob	ˈtɯɑbˈmiod	tɑøˈnɑesɩy

O Practice all the vowels and consonants discussed in the previous chapters in more complicated nonsense words such as the following:

ɣɑˈrot̪iɸ	ŋɔvøˈd̪eṇ	jæɮɯˈɓeɗ
beˈɟɛʒuð	ɢɑçyˈbɨg	syˈt’oʍɛɟ
ɲiˈḍyxɛn̪	ṣeʕɔˈpæz	ʎɛˈnøk’æx
θæˈɴɑkɯʃ	fiʁoˈceɬ	ʗiɹuˈɡod
ẓøˈχoqɔl	ħeβɯˈɟæt	wup’ɔˈɔem

Syllables and Suprasegmental Features 10

Throughout this book there have been references to the notion *syllable*, but this term has never been defined. The reason for this is simple: there is no agreed phonetic definition of a syllable. This chapter will discuss some of the theories that have been advanced and show why they are not entirely adequate. We will also consider **suprasegmental features**—those aspects of speech that involve more than single consonants or vowels. The principal suprasegmental features are stress, length, tone, and intonation. These features are independent of the categories required for describing segmental features (vowels and consonants), which involve airstream mechanisms, states of the glottis, primary and secondary articulations, and formant frequencies.

Syllables

The fact that syllables are important units is illustrated by the history of writing. There are many writing systems in which there is one symbol for each syllable. Perhaps the best known present-day example is Chinese. But only once in the history of mankind has anybody devised an alphabetic writing system in which syllables were systematically split into their components. About 4000 years ago the Greeks modified the Semitic syllabary so as to represent consonants and vowels by separate symbols. The later Aramaic, Hebrew, Arabic, Indic, and other alphabetic writing systems can all be traced back to the principles first and last established in Greek writing. It seems that everybody finds syllables to be comparatively easy units to identify. But people who have not been educated in an alphabetic writing system find it much more difficult to consider syllables as being made up of segments (consonants and vowels).

Although nearly everybody can identify syllables, almost nobody can define them. If I ask you how many syllables there are in "minimization" or "suprasegmental" you can easily count them and tell me. In each of these words there are five syllables. Nevertheless, it is curiously difficult to state an objective procedure for locating the number of syllables in a word or a phrase.

There are a few cases where people disagree on how many syllables there are in a word in English. Some of these are due to dialectal differences in the way that particular words are spoken. I would say that the word "predatory" has three syllables because I say [ˈprɛdətrɪ]. Other people who pronounce it as [ˈprɛdətɔrɪ] say that it has four syllables. Similarly, there are many words such as "bottling" and "brightening" that some people pronounce with syllabic consonants in the middle, so that they have three syllables, whereas other do not.

There are also several groups of words in which people do not differ in their pronunciation, but nevertheless differ in their estimates of the number of syllables. One group of words contains nasals that may or may not be counted as separate syllables. Thus words such as "communism, mysticism" may be said to have three or four syllables, depending on whether the final [m] is considered to be syllabic. A second group contains high front vowels followed by /l/. Many people will say that "meal, seal, reel" contain two syllables, but others will consider them to have one. A third group contains words in which /r/ may, or may not, be syllabic. Some people consider "hire, fire, hour" to be two syllables, whereas others (who pronounce them in exactly the same way) do not. Similar disagreements also arise over words such as "mirror" and "error" for some speakers. Finally there is disagreement over the number of syllables in a group of words that contain unstressed high vowels followed by another vowel without an intervening consonant. Examples are words such as "mediate, heavier, neolithic." Differences of opinion as to the number of syllables in these words may be due to differences in the way that they are actually pronounced, just as in the case of "predatory" cited above. But, unlike "predatory," it is often not clear if a syllable has been omitted on a particular occasion.

It is also possible that different people do different things when asked to say how many syllables there are in a word. Some people may pay more attention to the phonological structure of words than others. Thus many people will say that "realistic" has three syllables. But others will consider it to have four syllables because it is like the word "reality" which everybody agrees has four syllables. Similarly, "meteor" will be two syllables for some people, but three syllables for those who consider it is the same as the stem in "meteoric."

Judgments of the number of syllables in words such as "hire" and "hour" may also be affected by phonological considerations. Some people distinguish between "hire" and "higher," and pronounce "hour" so that it does not end in the same way as "tower." These people are likely to consider "hire" and "hour" to be monosyllables, and "higher" and "tower" to have two syllables. But others who do not differentiate between "hire" and "higher" and who pronounce "hour" in the same way as "tower" may say that each of these words has two syllables. Thus two speakers may pronounce "hire" in exactly the same way, but one will consider it to have one syllable, and the other two, because of the way in which they pronounce other words.

Having cited a number of words in which there are problems in determining the number of syllables that they contain, it is important to remember that there is no doubt about the number of syllables in the majority of words. Consider a random list of words (the first word on each three-hundredth page of *Webster's New World Dictionary*), "compline, gauger, maroon, radiometer, temperate." There is complete agreement on the number of syllables in each of these words except for the last ("temperate"). In the case of this word, the disagreement is not over what constitutes a syllable but whether the pronunciation is [ˈtɛmprɪt] or [ˈtɛmpərɪt].

In looking for an adequate definition of a syllable we need to do two things. We must account for the words in which there is agreement on the number of syllables, and we must also explain why there is disagreement on some other words. One way of trying to do this is by defining the syllable in terms of the inherent sonority of each sound. The **sonority** of a sound is its loudness relative to that of other sounds with the same length, stress, and pitch. Try saying just the vowels (i, e, ɑ, o, u]. You can probably hear that the vowel [ɑ] has greater sonority (due, largely, to its being pronounced with a greater mouth opening). You can verify this fact by asking a friend to stand some distance away from you and say these vowels in a random order. You will find that it is much easier to hear the low vowel [ɑ] than the high vowels [i, u].

We saw in Chapter 8 that the loudness of a sound mainly depends on its acoustic intensity (the amount of acoustic energy that is present). The sonority of a sound can be estimated from measurements of the acoustic intensity of a group of sounds that have been said on comparable pitches and with comparable degrees of length and stress. Estimates of this kind were used for drawing the bar graph in Figure 10.1. As you can see, the low vowels [ɑ] and [æ] have greater sonority than the high vowels [u] and [i]. The approximant [l] has about the same sonority as the high vowel [i]. The nasals [m, n] have slightly less sonority than [i], but greater sonority than a voiced fricative such as [z]. The voiced stops and all the voiceless sounds have very little sonority.

The degrees of sonority shown in Figure 10.1 should not be regarded as exact measurements. The acoustic intensity of different sounds may vary quite considerably for different speakers. Thus, in a particular circumstance one speaker may pronounce [i] with a greater sonority than [l], whereas another may not.

We can now see that one possible theory of the syllable is that peaks of

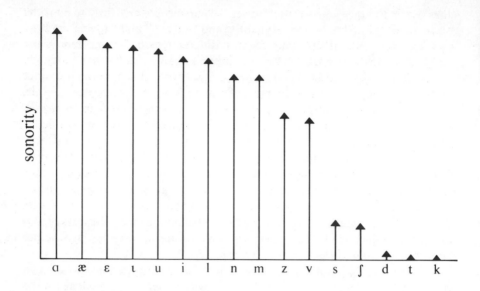

Figure 10.1 *The relative sonority of a number of the sounds of English.*

syllabicity coincide with peaks of sonority. This theory would explain why people agree on the number of syllables in the majority of words. In words such as "visit, divided, condensation" there are clear peaks of sonority. In these words each of the syllable peaks has much more sonority than the surrounding sounds. The theory also explains why there are disagreements over words such as "prism, error, seal, meteor." Different individuals may vary in the number of peaks of sonority that they have in some of these words. The final [m] in "prism" might have greater sonority than the preceding [z] for some people, but not for others. Similarly, the final [r] in "error," the [l] in "seal," and the second [i] in "meteor" might or might not constitute distinguishable peaks of sonority.

A sonority theory of the syllable will not, however, account for all the observed facts. It obviously fails in a word such as "spa." This word is one syllable, but it must be said to contain two peaks of sonority. It consists of three segments, the first and last of which have greater sonority than the second. A sonority theory also fails to account for the difference in the number of syllables in the phrases "hidden aims" and "hid names." Each of these phrases contains the same sequence of segments, namely, [hɪdneɪmz]. Therefore there are the same number of peaks of sonority. But the first phrase has three syllables, and the second has two.

There are also a number of words that many people can pronounce with or without one of the syllables. Typical of these words are "paddling, frightening, reddening." Each of these words can be said as two syllables, with the division between them as shown by the inserted period: [ˈpæd.lɪŋ,

ˈfraɪt.nɪŋ, ˈrɛd.nɪŋ]. Alternatively (still using an inserted period to show the syllable breaks), they can be said as three syllables, with a syllabic nasal or lateral in the middle: [ˈpæd.l̩.ɪŋ, ˈfraɪt.n̩.ɪŋ, ˈrɛd.n̩.ɪŋ]. Some people claim that they make a distinction between "lightning" (in the sky) [ˈlaɪt.nɪŋ] and "lightening" (making light) [ˈlaɪt.n̩.ɪŋ], and between "codling" (a little codfish) [ˈkɑd.lɪŋ] and "coddling" (a way of cooking an egg) [ˈkɑd.l̩.ɪŋ]. In all these cases a sonority theory of the syllable is inadequate. The variations in the number of syllables cannot be said to be due to variations in the number of peaks of sonority.

One way of avoiding this difficulty is to say that syllables are not marked by peaks in sonority but by peaks in **prominence**. The relative prominence of two sounds depends in part on what their relative sonority would have been if they had had the same length, stress, and pitch; but it also depends in part on their actual stress, length, and pitch. Then we can say that, for example, the [n] in "hidden aims" constitutes a peak of prominence because it has more stress or more length (or both) than the [n] in "hid names."

The problem with this kind of definition is that one cannot state a procedure for combining sonority, length, stress, and pitch so as to form prominence. There is no way in which one can measure the prominence of a sound. As a result, the notion of a peak of prominence becomes a completely subjective affair, so that it does not really throw any light on how one defines a syllable.

A completely different approach is to consider syllabicity not as a property of the sounds one hears but as something produced by the speaker. A theory of this kind was put forward by the psychologist R. H. Stetson. He suggested that every syllable is initiated by a **chest pulse**—a contraction of the muscles of the rib cage that pushes more air out of the lungs. Stetson made numerous observations of the actions of the respiratory system. But his claims about the actions of the muscles were nearly all deductions based on his observations of the movements of the rib cage and his measurements of the pressure of the air in the lungs. Unfortunately, subsequent direct investigations of the activity of the muscles themselves have failed to confirm his theory. At this point it seems extremely unlikely that every syllable is initiated by a chest pulse.

It does, however, seem possible that syllables are best defined in terms of the activities of the speaker. It may be that they can be defined in terms of some measurable combination of respiratory and laryngeal activity. Alternatively, syllables may be considered to be abstract units that exist at some higher level in the mental activity of a speaker. They may be necessary units in the organization and production of utterances. The support for this view comes from various sources. Consider, for example, the errors—the slips of the tongue—that people make when talking. Perhaps one of the commonest is the interchanging of consonants, so that "a malt whisky" becomes [ə ˈwɔlt ˈmɪski]. In virtually all cases of errors involving the interchange of consonants, it is not a matter of one consonant interchanging with any other consonant.

Instead, it is always a syllable initial consonant that interchanges with a syllable initial consonant or a syllable final consonant that interchanges with a syllable final consonant. Observations such as these are hard to explain unless we consider the syllable to be a significant unit in the production of speech. Further evidence of a similar kind is provided by descriptions of the sound patterns that occur in languages. We have seen in the earlier chapters that it is difficult to describe English without considering syllables as units.

In summary, we can say that there are two types of theories attempting to define syllables. First, there are those in which the definitions are in terms of properties of sounds, such as sonority (acoustic energy) or prominence (some combination of sonority, length, stress, and pitch). Second, there are theories based on definitions that are in terms of activities of the speaker, such as producing chest pulses or organizing the components of utterances. But as yet none of these theories is entirely satisfactory.

Stress

Stress is a suprasegmental feature of utterances. It applies not to individual vowels and consonants but to whole syllables—whatever they might be. A stressed syllable is pronounced with a greater amount of energy than an unstressed syllable.

English and other Germanic languages make far more use of differences in stress than most of the languages of the world. In many languages the position of the stress is fixed in relation to the word. Czech words nearly always have the stress on the first syllable, irrespective of the number of syllables in the word. In Polish and Swahili, the stress is usually on the penultimate syllable. In some languages stress is not a property of the word at all. All the syllables in a French word are about equally stressed. The only increase in stress that occurs in French comes on the last syllable of the phrase.

Variations in the use of stress cause different languages to have different rhythms. In French there is a great evenness to the rhythm, since only the last syllable in a phrase is different from any other. In comparison with English, French may be called a **syllable-timed** language, in that syllables, rather than only stressed syllables, tend to recur at regular intervals of time. Conversely, English and other Germanic languages may be called **stress-timed** languages, provided that we do not take this phrase to indicate anything more than a *tendency* for stresses to recur at regular intervals. As we saw in Chapter 5, there is no evidence to indicate that the timing of English utterances is completely determined by the stressed syllables.

Perhaps a better typology of rhythmic differences among languages would be to divide languages into those that have variable word stress (such as English and German), those that have fixed word stress (such as Czech, Polish, and Swahili), and those that have fixed phrase stress (such as French). This is, however, another area in which phoneticians must do more research before there is an agreed typology that can be set forth in a textbook such as this. There are many languages that do not seem to fit into any of these divisions.

In contrast to the nature of syllables, the nature of stress is fairly well understood. Stressed sounds are those on which the speaker expends more muscular energy. Usually this involves simply pushing out more air from the lungs by extra contraction of the muscles of the rib cage. Sometimes there may also be extra activity of the laryngeal muscles, so that there is an additional increase in pitch. There may also be increases in the muscular activity involved in the articulatory movements.

When there is an increase in the amount of air being pushed out of the lungs, there is an increase in the loudness of the sound produced. Some books define stress simply in terms of loudness, but this is not a very useful definition if loudness is considered to be simply a matter of the amount of acoustic energy involved. We have already noted that some sounds have more acoustic energy than others because of factors such as the degree of mouth opening.

A much more important indication of stress is the rise in pitch that occurs when there is an increase in the flow of air out of the lungs. You can check for yourself that the increase in airflow causes a rise in pitch even without an increase in the activity of the laryngeal muscles. Ask a friend to touch the lower part of your chest while you stand against a wall with your eyes shut. Now say a long [a] on a steady pitch and have your friend push against your chest at an unexpected moment. You will find that at the same time as there is an increase in the flow of air out of your lungs (as a result of your friend's push), there will also be an increase in the pitch of the vowel.

Length

Another area in which languages may differ is in the way that they vary the lengths of segments. In English, variations in lengths are completely allophonic. We saw, for example, that the vowel in "bad" is predictably longer than the vowel in "bat," because, other things being equal, vowels are always longer before voiced consonants than before voiceless consonants.

In other languages variations in length may be used contrastively. Long vowels contrast with short vowels in many languages, for example, Danish, Finnish, Arabic, Japanese. Korean examples are given in Table 10.1. Length may be shown by [ː] placed after the symbol or by doubling the symbol.

Contrasts between long and short consonants are not so common, but they do occur. Luganda has contrasts such as ['kkúlà], meaning "treasure," and [kúlà], meaning "grow up." Italian has contrasts such as "nonno" ['nonnɔ] (grandfather) versus "nono" ['nonɔ] (ninth), and "folla" ['folla] (crowd) versus "fola" ['fola] (fable). Long consonants (or vowels) that can be analyzed as double consonants (or vowels) are called **geminates**.

Table 10.1

Contrasts in vowel length in Korean.

il	(day)	iːl	(work)
seda	(to count)	seːda	(string)
sɛm	(fountain)	sɛːm	(jealousy)
pam	(night)	paːm	(chestnut)
tol	(birthday)	toːl	(stone)
kul	(oyster)	kuːl	(tunnel)
tɯŋ	(grade)	tɯːŋ	(back)

The Italian geminate consonants are like the contrasts between English consonants in "white tie" [waɪt taɪ], "why tie" [waɪ taɪ], and "white eye" [waɪt aɪ]. The difference is that in Italian a long consonant can occur within a single morpheme (a grammatical term for the smallest meaningful unit). But in English, geminate consonants can occur only across word boundaries, as in the previous examples, or in a word containing two morphemes, such as "unknown" [ˈʌnˈnoʊn] or "guileless" [ˈgaɪlləs].

Probably one of the most interesting languages in the way that it uses length is Japanese. Japanese may be analyzed in terms of the classical Greek and Latin unit called a **mora**. A mora is a unit of timing. Each mora takes about the same length of time to say. The most common type of Japanese mora is formed by a consonant followed by a vowel. Japanese words such as [kakemono] (scroll) and [su̥kiyaki] (beef stew) each consist of four morae of this type. Note that in the latter word the high vowel /u/ is voiceless because it occurs between two voiceless consonants; but it still takes the same length of time as the vowels in the other syllables. Another type of mora is a vowel by itself, as in the word [iki] (breath). This word has two morae, each of which takes the same length of time to say. A consonant cannot occur after a vowel within a mora, but it too can form a mora by itself. The word [nippoŋ] (Japan) must be divided into four morae [ni p po ŋ]. Although it has only two vowels, it takes the same length of time to say [nippoŋ] as it does to say [kakemono] or [su̥kiyaki].

Pitch

The pitch of the voice is determined by several factors. The most important is the tension of the vocal cords. If the vocal cords are stretched, the pitch of the sound will go up. Altering the tension of the vocal cords is the normal way of producing most of the pitch variations that occur in speech. In addition, as we saw in the section on stress, an increase in the flow of air out of the lungs will also cause an increase in pitch, so that stressed sounds will usually have a higher pitch. Finally, variations in pitch occur in association with the variations in the position of the vocal cords in different phonation types. Thus creaky voice usually has a low pitch as well as a particular voice quality.

Many different kinds of information can be conveyed by variation in pitch. As is the case with other aspects of speech sounds, some of this information simply indicates the personal characteristics of the speaker. The pitch of the voice usually indicates whether the speaker is male or female and, to some extent, his or her age. In addition, it conveys a great deal of nonlinguistic information about the speaker's emotional state—whether he is calm or angry, whether he is happy or sad. As yet, nobody knows if the pitch changes conveying this sort of information are universal. But it is apparent that speakers of many different languages have similar inflections when conveying similar emotional information.

There also seem to be some universal aspects to the ways in which languages use pitch differences to convey linguistic information. All languages use pitch to mark the boundaries of syntactic units. In nearly all languages the completion of a grammatical unit such as a normal sentence is signaled by a falling pitch. The last syllable (or the last stressed syllable) is on a lower pitch than it would have been if it had been nonfinal. Conversely, incomplete utterances, such as mid-sentence clause breaks where the speaker intends to show that there is something still to come, often have a basically rising intonation. There are, of course, exceptions to these two generalizations. In some styles of English, for example, it is possible to have a rising intonation on many sentences. But the use of a falling pitch to mark noninterrogative sentences occurs in by far the majority of utterances.

Syntactic information is the only linguistic information conveyed by pitch in English and most other Indo-European languages. But in many languages pitch variations have another function. Differences in pitch can be used to change the meaning of a word. For example, in Chinese the consonant-vowel sequence [ma] pronounced with a high and level pitch means "mother," but the same sequence pronounced with a high falling pitch means "scold."

Pitch variations that affect the meaning of a word are called **tones**. The meaning of a word depends on its tone in the majority of the languages in the world. All languages also use intonation, which is the use of pitch variations to convey syntactic information. The intonation patterns are superimposed on the tones in a way that we will discuss later.

The simplest kind of tone language is that in which there are only two possible tones, high and low. In many Bantu languages, such as Shona (spoken in Rhodesia), Zulu, or Luganda, every vowel may be classified as being on a high or on a low pitch. Thus in Shona the sequence [kùtʃérá] meaning "to draw water" has a low tone on the first syllable and a high tone on the second and third syllables. But when this sequence is [kùtʃèrà] with low tones on each syllable, it means "to dig."

Tones may be transcribed in many different ways. One of the simplest systems is to mark a high pitch by an acute accent over the vowel [á] and a low pitch by a grave accent [à]. Middle pitches can be left unmarked. This is the kind of transcription I have been using in the examples cited in some of the tables illustrating sounds not found in English (see, for example, Tables

6.2, 7.5). In a language with three tones, such as Yoruba (spoken in Nigeria), the mid tone would be left unmarked. In this way we could transcribe a three-way opposition such as occurs in Yoruba: [ó wá] (he comes), [ó wa] (he looked), [ó wà] (he existed).

Speakers of English often find it hard to consider the tone as an important, meaningful part of a word. But for speakers of a tone language, a difference in tone is just as significant as a difference in consonant or vowel quality. If you are trying to say "he looked" in Yoruba, and you say [ó wà] instead of [ó wa], it will sound just as odd as if you had said "he licked" instead of "he looked" in English.

Contrastive tones are usually marked over the vowel in a tone language. But they are often properties of the syllable as a whole. They can also occur on voiced consonants that can be regarded as syllabic. The Igbo (spoken in Nigeria) for "I'm beautiful" is [ḿ mà ḿmá]. Occasionally tones occur on consonants that are not normally syllabic. In the section on length in this chapter I transcribe the Luganda word for "treasure" as [ˈkkúlà], with a low tone mark before the first [k]. Obviously the silence preceding a voiceless consonant cannot be said on a low pitch. Only voiced sounds can have a high or a low pitch. This tone had to be transcribed simply because (for reasons to be explained later) it is a necessary unit when considering the sound pattern of Luganda as a whole.

Tone languages make two slightly different uses of pitch within a word. In the examples given so far, differences in pitch have affected the lexical (dictionary) meaning of a word. But many, if not most, tone languages also use pitch differences to make changes in grammatical (morphological) meaning. Thus in Igbo the idea of possession—roughly the equivalent of "of" in English—may be expressed by a high tone. This high tone appears, for example, in the phrase meaning "the jaw of a monkey." The word for "jaw" is [àgbà] with two low tones. The word for "monkey" is [èŋwè], also with two low tones. But the phrase "The jaw of a monkey" is [àgbá èŋwè], with a high tone on the second syllable of the word for "jaw." Thus the English word "of" can sometimes be represented simply as a high tone on a particular syllable in Igbo.

Another example of the grammatical use of tone occurs in the tense system of Bini (spoken in Nigeria), as shown in Table 10.2. In what may be called the Timeless tense (indicating a habitual action) there is a low tone on both the pronoun and the verb. In what may be called the Continuous tense (indicating an action in progress) there is a high tone on the pronoun, a low tone on monosyllabic verbs, and a tone going from low to high on disyllables. In the past tense there is a low tone on the pronoun, a high tone on monosyllabic verbs, and high to low on disyllables.

Before considering more complicated tonal systems, you should check that you can pronounce correctly all the tones that have to be pronounced in the examples cited in the previous paragraphs. You should, of course, say the high tones on a pitch in the upper part of your own pitch range, and the

Table 10.2

The use of tone in part of the tense system of Bini.

Tense	Monosyllabic verbs		Disyllabic verbs	
Timeless	ì mà	(I show)	ì hrùlè	(I run)
Continuous	í mà	(I am showing)	í hrùlέ	(I am running)
Past	ì má	(I showed)	ì hrúlè	(I ran)

low tones on a pitch in the lower part. If you are working with a friend or with recordings of a speaker of a tone language, be careful *not* to imitate his exact pitches, unless he has just the same pitch range as you normally do. Contrastive tones must always be considered relative to the presumed mean pitch of the speaker. (One of my problems in doing fieldwork with speakers of tone languages is that they often say I am mispronouncing a word when I imitate them fairly exactly. I have rather a deep voice, and my repetitions are apt to be misunderstood unless I make a distinct effort to say them not in the same way as the speaker, but on a somewhat lower pitch.)

Languages in which most of the tones can be described in terms of points within a pitch range are called **register tone languages**. Luganda, Zulu, and Hausa are examples of register tone languages in each of which there are basically just two tones, high and low. Yoruba is an example of a register tone language with three tones, high, mid, and low. Additional gliding tones do occur in Yoruba (and in most other register tone languages), but they can be shown to be the result of combining two of the register tones within a single syllable. Register tone languages with four tones are somewhat more uncommon. Egede and Kutep (both spoken in Nigeria) have tones that can be distinguished as being top, high, mid, and low.

The tones of some languages cannot be conveniently described in terms of single points within a pitch range. In Mandarin Chinese there are four tones, three of which involve gliding movements. Tones of this kind are called contour tones. **Contour tone languages** are those in which a number of the tones have to be specified in terms of gliding pitch movements, rather than in terms of single points. In addition to Chinese, many of the languages of Southeast Asia (e.g., Thai and Vietnamese) are contour tone languages.

The transcription system we have been using is suitable for most register tone languages. It must, of course, be expanded to incorporate languages with four tones, perhaps by marking the lower of the two mid tones with a horizontal bar [ā] and leaving the upper one unmarked. But it cannot be used to specify accurately the tones of a contour tone language.

One way of representing contour tones is to consider five equally spaced points within the normal pitch range of a speaker's voice: (1) low, (2) half-low, (3) middle, (4) half-high, and (5) high. We can then describe a contour tone as a movement from one of these points to another. We can represent this information graphically. If we draw a vertical line to indicate the normal range of a speaker's voice, we can plot a simplified graph of the pitch to the left of this line. In this way we can form a letterlike symbol which represents the tone.

The four "tone letters" that are required for describing Mandarin Chinese are shown in the fourth column of Table 10.3. Each consists of a reference line to the right, preceded by a line indicating the pitch of the tone. Thus tone 1 is a high level tone remaining at pitch level 5. Tone 2 is a rising tone, going from pitch level 3 to pitch level 5. Tone 3 begins by falling from pitch level 2 to the lowest possible level and then rises to pitch level 4. Tone 4 falls from pitch level 5 all the way to pitch level 1. It is usually impractical to use tone letters in a transcription of a language. A convenient system is to describe each tone in a particular language by means of tone letters and then use superscript numbers, as in column five in Table 10.3.

Table 10.3

Tonal contrasts in Mandarin Chinese.

Tone number	Description	Pitch	Tone letter	Example	Gloss
1	high level	55	˥	ma^1	mother
2	high rising	35	˦	ma^2	hemp
3	low falling rising	214	˩	ma^3	horse
4	high falling	51	˥	ma^4	scold

Table 10.4

Tonal contrasts in Thai.

Tone number	Description	Pitch	Tone letter	Example	Gloss
1	low falling	21	˩	naa^1	(a nickname)
2	high falling	51	˥	naa^2	face
3	high rising	45	˦	naa^3	aunt
4	low falling rising	215	˩	naa^4	thick
"common"	mid falling	32	˧	naa	field

Other tone letters designed in the same way can be used for the description of tones in other languages. The tones of Thai are illustrated in Table 10.4. Note how the numbers that are conventionally used in specifying Thai tones do not have the same values as those conventionally used for Mandarin Chinese in Table 10.3. Tone 1 in Thai is a falling tone, whereas in Mandarin Chinese it is a high-level tone. In Thai there is also a fifth tone, designated the common tone, which is left unmarked in transcriptions.

Even in a tone language the pitch of the voice changes continuously throughout sequences of voiced sounds. There are seldom sudden jumps from one pitch level to another. As a result, assimilations occur between tones in much the same way as they do between segments. When a high tone precedes a low tone, then the low tone will usually begin with a downward pitch change. Conversely, a high tone following a low tone may begin with an upward pitch movement. Considering two adjacent tones, it is usually the first that affects the second rather than the other way around. There seems to be a tendency in the languages of the world for tone assimilations to be perseverative—the tone of one syllable hanging over into that of later syllables—rather than anticipatory—the tone of one syllable changing because it anticipates that of the syllable yet to come.

Changes of tone due to the influence of one tone on another are called **tone sandhi**. Sometimes these changes are simple assimilations. For example, in Mandarin Chinese the form meaning "south" is usually [nan²] with a high, rising tone. But when it occurs between two high tones, then it, too, is pronounced with a high tone. The phrase meaning "southeast wind" is [doŋ¹nan¹feŋ¹] (literally "east-south wind") with high tones throughout.

In another case of tone sandhi in Mandarin Chinese, tone 3, the low falling-rising tone, is changed into tone 2, the high, rising tone. This occurs whenever one tone 3 word is followed by another tone 3 word. Thus the word meaning "very" is [hao³] with a falling-rising tone. But in the phrase meaning "very cold!" it is pronounced as [hao² leeŋ³]. In this way Mandarin Chinese avoids having two falling-rising tones one after the other.

As I mentioned earlier, tone languages also use intonational pitch changes. One of the main functions of these pitch changes is to divide utterances into syntactic units such as sentences. This is often accomplished by means of **downdrift**, the successive lowering of tones within a syntactic unit.

In Hausa, downdrift involves the falling of the mean pitch level throughout the sentence. Both high tones and low tones at the beginning of a sentence are higher than they are at the end. A high tone at the end of a Hausa sentence may even have about the same absolute pitch as a low tone had at the beginning of the same sentence.

In other languages the downdrift may take a slightly different form. The low tones may remain at about the same level throughout the sentence, so that the downdrift affects only the high tones. In Luganda there is a rule whereby high tones are lowered slightly whenever they are preceded by a low tone within the same sentence. This was the reason why I had to mark the low tone at the beginning of ['kkúlà] "treasure," even though it could not be pronounced. The high tone in this word is slightly lower than it would have been if this (silent) low tone had not been there.

To summarize, variations in pitch are used in a number of different ways. In the first place they convey nonlinguistic information about the speaker's emotional state and, to some extent, personal physiological characteristics. Second, in all languages, differences in pitch convey one or more kinds of linguistic information. The linguistic uses of pitch are: intonation (the distinctive pitches in a phrase), which in all languages conveys information about the syntactic components of the utterance, and tone (the distinctive pitches within a word), which may convey both lexical information about the meaning of the word and the grammatical function of the word. Those languages that may be classified as tone languages can be divided into register tone languages, in which most tones can be specified in terms of single points within a speaker's pitch range, and contour tone languages, in which many of the tones involve gliding pitch movements.

EXERCISES

A People differ in their judgments of the number of syllables that there are in the following words. Ask several people (if possible including some children) to say these words and then tell you how many syllables there are in each of them. Try to explain, for each word, why people may differ in their judgments, even if the people you ask are all in agreement.

laboratory _____

spasm _____

oven _____

prisoner _____

million _____

merrier _____

feral _____

B List four words for which the sonority theory of syllabicity is inadequate in accounting for the number of syllables that are present.

_____

_____

C Make a list of ten words chosen at random from a dictionary. In how many cases is there no doubt as to the number of syllables that they contain? Explain the reasons for the doubt in the case of the others.

_____

_____

_____

_____

_____

D Look at dictionaries or introductory textbooks on four or five foreign languages not mentioned in this chapter. Try to state whether they have variable word stress, fixed word stress, or whether stress does not seem to be a property of the word.

_____

_____

E Again by looking at dictionaries or introductory textbooks, find examples of tone languages not mentioned in this chapter. For each language try to state how many contrasting tones it has, exemplifying the distinctions between each of them with minimal pairs if possible.

F In Luganda, many words fall into one or the other of two classes, each with a different pattern of permissible tones, as exemplified in the lists below:

I		II	
èkítábó	(a book)	àkàsózì	(a hill)
òmúːntú	(a man)	òmùkázì	(a woman)
òlúgúːdó	(a road)	èm̀bwáː	(a dog)
òkúwákáná	(to dispute)	òkùsálà	(to cut)

Describe the permitted sequences of tones in each class. (In fact, Class II is more complicated than is indicated by the data given here.)

G Roughly speaking, when making a declarative statement in Luganda the initial vowel is dropped and the tones in class I words become as shown below:

kìtábó	(it is a book)
mùːntú	(he is a man)
lùgúːdó	(it is a road)

State the rule affecting the tones in this grammatical construction.

PERFORMANCE EXERCISES

A Practice saying nonsense words with long and short vowels. Say partially English phrases such as those shown below. Try to make the length of each vowel independent of the quality—so that [bɪb] is as long as [bib]—and of the following consonant—so that [bip] is as long as [bib]. The syllables are included within a phrase so that you can make sure that you keep the overall rate of speech constant.

ˈseɪ	ˈbiːb	əˈgɛn
ˈseɪ	ˈbib	əˈgɛn
ˈseɪ	ˈbɪːb	əˈgɛn
ˈseɪ	ˈbɪb	əˈgɛn
ˈseɪ	ˈbiːp	əˈgɛn
ˈseɪ	ˈbip	əˈgɛn
ˈseɪ	ˈbɪːp	əˈgɛn
ˈseɪ	ˈbɪp	əˈgɛn

B Repeat this exercise with other syllables such as those shown below. Continue using a frame such as "say _____ again."

buːd
bud
bɔːd
bɒd
buːt
but
bɔːt
bɒt

C Learn to differentiate between single and double, or geminate, consonants. Say:

eˈpɛm	oˈnun	øˈzys
epˈpɛm	onˈnun	øzˈzys
ˈepɛm	ˈonun	ˈøzys
ˈeppɛm	ˈonnun	ˈøzzys

D Take a sentence that can be said with strong stresses recurring at roughly regular intervals, such as:

ˈWhat is the ˈdifference in ˈrhythm between ˈEnglish and ˈFrench?

Say this sentence with as regular a rhythm as you can, while tapping on the stressed syllables. You should be able to say it slowly, at a normal speed, and fast, in each case tapping out a regular rhythm. Now try saying it as a Frenchman just learning to speak English might say it, with each syllable taking about the same length of time. Make regular taps, one corresponding to each syllable throughout the sentence. Say it slowly, at a normal speed, and fast in this way.

E One of the best ways of learning about suprasegmental features is to learn to say a short sentence backwards. To do this properly you have to reverse the intonation pattern of the sentence, make the aspiration come before rather than after voiceless stops, and take into account all the variations in vowel and consonant length due to the phonetic context. If you can make a recording of yourself on a stereo or a full-track tape recorder, you will be able to judge how successfully you can do this by playing the recording backward, so that the reversed sentence should sound as if it had been said normally. Begin with a fairly easy phrase such as:

Mary had a little lamb.

Then go on with a more difficult one such as:

Whose fleece was white as snow.

In each case it is best to begin by making a narrow transcription of the phrase, including the intonation pattern, and then to write this in the reverse order.

F Practice tonal contrasts by learning to say the following words in Bariba, a West African language. The dialect illustrated has four tones—top [′], high (no mark), mid [¯], and low [`].

yaá	(there's meat)
yaa	(meat)
waā	(a snake)
boo gé ga gu	(that goat died)
boo gè ga gu	(the goat that died)
ko n duē	(I'll play)
ko n dūē	(I'll buy some)
na tim mɔ	(I have some honey)
ma tì m̃ mɔ	(I have some medicine)
na boo mɔ	(I have a goat)
na bòo mɔ	(I have a water pot)
na bòò mɔ	(I have an ulcer)
ko n naā sōrī	(I'll tether the cow)
ná rà naā sòrì	(I tether the cow)

G Cantonese Chinese has a different tone system from Mandarin Chinese (shown in Table 10.3). Say each of the following rows of Cantonese syllables with the tone indicated by the description on the left.

Pitch	Tone letter	Example	Gloss	Example	Gloss
55	˥	ma	(interrogative)	fu	rich
35	˦	ma	mother	fu	office
33	˧			fu	husband
21	˨	ma	hemp	fu	support
23	˧	ma	horse	fu	wife
22	˨	ma	scold	fu	father

Linguistic Phonetics 11

Each of the segments in a word can be described as being the sum of a number of components or features. Thus the consonant [m] at the beginning of the word "man" can be said to have the feature of being voiced, the feature of being made at the bilabial place of articulation, the feature of being a nasal, and so on. This chapter will consider some of the features of sounds that are important in making linguistic descriptions.

There is still some disagreement on the exact form of the set of features required for the description of the sound patterns that occur in languages. Accordingly, we will consider two different possibilities—a set of features known as the prime features, most of which are based on traditional categories, and a set of features proposed by Noam Chomsky and Morris Halle.

Linguistic Processes

When we consider utterances in a language, we must take into account both the speaker's point of view and the listener's point of view. The speaker would like to convey his meaning with the least possible articulatory effort. He will therefore tend to produce utterances with a large number of assimilations, with some segments left out, and with the differences between other segments reduced to a minimum. Producing utterances in this way requires the speaker to follow a principle of maximum **ease of articulation**. But the listener would like to be able to understand the meaning with the least possible effort on his part. He would therefore prefer utterances that have sounds that remain constant and distinct from one another. He would like the sound pattern of the language to be in accord with the principle of maximum **perceptual separation**.

The principle way of reducing articulatory effort is by making maximum use of coarticulations between sounds. As a result of coarticulations, languages change. For example, in Old English the words for "chin" and "chip" used to begin with velar stops so that they were pronounced something like [kin] and [kip]. Due to the coarticulation between this stop and the following front vowel, the [k] changed into the affricate [tʃ], resulting in the present pronunciations [tʃɪn] and [tʃɪp]. Similarly, in an earlier form of the language words such as "nation, station" contained [s], so that they were pronounced [ˈnasion] and [ˈstasion]. As a result of coarticulation, the [s] became [ʃ], and the unstressed vowel became [ə]. (The "t" was never pronounced in English. It is due to the introduction of Latinized spellings.)

Further examples are not hard to find. Coarticulations involving a change in the place of the nasal and the following stop occur in words such as "improper" and "impossible." In words such as these the [n] that occurs in the prefix "in-" (as in "intolerable" and "indecent") has changed to [m]. These changes, which occurred before these words were borrowed into English, are even reflected in the spelling. There are also coarticulations involving the state of the glottis. Words such as "resist" and "result" are pronounced as [rəˈzɪst] and [rəˈzʌlt], with a voiced consonant between the two vowels. The stems in these words originally began with the voiceless consonant [s], as they still do in words such as "consist" and "consult." In all these and in many similar historical changes, one or more segments are affected by adjacent segments so that there is an economy of articulation.

The principle of maximum perceptual separation can be regarded as a tendency toward extravagance (for the sake of the listener) rather than economy (for the sake of the speaker). Perceptually what matters is that sounds that affect the meaning of a word should be as distinct from one another as possible. This can be achieved by maximizing the perceptual distance between the sounds that occur in a contrasting set, such as the vowels in stressed monosyllables (as in "beat, bit, bet, bat," etc.). Thus the principle of maximum perceptual separation does not usually result in one sound affecting an adjacent sound, as occurs with the principle of maximum ease of articulation. Instead, perceptual separation affects the set of sounds that potentially can occur at a given position in a word, such as in the position that must be occupied by a vowel in a stressed monosyllable.

We have already noted some of the ways in which languages tend to maximize the perceptual separation between sounds. As we saw in Chapter 9, this tendency explains why some vowel systems are more likely to occur than others. If the vowels of a language are to be maximally distinct, the formant frequencies will be such that the vowels are as far apart as possible when plotted on a vowel chart. Consequently there is a natural tendency in languages for vowels to be spaced at approximately equal distances apart and for them to be on the outside of the possible vowel area. This tendency is most evident in languages with a comparatively small number of vowels. There are hundreds of languages that have only five contrasting vowels (e.g., Spanish, Hausa, Japanese, and Swahili, to name four completely unrelated languages). In all these languages the vowels are roughly evenly distributed so that there are at least two front vowels and two back vowels. There is no language in which there are only five vowels all of which are front vowels. But there are, of course, many languages like English that have five front vowels and an approximately similar number of back vowels.

If there is a possibility for a pair of contrasting sounds to occur in the same place within a word, then there will be a tendency for the perceptual distance between them to be increased. Conversely, whenever a language does not distinguish between two sounds, the actual sound produced will tend to be in between the two possibilities. Thus, as we have seen, English distinguishes between voiced and voiceless stops as in "pie, buy." But this distinction cannot occur after /s/. Consequently the stop in "spy" is in between these two possibilities.

Other examples of this phenomenon have also been mentioned. We saw that before [ŋ] English does not distinguish between tense and lax vowels. Consequently the vowel that occurs in, for example, "sing," has a quality in between that of [i] and [ɪ]. Similarly, there is no distinction between tense and lax vowels before [r]. The vowel in "here" in most forms of American English is also intermediate between [i] and [ɪ].

The principle of maximum perceptual separation also accounts for some of the differences between languages. French has two high rounded vowels, [u] as in "tout" [tu] (all), and [y] as in "tu" [ty] (you). These two possibilities are kept distinct by one being definitely a front vowel, and the other definitely a back vowel. But English does not have this opposition. Consequently the high rounded vowel that occurs in, for example, "who, two," varies considerably. In some dialects (e.g., most forms of American English) it is a central or back vowel, and in others (e.g., some forms of Scottish English) it is a front vowel. As far as this vowel is concerned, what matters most in English is that it should be high and rounded. Whether it is front or back is less important.

As a final example, consider the difference between bilabial fricatives and labiodental fricatives. In English there is no phonemic distinction between [ɸ] and [f] or between [β] and [v]. Consequently there is no need to maintain a perceptual distinction between these two possibilities. In saying a word such as "fin," the upper lip is seldom lifted out of the way. The friction is often formed between the lower lip and both the upper teeth and the upper lip. But in the West African language Ewe, where there is a contrast between words such as [éɸá] (he polished) and [éfá] (he was cold), the distinctions between bilabial and labiodental fricatives are maximized. In making the labiodental fricatives, the upper lip is actively raised so that friction can occur only between the upper teeth and the lower lip.

All these examples illustrate the way languages maintain a balance between the requirements of the speaker and those of the listener. On the one hand there is the pressure to make changes that would result in easier articulations from a speaker's point of view. On the other hand there is the pressure from the listener's point of view that requires that there should be sufficient perceptual contrast between sounds that are able to affect the meaning of an utterance.

The Prime Feature System

A **prime feature** is a measurable property that can be used to classify the sounds of a language. For example, the prime feature Nasal classifies English phonemes into those that are [+nasal], that is, /m,n/, and those that are [−nasal], that is, all other English phonemes.

The set of prime features can be used to specify sounds that act together in phonological rules. We began using features in this way in Chapter 4 when we stated rules accounting for the allophones of English phonemes. In these rules, features such as Nasal and Voice were used to classify natural classes of sounds. Thus [−voice] was used as a specification of the English phonemes /p, t, k, f, θ, s, ʃ/. These phonemes were grouped together in several phonological rules, for example, in the rule stating that when any of them occurs at the end of a word, the preceding vowel is shortened.

Each of the prime features specifies a single measurable property. Thus the feature Nasal, for example, specifies the degree of lowering of the soft palate. Every sound can be partially described in terms of how much, if any, lowering of the soft palate occurs during its production. In this sense, each feature is like a physical scale. Every speech sound can be described in terms of the set of properties specified by the feature. The physical scales corresponding to the prime features will be discussed in detail in the next chapter.

Some of the prime features that are important in linguistic descriptions of English segments are listed in the first column of Table 11.1. As you can see, they are all familiar terms that are interpretable on the basis of the definitions given earlier. The traditional categories that we have been discussing throughout this book are very like the set of prime features.

The simplest of the prime features that may be used for classifying English sounds is the feature Voice. All English segments may be classified as being [+voice] or [−voice]. When a feature can be used to classify sounds in terms of two possibilities in this way, it is said to be a **binary feature**.

The second prime feature required for classifying English sounds is the feature Place. This is a **multivalued feature**, in that sounds have to be classified in terms of more than two possibilities. Five categories are needed for English; some additional categories will be needed in the classification of the sounds of other languages. For example, in Ewe there are phonemic contrasts between the bilabial fricatives [ɸ, β] and the labiodental fricatives [f, v]. Accordingly, when classifying the oppositions that occur in this language, we

Table 11.1

Some of the prime features required for classifying English segments.

Feature name	Classificatory possibilities	English segments
Voice	[+voice]	b, d, g, m, n, v, ð, z, ʒ, w, r, l, j (and all vowels)
	[−voice]	p, t, k, f, θ, s, ʃ
Place	[labial]	p, b, m, f, v
	[dental]	θ, ð
	[alveolar]	t, d, n, s, z, l, r
	[palatal]	ʃ, ʒ, j (and front vowels)
	[velar]	k, g, w (and back vowels)
Stop	[stop]	p, t, k, b, d, g, m, n
	[fricative]	f, θ, s, ʃ, v, ð, z, ʒ
	[approximant]	w, r, l, j (and all vowels)
Nasal	[+nasal]	m, n
	[−nasal]	(all other segments)
Lateral	[+lateral]	l
	[−lateral]	(all other segments)
Sonorant	[+sonorant]	m, n, r, l (and all vowels)
	[−sonorant]	p, t, k, b, d, g, f, θ, s, ʃ, v, ð, z, ʒ, w, j
Height	[maximum]	(all consonants except w, j)
	[4 height]	i, u, w, j
	[3 height]	e, ɪ, o, ʊ
	[2 height]	ɛ, ɔ
	[1 height]	æ, ɑ
Back	[+back]	u, o, ʊ, ɔ, ɑ, w, k, g
	[−back]	i, e, ɪ, ɛ, æ (and all other consonants)
Syllabic	[+syllabic]	(all vowels)
	[−syllabic]	(all consonants, including w, j)

will need the separate categories [bilabial] and [labiodental]. In English we can classify the sounds /p, b, m, f, v/ simply as [labial] because all these sounds act together as a single natural class.

The prime feature Stop is another multivalued feature. It specifies three possibilities in English. In the category [stop] are all those sounds in which there is a complete coming together of two articulators. In addition to the oral stops /p, t, k, b, d, g/, the nasals /m,n/ fall into this category. The nasal [ŋ] would also have been included if we had regarded it as a separate phoneme. The sounds classified as [fricative] are those in which there is a slightly lesser degree of coming together of two articulators. All other sounds have an even lesser degree of approximation of two articulators and are classified as [approximant].

The features Nasal and Lateral are both binary features. The application of each of them to the classification of English segments is as shown in Table 11.1 and needs no further comment for the moment.

The feature Sonorant is different from the features we have been considering so far. It refers to an auditory (as opposed to an articulatory) property of the sounds being classified. This feature specifies the amount of acoustic energy in a sound. It separates out those segments that are able to be syllabic.

The next two features, Height and Back, are primarily concerned with the classification of vowels. In the analysis of English suggested here, vowels can be assigned any one of four vowel heights. Consonants are assigned maximum height values. Both vowel and consonants can be classified in terms of binary values of the feature Back in English.

The final feature in Table 11.1, Syllabic, separates vowels from consonants. It thus classifies [i] and [u] as being distinct from [j] and [w]. Of course, segments that are classified as being [−syllabic], that is, consonants, may become [+syllabic] in particular circumstances. As with all the other features listed in Table 11.1, the value assigned to a particular segment is simply that which is appropriate in the phonological specification of English words.

There are many prime features in addition to those noted in Table 11.1. In this preliminary overview of the prime features, we have been mainly concerned with how features can be used to classify segments that distinguish English words. In the next chapter we will consider formal definitions of these features. We will also consider additional prime features that are necessary in the description of other languages. In the remainder of this chapter we will examine the set of features proposed by Chomsky and Halle. We will consider both their definitions of the features and the applicability of their features to the description of English and other languages.

The Chomsky-Halle Feature System

Some of the definitions of features given by Noam Chomsky and Morris Halle in *The Sound Pattern of English* (New York: Harper and Row, 1968) are quoted in the inset paragraphs in this section. Many of their features are very similar to the prime features and need not be considered in detail here. In their system, however, every feature must have only binary values when classifying sounds. The main result of this constraint is that they require different features for classifying those aspects of sounds specified by the multivalued prime features Place, Stop, and Height.

Chomsky and Halle use six features to specify the place of articulation of a sound. We may begin by considering their feature:

Anterior—Nonanterior

"Anterior sounds are produced with an obstruction that is located in front of the palato-alveolar region of the mouth; nonanterior sounds are produced without such an obstruction. The palato-alveolar region is that where the ordinary English [š] is produced." (The [š] is equivalent to the IPA [ʃ].)

This feature divides sounds into those made in the front of the mouth, such as [p, t], as opposed to those made farther back, such as [tʃ, k] (or [č, k] as Chomsky and Halle would write).

Sounds differing in place of articulation are further divided by the feature:

Coronal–Noncoronal

"Coronal sounds are produced with the blade of the tongue raised from its neutral position; noncoronal sounds are produced with the blade of the tongue in the neutral position."

The blade of the tongue is raised from its neutral position for alveolar and palato-alveolar sounds such as [t] and [tʃ]. Accordingly, the two features Anterior and Coronal divide sounds as shown in Figure 11.1.

[−Coronal]	[+Coronal]		[−Coronal]
p	t	tʃ	k
b	d	dʒ	g
f	s	ʃ	x
v	z	ʒ	ɣ
m	n		ŋ
	[+Anterior]		[−Anterior]

Figure 11.1   *The use of the features Coronal and Anterior.*

Further division of places of articulation is achieved by the feature:

Distributed–Nondistributed

"Distributed sounds are produced with a constriction that extends for a considerable distance along the direction of the air flow; nondistributed sounds are produced with a constriction that extends only for a short distance in this direction."

This feature is used to make distinctions among fricatives. It separates the bilabial fricatives [ɸ, β], in which the fricative articulation is distributed along the surface of the lips, from the labiodental fricatives [f, v], in which the articulation involves the sharp edge of the lower teeth. It could also be used to separate the dental fricatives [θ, ð], which involve the tip of the tongue and the edge of the upper teeth, from the alveolar fricatives [s, z], in which the tongue forms a longer articulatory channel. Similarly, the retroflex fricatives [ṣ, ẓ] have a short articulatory channel formed by the tip of the tongue, whereas in the palato-alveolar fricatives [ʃ, ʒ] the articulation is distributed over a longer channel in which the blade of the tongue is involved. Accordingly, the three features we have considered so far may be used to specify seven places of articulation as shown in Figure 11.2.

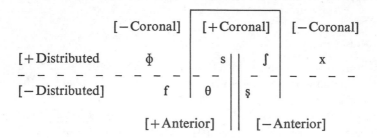

Figure 11.2 *The use of the features Distributed, Coronal, and Anterior.*

The distinction between palatal sounds such as [ç, c] and the corresponding velar sounds [x, k] involves another feature:

Back–Nonback

"Back sounds are produced by retracting the body of the tongue from the neutral position; nonback sounds are produced without such a retraction from the neutral position."

In addition to distinguishing palatal consonants from velar consonants, this feature also distinguishes between front vowels such as [i, e, æ] and back vowels such as [u, o, ɔ].

The two features used for distinguishing velar, uvular, and pharyngeal consonants also play a major role in classifying vowels:

High–Nonhigh

"High sounds are produced by raising the body of the tongue above the level that it occupies in the neutral position; nonhigh sounds are produced without such a raising of the tongue body."

Low–Nonlow

"Low sounds are produced by lowering the body of the tongue below the level that it occupies in the neutral position; nonlow sounds are produced without such a lowering of the body of the tongue."

These two features are obviously the converse of each other, so that it is impossible for a segment to be both [+high] and [+low]. Insofar as consonants are concerned, the relationship between these features and some of the other Chomsky-Halle features is shown in Figure 11.3. We can also summarize the specification of different places of articulation as shown in Table 11.2. The values [α] and [−α] have been used in the column for the

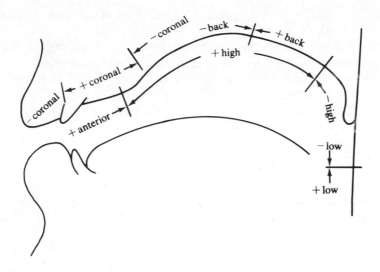

Figure 11.3 *A representation of the Chomsky-Halle binary features for place of articulation in terms of an articulatory diagram. It is assumed that there are no secondary articulations.*

Table 11.2

The relationships among the terms within the place of articulation feature as used in this book and some Chomsky-Halle features.

	Anterior	Coronal	High	Back	Low	Distributed
Bilabial	+	−	−	−	−	+
Labiodental	+	−	−	−	−	−
Dental	+	+	−	−	−	+α
Alveolar	+	+	−	−	−	−α
Retroflex	−	+	+	−	−	−
Palato-alveolar	−	+	+	−	−	+
Palatal	−	−	+	−	−	
Velar	−	−	+	+	−	
Uvular	−	−	−	+	−	
Pharyngeal	−	−	−	+	+	
Glottal	−	−	−	+	+	

feature Distributed. This is another way of saying that if the feature occurs with the value [+] in one circumstance, then it must occur with the value [−] in the other. [α] is a variable which may be either [+] or [−]. Whichever value is assigned on the specification of dental sounds, the opposite value must be assigned in the specification of alveolar sounds. This is appropriate only in those cases in which the difference between dental and alveolar sounds is that one of them has the articulation distributed along the blade of the tongue, and the other uses the tip of the tongue. If both use the tip of the tongue (as occurs in the formation of [ṭ] and [t] in Malayalam), this system cannot be applied.

The Chomsky-Halle features High, Low, and Back can be used to classify vowels as shown in Figure 11.4. Mid vowels are classified as being [−high] and [−low]. Since the definitions of the features High and Low prohibit a sound from being simultaneously [+high] and [+low], vowels must be classified in terms of not more than three possible vowel heights.

	[−Back]	[+Back]	
[+High]	i	u	
[−High]	e	o	[−Low]
	æ	ɔ	[+Low]

Figure 11.4   *The use of the features High, Back, and Low in classifying vowels.*

There is also a feature that specifies the position of the lips:

Rounded–Nonrounded

"Rounded sounds are produced with a narrowing of the lip orifice; non-rounded sounds are produced without such a narrowing."

In Figure 11.4 the feature Round was not needed as in English it has the same values as the feature Back, [+back] vowels being [+round] and [−back] vowels [−round]. If these two features had different values, the set of vowels that would be specified is as shown in Figure 11.5.

	[−Back] [+Round]	[+Back] [−Round]	
[+High]	y	ɯ	
[−High]	ø	ɤ	[−Low]
	œ	ʌ	[+Low]

Figure 11.5   *The classification of vowels when the features Round and Back have different values.*

Further differences between vowels can be specified by means of the feature:

Tense—Nontense

"[This feature] specifies the manner in which the entire articulatory gesture of a given sound is executed by the supraglottal musculature. Tense sounds are produced with a deliberate, accurate, maximally distinct gesture that involves considerable muscular effort; nontense sounds are produced rapidly and somewhat indistinctly. In tense sounds, both vowels and consonants, the period during which the articulatory organs maintain the appropriate configuration is relatively long, while in nontense sounds the entire gesture is executed in a somewhat superficial manner."

In practice this feature is often used to distinguish between centralized and noncentralized vowels as shown in Figure 11.6.

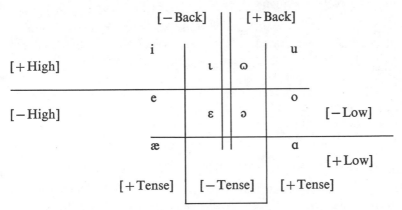

Figure 11.6 *The use of the feature Tense to distinguish [+tense] vowels, which are on the periphery of the vowel area, and the corresponding [—tense] (lax) vowels, which are slightly lower and more central.*

Chomsky and Halle use five features to account for some of the different manners of articulation. Their definitions of the features Nasal and Lateral are:

Nasal—Nonnasal

"Nasal sounds are produced with a lowered velum which allows the air to escape through the nose; nonnasal sounds are produced with a raised velum so that the air from the lungs can escape only through the mouth."

Lateral—Nonlateral

"Lateral sounds are produced by lowering the mid section of the tongue at both sides or at only one side, thereby allowing the air to flow out of the mouth in the vicinity of the molar teeth; in nonlateral sounds no such side passage is open."

These features are virtually the same as the corresponding prime features.

The Chomsky-Halle feature Strident is also very similar to the prime feature Sibilant, as may be seen from the definition:

Strident–Nonstrident

"Strident sounds are marked acoustically by greater noisiness than their nonstrident counterparts."

Instead of the prime feature Stop, which has the classificatory possibilities [stop], [fricative], and [approximant], they define a feature:

Continuant–Noncontinuant (Stop)

"In the production of continuant sounds, the primary constriction in the vowel tract is not narrowed to the point where the air flow past the constriction is blocked; in stops the air flow through the mouth is effectively blocked."

Using a Chomsky-Halle feature system, only stops and nasals are [−continuant]. Fricatives and all other sounds are [+continuant].

They also have a feature:

Instantaneous Release–Delayed Release

"During the delayed release, turbulence is generated in the vocal tract so that the release phase of affricates is acoustically quite similar to the cognate fricative. The instantaneous release is normally accompanied by much less or no turbulence."

Table 11.3 shows how these five features can be combined to specify

Table 11.3

The use of some Chomsky-Halle features to specify some different manners of articulation.

Traditional phonetic description			Symbol	Feature specification				
				Nasal	Contin-uant	Delayed release	Strident	Lateral
voiced	alveolar	nasal	n	+	−	−	−	−
		stop	d	−	−	−	−	−
		affricate	dz	−	−	+	+	−
	dental	affricate	dð	−	−	+	−	−
		fricative	ð	−	+	−	−	−
	alveolar	fricative	z	−	+	−	+	−
		lateral	l	−	+	−	−	+
		lateral fricative	ɮ	−	+	−	+	+

some dental and alveolar consonants. Note how the feature Strident can be used to distinguish between dental and alveolar fricatives and between dental and alveolar affricates.

Chomsky and Halle define a number of other features that will account for additional manners of articulation and different types of phonation. We will note only the feature:

Voiced–Nonvoiced

Their definition of this feature is somewhat complex in that they wish to regard some sounds as voiced even though the vocal cords are not actually vibrating. In some stop consonants the vocal cords may be in a position in which they could vibrate, but the flow of air is not sufficient to cause vibration. Accordingly, voiced sounds are defined as those in which the vocal cords are in a position such that they will vibrate if there is an appropriate airstream. Voiceless (or nonvoiced) sounds are those in which the glottal opening is so wide that there can be no vibration.

Finally we must consider the features that Chomsky and Halle suggest for dividing sounds into major classes such as consonants and vowels. Chomsky and Halle suggest a feature:

Consonantal–Nonconsonantal

"Consonantal sounds are produced with a radical obstruction in the midsagittal region [the midline] of the vocal tract; nonconsonantal sounds are produced without such an obstruction."

A radical obstruction is a narrowing of the vocal tract greater than that which occurs in semivowels. They also propose a feature:

Vocalic–Nonvocalic

"Vocalic sounds are produced with an *oral* cavity in which the most radical constriction does not exceed that found in the high vowels [i] and [u] and with vocal cords that are positioned so as to allow spontaneous voicing; in producing nonvocalic sounds one or both of these conditions are not satisfied."

Using these two features we can divide sounds into some appropriate natural classes as shown in Figure 11.7.

Vowels are classified as those sounds that are [+vocalic] and [−consonantal]. True consonants are the reverse: [−vocalic] and [+consonantal]. Semivowels have neither a free passage through the vocal tract, nor a radical obstruction, so they are [−vocalic] and [−consonantal]. The sounds [h] and [ʔ] are both voiceless and are therefore [−vocalic]. But since neither of them contains an obstruction within the vocal tract, which is defined as the air passages *above* the glottis, they are also [−consonantal]. Conversely, the sound [l] is voiced and has a free passage for the airstream; but it has a

	[−Consonantal]	[+Consonantal]
[+Vocalic]	Vowels	[l]
[−Vocalic]	[w, j, ɥ, h, ʔ]	True consonants

Figure 11.7 *The result of dividing sounds into major classes by means of the features Consonantal and Vocalic.*

radical obstruction in the *midline* of the vocal tract. It is therefore [+vocalic] and [+consonantal].

Chomsky and Halle have one more feature that is useful for separating sounds into major classes:

Sonorant–Nonsonorant (Obstruent)

"Sonorants are sounds produced with a vocal tract cavity configuration in which spontaneous voicing is possible; obstruents are produced with a cavity configuration that makes spontaneous voicing impossible."

This definition differs from that given for the prime feature Sonorant in that it is in physiological terms, rather than in terms of a measurable acoustic property (the intensity, or acoustic energy, that is present). Sounds that have what Chomsky and Halle call "spontaneous voicing" include vowels, semi-vowels, nasals, and laterals. Chomsky and Halle state that other sounds, such as stops and fricatives, can be voiced only if the position of the vocal cords is suitably adjusted. All such sounds can have only nonspontaneous voicing and are therefore [−sonorant]. Sounds having similar vocal tract configurations to those in vowels include [h] and [ʔ]. They are therefore [+sonorant].

Table 11.4 shows part of the classification of the phonemes of English given by Chomsky and Halle in *The Sound Pattern of English*. Review the definitions of their features and check that you can understand the reason for the assignment of each value in this table. The blanks in the table occur where the specification of a particular value is irrelevant in the classification of the phonemes of English. These blanks could be filled in by rules. For example, all sounds which are [+vocalic] are also [−strident].

Table 11.4

The classification of some English phonemes in terms of the Chomsky-Halle features.

	p	t	k	f	θ	s	ʃ	m	n	l	r	h	w	j	i	ɪ	eɪ	ɛ	æ
Vocalic	−	−	−	−	−	−	−	−	−	+	+	−	−	−	+	+	+	+	+
Consonantal	+	+	+	+	+	+	+	+	+	+	+	−	−	−	−	−	−	−	−
High	−	−	+	−	−	−	+	−	−	−	−	−	+	+	+	+	−	−	−
Back	−	−	+	−	−	−	−	−	−	−	−	−	−	+	−	−	−	−	−
Low	−	−	−	−	−	−	−	−	−	−	−	+	−	−	−	−	−	−	+
Anterior	+	+	−	+	+	+	−	+	+	+	−	−	−	−	−	−	−	−	−
Coronal	−	+	−	−	+	+	+	−	+	+	+	−	−	−	−	−	−	−	−
Round													+	−	−	−	−	−	−
Tense													−	−	+	−	+	−	−
Voice	−	−	−	−	−	−	−	+	+	+	+	−							
Continuant	−	−	−	+	+	+	+	−	−	+	+	+							
Nasal	−	−	−	−	−	−	−	+	+	−	−	−							
Strident	−	−	−	+	−	+	+	−	−	−	−								

EXERCISE

Without looking at Table 11.4, classify the phonemes of English in Table 11.5 in terms of the Chomsky-Halle feature system.

Table 11.5

Classify these English phonemes in terms of the Chomsky-Halle features, preferably without looking at Table 11.4.

	b	d	g	v	ð	z	ʒ	u	ɷ	oɷ	ɔ	ɑ
Vocalic												
Consonantal												
High												
Back												
Low												
Anterior												
Coronal												
Round												
Tense												
Voice												
Continuant												
Nasal												
Strident												

You should have specified the first seven columns in Table 11.5 (i.e., all the consonants) exactly the same as the first seven columns in Table 11.4, except that row ten (the feature Voice) should be + throughout, instead of −. The last five columns in Table 11.5 (i.e., the vowels) should be the same as the last five columns in Table 11.4, except that the fourth row (the feature Back) should be + throughout, and the eighth row (the feature Round) should be + for all except the last column (the vowel /ɑ/). In the penultimate column (the vowel /ɔ/), the value for the feature Low is also +.

PERFORMANCE EXERCISES

The material at the end of this and the following chapter is intended to help you review many of the sounds that have been described in previous chapters. It consists of real words in some different languages. If possible, you should compare your pronunciation of words with that of a native speaker. Where native speakers are not available—as, for example, in the case of Zulu for most courses in phonetics in Britain and America—try to pronounce the words just on the basis of the transcription provided. You might begin your review by trying to pronounce the data given in the following tables, which provide material on specific languages:

6.1	Amharic	(ejectives)
6.2	Uduk	(ejectives and implosives)
6.3	Zulu	(clicks)
6.5	Thai	(stops)
6.6	Hindi	(stops)
7.1	Malayalam	(places of articulation)
7.2	Quechua	(palatal, velar, and uvular plosives and ejectives)
7.3	Margi	(prenasalized stops)

A Navaho (United States)

t'áá?	(just)
tsíí‡	(haste)
ts'in	(bone)
tʃ'ah	(hat)
diṍő?	(prairie dog)
t‡ah	(ointment)
t‡'óó‡	(rope string)
?ak'os	(neck)
‡itsxʷo	(yellow-orange)
xaɩh	(winter)

B Italian

ˈɲomi	"gnomi"	(gnomes)
ˈɲokki	"gnocchi"	(dumplings)
laˈsaɲɲa	"lasagna"	(lasagna)
ˈfiʎʎə	"figlio"	(son)
faˈmiʎʎa	"famiglia"	(family)
ˈzbaʎʎə	"sbaglio"	(mistake)

C German

ˈvɔxə	"Woche"	(week)
ˈʔaxtɔŋ	"Achtung"	(attention)
maxt̩	"Macht"	(power)
ʃlɛçt	"schlecht"	(bad)
ɩç	"Ich"	(I)
mɩlç	"Milch"	(milk)

D Burmese

mà	(healthy)
m̥à	(order)
nà	(pain)
n̥à	(nostril)
la	(moon)
l̥á	(beautiful)
ŋâ	(fish)
ŋ̥â	(rent)

E Ewe (Ghana)

èβè	(the Ewe language)
èvè	(two)
éɸá	(he polished)
éfá	(he was cold)
èβló	(mushroom)
évló	(he is evil)
éɸlè	(he bought)
éflɛ́	(he split off)

F Zulu

lòndá	(preserve)
ɮùɮá	(roam loose)
ɬòɬá	(prod)
gↄòbá	(pound)
ↄòↄá	(narrate)
cʎ'ècʎ'á	(tattoo)
gʘòká	(dress up)
ʘàʘá	(explain)

G French

byʁo	"bureau"	(office)
ʁy	"rue"	(street)
katχ̟	"quatre"	(four)
lɛtχ̟	"lettre"	(letter)

The Prime Features 12

In the previous chapter it was noted that features describe physical properties of sounds. We discussed the definitions of the Chomsky-Halle features, but no formal definitions were given of the properties corresponding to the prime features. Nor were there any examples of their being considered as physical scales, nor statements about measurements of sounds in terms of them.

Linguistic Specifications and Physical Measurements

When we describe the sounds of a language we want to do so in a way that is independent of any particular speaker of that language. Thus if we wanted, for example, to describe the English vowel [u] as in "who," we would say (among other things) that it has almost a maximal degree of lip rounding. If we wanted to make this description more precise, we might try to state the degree of the feature Round that occurred during this sound. But there would be no point in trying to state the degree of this feature in terms of, say, a measurement of the number of millimeters between the lips of a particular speaker. The speech organs of different individuals vary considerably, and all physical measurements of speech sounds can refer only to a particular individual.

Generally speaking, the phonetic characteristics of a sound cannot be determined by measuring the absolute values of the physical phenomena involved. Instead, we must state the percentage values of the range that is possible for each speaker. With my particular vocal tract, the first formant range in vowels is from about 230 Hz. to 475 Hz. My soft palate seems to move over a range of about 15 mm. In your case these ranges may be smaller or larger. But for both of us, when we are pronouncing vowels that have about the same degree of Height, then our first formants will have about the same percentage value of our possible range. Similarly, when we both say a sound that has a comparable degree of nasality, then the percentage lowering of the soft palate will be about the same for both of us. Putting this another way, if the feature Place (of articulation) is defined in terms of distance from the glottis, then in both my case and in the case of a ten-year-old child, the alveolar consonant in "tie" will have a Place value of about 85 percent. But in my case, 85 percent of the way along the vocal tract will be 160 mm. from the glottis, whereas in the child's case it may be only 130 mm.

A **systematic phonetic description** of a language is one in which the segments in an utterance are specified in terms of the percentage values of the features. These percentage values are independent of the behavior of any individual speaker of the language. Consequently, when we describe a language, rather than a particular speaker of the language, the percentage values are the most detailed phonetic descriptions that can be made. When we observe an actual utterance, we can measure certain physical events. These measurements will reflect both the phonetic quality of the sounds of the language and the aspects of the utterance that are due to its having been made by a particular person.

So far we have been concentrating on the use of features in phonetic, as opposed to phonemic, descriptions of languages. But features can also be used to classify the ways in which sounds can cause contrasts in meaning. Thus the vowel /i/ as in "feed" can be classified as being distinct from the vowel /u/ as in "food" simply by stating that /i/ is [−back] in contrast with /u/, which is [+back]. If we are just discussing the phonological oppositions that can occur in English, we do not want to state the percentage values of the feature Back in these vowels. From this point of view, all that matters is that they contrast with one another by having opposing values of the feature Back.

When classifying the phonemes of a language, there are often only two possible values of a feature. Thus all English phonemes can be classified as being [+voice] or [−voice], [+nasal] or [−nasal], [+lateral] or [−lateral], [+sonorant] or [−sonorant], [+back] or [−back], and [+syllabic] or [−syllabic]. But even when simply classifying English phonemes, some features are multivalued. As we saw in the previous chapter, English phonemes can be classified in terms of five values of the feature Place: [labial], [dental], [alveolar], [palatal], and [velar]. These terms form a set of mutually exclusive items. Similarly, both the features Stop and Height have more than two possible values.

It is important to distinguish between the two ways in which features can be used. First, each feature can be used to *describe* the phonetic quality of a sound. When it is being used in this way, a feature specifies a continuous scale and has a percentage value. Second, each feature can be used to *classify* the phonological oppositions—the phonemes—that occur in a language. When it is being used in this way, the possible values that can occur constitute a set of discrete terms. If, in a given language, the phonemes can be classified by stating only two contrasting values of a feature, then the terms [+] and [−] are used. If more than two possible values contrast, then the values are given names, such as, for the feature Height, [high], [mid], and [low]. These points are summarized in Table 12.1.

Table 12.1

Different uses of features.

Level of description	Use of features	Discrete or continuous	Method of use
phonemic	classify	discrete items in a set	[+] or [−] if two possibilities; named terms if more possibilities
phonetic	describe	continuous scale	percentage values

The Set of Prime Features

The complete set of prime features is shown in Table 12.2. The first column lists the name of the feature, and the second column gives a short description of the measurable property corresponding to the feature. Our instrumental technology has not advanced sufficiently to measure all aspects of speech equally. But subject to that limitation, it is nevertheless possible for the phonetician to measure phonological features in terms of physiological and acoustic parameters.

The third column lists the set of phonological possibilities that can occur when the feature is being used to classify phonemes. When the name of a feature is being used in this way, it is placed in between square brackets. The next four columns exemplify phonemic contrasts in which this feature is used. The final column lists the percentage values that occur in the particular phonetic circumstances of the examples given. Using values such as these, it is theoretically possible to express with reasonable accuracy a picture of the physical events taking place. But I cannot claim to have done this in Table 12.2, which exemplifies such a wide range of contrasts. Many of the figures in the last column are estimates, since no instrumental data are available on some of the languages cited. Each feature will be discussed in turn in this section, considering both the set of terms required to classify phonemes, and some of the percentage values that occur.

1 Glottalic

This feature specifies the airstream mechanism by quantifying the movement, if any, of the glottis. From a phonemic point of view there are three possibilities: [ejective]—glottis moving upward; [pulmonic]—no movement

Table 12.2

The prime features.

Feature name	Abbreviated definition of physical scale	Phonological terms	Exemplification				% value
			symbols	language	word	gloss	
1 Glottalic	Rate of upward movement of the glottis	[ejective]	t'	Uduk	t'è	lick	100
		[pulmonic]	t	Uduk	tèr	collect	50
		[implosive]	ɗ	Uduk	dek	lift	0
2 Velaric	Degree of suction of air in mouth	[+click]	ʇ	Zulu	ǀàǀá	climb	100
		[−click]	t	Zulu	tátù	third	0
3 Voice	Degree of approximation of the arytenoid cartilages	[glottal stop]	ʔ	Javanese	buka?	open	100
		[laryngealized]	ɓ̰	Hausa	ɓèráː	rat	80
		[voice]	b	Hausa	bèrà	girl	60
		[murmur]	b̤ɦ	Hindi	b̤ɦal	forehead	20
		[voiceless]	p	Hindi	pal	take care of	0
4 Aspiration	Time of onset of voicing with respect to release of the articulation	[aspirated]	pʰ	Thai	pʰàː	split	100
		[unaspirated]	p	Thai	pàː	forest	50
		[voiced]	b	Thai	bàː	shoulder	0
5 Place	Distance from the glottis to the first constriction of the vocal tract	[bilabial]	β	Ewe	ɛ̀βɛ̂	Ewe	100
		[labiodental]	v	Ewe	ɛ̀vɛ̂	two	95
		[dental]	t̪	Malayalam	kuʈʈi	stabbed	90
		[alveolar]	t	Malayalam	kuʈʈi	peg	85
		[retroflex]	ʈ	Malayalam	kuʈʈi	child	80
		[palato-alveolar]	ʃ	English	ʃip	sheep	75
		[palatal]	c	Quechua	caka	bridge	70
		[velar]	k	Quechua	kara	expensive	60
		[uvular]	q	Quechua	qara	skin	50
		[pharyngeal]	ħ	Arabic	had	someone	30
		[glottal]	ʔ	Arabic	ʔatħa	God	0
6 Labial	Degree of approximation of the centers of the lips	[+labial]	k͡p	Igbo	ák͡pà	bag	100
		[−labial]	k	Igbo	áká	hand	0

	Feature	Definition		Language				
7	Stop	Degree of approximation of the articulators	[stop]	English	t	taɪ	tie	100
			[fricative]	English	s	saɪ	sigh	90
			[approximant]	English	h	haɪ	high	0
8	Nasal	Degree of lowering of the soft palate	[+nasal]	English	n	noʊ	know	100
			[−nasal]	English	d	doʊ	dough	0
9	Lateral	Amount of airstream flowing over the side of the tongue	[+lateral]	English	l	loʊ	low	100
			[−lateral]	English	d	doʊ	doe	0
10	Trill	Degree of vibration of an articulator	[+trill]	Spanish	r	pero	dog	100
			[−trill]	Spanish	r	pero	but	0
(11	Tap)	Rate of articulatory movement?	[+tap]	Tamil	ɾ	aːɾəm	saw	100
			[−tap]	Tamil	ɹ	meːɾə	depth	0
12	Sonorant	Amount of acoustic energy	[+sonorant]	English	i	ˈsʌnɪəɹ	sunnier	80
			[−sonorant]	English	j	ˈʌnjən	onion	70
13	Sibilant	Amount of high frequency (over 3000 Hz.) energy	[+sibilant]	English	s	sɪn	sin	100
			[−sibilant]	English	θ	θɪn	thin	20
14	Grave	Ratio of low to high frequency energy	[+grave]	English	f	pɪn, kɪn	pin, kin	90
			[−grave]	English	θ	tɪn	tin	60
15	Height	Inverse of frequency of the first formant	[4 height]	Danish	i	viːðə	know	95
			[3 height]	Danish	e	veːðə	wheat	65
			[2 height]	Danish	ɛ	vɛːðə	wet	50
			[1 height]	Danish	æ	væːðə	wade	10
16	Back	Difference between frequency of formant two and formant one	[+back]	English	u	hu	who	80
			[−back]	English	i	hi	he	5
17	Round	Inverse of distance between corners of the lips	[+round]	French	y	ly	read	90
			[−round]	French	i	li	bed	0
18	Wide	Degree of advancement of tongue root	[+wide]	Igbo	i	óbi	heart	100
			[−wide]	Igbo	i̩	ọ̀bị	poverty	20
19	Rhotacized	Lowering of the frequency of the third formant	[+rhotacized]	English	ɹe	bɜɹd	bird	100
			[−rhotacized]	English	ɹ	bɪd	bid	0
20	Syllabic	(No agreed physical scale)	[+syllabic]	English	n̩	sʌdn̩	sudden	100
			[−syllabic]	English	n	sʌn	sun	0

of the glottis; and [implosive]—glottis moving downward. Most languages are like English in that they do not have any phonemic contrasts involving this feature. But there are several (for example, Amharic and Navaho) in which there are two contrasting possibilities. In these languages there is no need to use terms such as [ejective] and [pulmonic]. The contrasting phonemes can be classified simply as [+glottalic] and [−glottalic]. There are, however, a few languages like Uduk in which there are three-way contrasts, so that the terms shown in Table 12.2 have to be used.

There is very little phonetic data available on glottalic movements in any language. For the moment we will assume—probably incorrectly—that the maximum possible upward rate is the same but in the opposite direction as the maximum possible rate downward. If the physical scale corresponding to this feature is defined in terms of the rate of upward movement of the glottis, maximal ejectives may be said to have values of 100 percent. Maximal implosives, which have the most rapid downward movement, are 0 percent Glottalic. Pulmonic sounds that have neither an upward nor a downward movement are half way on this scale and have a value of 50 percent of this feature.

In making a phonetic description of a sound the three phonological possibilities [ejective], [pulmonic], and [implosive] will not be sufficiently specific. Sounds may be weakly or strongly ejective or weakly or strongly implosive. For example, in my, and many other people's, English, the /t/ at the end of "cat" may be weakly ejective, particularly if this word is sentence final. Phonemically this sound would not be classified as an ejective, since it does not contrast with another sound that is identical but nonejective. But a phonetic specification of this sound in this particular position might indicate that the percentage value of this feature was, say, 75 percent. Similarly, many languages (e.g., Vietnamese, Zulu, and American Indian languages such as Maidu) have fully voiced stops /b, d/ that need not be classified as [implosive], but that are often, from the point of view of the phonetic specification, weakly implosive and could be specified as, say, 25 percent Glottalic.

2 Velaric

This feature specifies the degree of use of the velaric airstream mechanism in a sound. The phonological possibilities for classifying sounds are simply [+click] and [−click]. This feature will be used in a binary way for classifying the sounds of Zulu and other languages spoken in southern Africa. It will also, of course, have large values (perhaps 100 percent = maximum use of Velaric suction) in the phonetic specification of the click sounds in these languages.

As we saw earlier, Yoruba and other languages spoken in West Africa employ a velaric airstream mechanism in producing the labial velar stops [k͡p, g͡b]. This feature is not used in classifying these sounds. But in a systematic phonetic account of sounds in these languages, there will have to be some mention of the degree of Velaric suction that occurs.

3 Voice

This feature specifies the different types of phonation discussed in Chapter 6. The physiological scale corresponding to it is the degree of approximation of the arytenoid cartilages. If you look back at Figure 6.4, you will see how this definition can be applied. The distance between the arytenoid cartilages (near the edges of the vocal cords in the lower part of each picture) is greatest for voiceless sounds, slightly less for murmured (breathy voiced) sounds, less still for voiced sounds, and even less for laryngealized sounds, in which these parts of the vocal cords are held tightly together. In a glottal stop, which is not shown in Figure 6.4, the distance between the arytenoid cartilages is at its minimum.

This feature might be more appropriately named Glottal Stricture. The name Voice is retained largely so that we can classify sounds as being simply [+voice] or [−voice] in the majority of the languages in the world. As was indicated in Table 12.1, there is no need to use named values such as [voiceless] when contrasting only two possibilities.

The number of phonological terms named in Table 12.2 is somewhat arbitrary. Since the feature Voice operates over a continuous physical scale —the distance between the arytenoids—it could have been divided into a larger or smaller number of categories. Five different values are listed and exemplified in Table 12.2, all of which are used in Beja, a language spoken in the Sudan. But most languages contrast only two possibilities, as in English; or three possibilities, as in Hindi, where sounds can be [voiced], [murmured], or [voiceless], or as in Hausa, [laryngealized], [voiced], or [voiceless].

4 Aspiration

This feature specifies when the voicing starts with respect to the timing of the articulation. If you refer to Figure 6.5 you will see how voice onset time can be measured. This feature can specify a three-way opposition, in that sounds can be [aspirated] or [unaspirated] or [voiced]. These three possibilities are needed in classifying the phonemes in languages such as Thai and Burmese. This feature is not needed for classifying the sounds of English, but in describing the phonetic quality of English sounds, we will have to specify different percentages of this feature in different circumstances. If it were not for the convenience of retaining the traditional term aspiration, this feature might have been called Voice Onset Time. Sounds that are voiced throughout the articulation will be said to have a value of 0 percent, those in which the voicing starts at the time of the release of the articulation will have a value of 50 percent, and those in which the voicing starts considerably later will be 100 percent Aspirated.

5 Place

The feature Place in Table 12.2 specifies the distance from the glottis to the first maximum constriction of the vocal tract. This implies that double articulations such as labial velar and labial palatal are not considered to be separate places of articulation as they were considered in Chapter 7, but have to be specified by means of an additional feature (such as labial). We could have listed them as additional places of articulation, but it would then have been difficult to have defined this feature in terms of a single physical scale.

Again as with all the other features, every speech sound must have one, and only one, value of this feature. The value that occurs in a particular circumstance may be intermediate between two of the named values. But this eventuality does not arise in classifying the sounds of any languages. In these circumstances the values named in Table 12.2 form a mutually exclusive set of possibilities.

No language uses contrasts among more than six places of articulation, so it may be argued that for classifying the sounds of any language we need no more than six named values of this feature. But all possible pairs of adjacent terms—for example, [bilabial] and [labiodental], [labiodental] and [dental], etc.—contrast in at least one language. Consequently there is no simple way of describing the six values that would be appropriate for classifying the sounds in all the languages of the world. There is no agreed subset of the eleven named values that can be appropriately used.

Note that even vowels have to be assigned values of this feature, although they can be fully classified in terms of features 15 through 18. In low front and central vowels the actual value is somewhat indeterminate. But as you can see by looking at the place of maximum vocal tract constriction in Figure 1.10, all back vowels, and high front and central vowels have an easily definable value of the feature Place. As we saw in the section on palatalization, the articulatory place of some of these vowels often influences the articulatory place of the adjacent consonant.

6 Labial

This feature is used to classify sounds such as [k͡p, t͡p, w, ɥ]. In these sounds there is an articulation at the lips that is of the same magnitude as an articulation elsewhere in the vocal tract. The sounds [p, b, m] can also be (redundantly) classified as [+labial]. The physical scale corresponding to this feature is the degree of approximation of the centers of the lips.

7 Stop

The physical scale corresponding to this feature is the degree of the articulatory closure. It overlaps with the feature Labial in the case of sounds with a primary articulation at the lips.

The phonological possibilities for this feature are [stop], [fricative], and [approximant]. The last term is used to designate all sounds that are not classified as [stop] or [fricative]. It usually includes sounds such as central and lateral approximants and vowels. But remember that the list of phonological terms used for classifying sounds with respect to a given feature is simply the list of terms that we need for dividing sounds up into groups that act together in phonological rules. In one language, for example, English, the segment /l/ may be classified as [approximant] because it acts in the same way as other approximants. But in another language, for example, Luganda, it may be more appropriate to classify /l/ as [stop] because of the sound patterns that occur in that language. Similarly trills, taps, and flaps are often classified as [stop], but in a particular language they might be [approximant] or [fricative]. At the phonetic level the only sounds that will be 100 percent Stop are those in which there is a complete closure, such as the consonants in "pie, buy, my." Other sounds will have a certain percentage value of the scale specifying minimum to maximum articulatory closure.

Considering its physical definition, this feature might have been called Articulatory Stricture. But the name Stop is preferable for reasons similar to those given for preferring Voice to Glottal Stricture. It is often convenient to classify sounds simply as [+stop] as opposed to [−stop]. The latter value can be used with its conventional meaning of specifying all sounds, including fricatives, that are not stops.

8 Nasal

Throughout the majority of this book we have been using the term nasal to mean, implicitly, nasal stop and the term stop to imply oral stop. This is a common phonetic usage of these two terms. But we cannot use the two terms in this way when we are specifying sounds by means of features that have to be definable in terms of physical scales. The scale corresponding to the feature Nasal is the degree of lowering of the soft palate. Sounds such as /m, n/ may be classified as [+nasal, +stop], sounds such as /p, b, t/ as [−nasal, +stop], sounds such as /l, r, o/ as [−nasal, −stop], and sounds such as /õ, ẽ/ as [+nasal, −stop].

9 Lateral

The terms [+lateral] and [−lateral] are completely straightforward, and there is no problem in using them in classifying sounds. Simply because sounds are so obviously either central or lateral, it is difficult to think of this feature in terms of a physical scale. But the degree of laterality can be defined as the proportion of the airstream that is flowing over the side of the tongue. About the maximal airflow over the sides of the tongue occurs in [l] as in "lie," which will have a phonetic value of close to 100 percent. Apart from /l/ sounds, all sounds in English have a value of 0 percent of this feature. But in some languages there are sounds in which neither the tip nor the sides of the tongue are touching the roof of the mouth. A sound of this kind may be auditorily intermediate between [ɹ] and [l]. It occurs sometimes in languages, such as Japanese, that do not distinguish /r/ and /l/.

10 Trill

The scale corresponding to this feature is the degree of Vibration of an articulator. It seems, however, that an articulator is either vibrating or it is not vibrating. In the case of this feature, therefore, each sound has a value of 0 percent or 100 percent. Intermediate values do not seem to be possible.

11 Tap

I listed this feature in parentheses in Table 12.2 because there is no agreed way of giving a feature specification of taps or flaps such as [ɾ, ʈ]. A possible physical scale is the rate of movement of an articulator. This feature will serve as a reminder that the whole area of the feature specification of trills, taps, and flaps needs more discussion than is appropriate in this book.

12 Sonorant

This is the first feature we have considered that is defined in terms of an acoustic, as opposed to a physiological, scale. It can be defined in accordance with the earlier discussion of sonority as the amount of acoustic energy that is present during a sound. In classifying the sounds of English, all the vowels are [+sonorant], and so are the consonants /m, n, l, r/. As we saw in Figure 10.1, all these sounds have a comparatively large amount of acoustic energy.

These sounds have no simple articulatory property in common. Nor are they readily definable in terms of combinations of other features. They act together as a class precisely because they have an acoustic property in common. We need the feature Sonorant in phonological rules that explain, for example, why the sounds at the ends of "spasm, prison, simple" and—in most forms of American English—"hinder" are syllabic. Sounds that are [+sonorant] become [+syllabic] when they occur at the end of a word after a sound that is [stop] or [fricative].

13 Sibilant

This feature specifies the amount of high-frequency energy that is present. In English, it separates out the fricatives /s, ʃ, z, ʒ/ from the fricatives /f, θ, v, ð/. Following the discussion of fricative sounds in an earlier chapter, we can now say that this division can be used to explain some of the differences in English plurals. Words ending in sounds that are [+sibilant], for example, "kiss, maze, rush, judge," form plurals by adding a suffix such as [ɪz]. But words ending in sounds that are [−sibilant], for example, "cat, dog, shoe, farm," add [s] or [z].

It is perfectly possible to describe the way the plural is formed in English in terms of features with articulatory definitions. We could say that an extra vowel is inserted after words ending in sounds that are [fricative] and either [alveolar] or [palato-alveolar] and before a suffix that is [fricative] and [alveolar]. This is a cumbersome but adequate description of what happens.

But it does not *explain* why the plurals of both "miss" and "wish" have an additional vowel, but the plural of "moth" does not. On an articulatory basis there is no reason why words ending in alveolar fricatives behave like those ending in palato-alveolar fricatives, but differently from those ending in dental fricatives. It is only when we use acoustically-based features that we see that there is an additional relationship between [s] and [ʃ] that does not occur between [s] and [θ]. The sounds [s] and [ʃ] act together because they are both [+sibilant].

14 Grave

This is another acoustically-based feature that is required to explain some of the sound patterns that occur in languages. It specifies the amount of acoustic energy in the lower, as opposed to the upper, frequencies. Thus [p] and [k] are followed by a comparatively low frequency burst of aspiration and are [+grave], whereas [t], in which the energy in the aspiration is at a much higher frequency, is [−grave]. This feature is important mainly in classifying stops and fricatives. The similarity between [+grave] sounds explains alternations and historical sound changes such as the Old English velar fricative [x] becoming Modern English labiodental [f] in "rough, tough." There is no articulatory reason why this change should have occurred. It is just that [x] and [f] sound alike because they are both [+grave].

15 Height

The major function of this feature is in the classification and description of vowels. As we saw in the chapter on acoustic phonetics, the physical scale corresponding to vowel Height is the inverse of the frequency of the first formant. In most consonants the first formant is either not observable or at a very low frequency.

This feature can seldom be used in a binary way. There are comparatively few languages in the world that require the specification of only two vowel heights. It is possible in Eskimo and some forms of Arabic that have only the three vowels /i, a, u/. But most languages need at least three values. Danish contrasts four values of vowel Height. The percentage values corresponding to the phonetic specification of these vowels are represented in Figure 9.5, which shows the relative values of the mean formant frequencies in these vowels.

16 Back

This feature may be defined in terms of the inverse of the difference between the frequency of formant two and that of formant one. Its application to the specification of vowels is completely straightforward (see Chapters 8 and 9). Its specification in the case of consonants is considerably more complex. The frequency of the first formant will be at a minimum in most consonants in which there is an articulatory closure, but the frequency of the second formant varies considerably. Some general guidelines are available from the discussion of formant transitions. But there is insufficient data for this topic to be considered further in this book.

The vowels of most languages can be classified in terms of the binary values [+back] and [−back]. It has, however, been suggested that it is sometimes convenient to use the phonological possibilities [front], [central], and [back]. Percentage values vary considerably, as can be seen from the vowel charts in Figure 9.5.

17 Round

The third feature required in the specification of vowels is the degree of rounding of the lips. The physical measure corresponding to this feature is the distance between the corners of the lips. In a language such as English the feature Round is not needed for classifying the vowels. English vowels that are [+back] are predictably [+round], except for the vowel with the lowest vowel height (/ɑ/ as in "father"), which is [−round]. Danish vowels, however, have to be classified in terms of the values [+round] and [−round]. As we saw in Chapter 9, Danish has the front vowels /y/ and /ø/ that differ from /i/ and /e/ simply by added lip rounding.

The feature Round differs from the feature Labial in that it specifies the horizontal distance between the corners of the lips, whereas Labial specifies the vertical distance between the centers of the lips. These two features act independently. It is quite possible for [b] to be made with or without labialization. The addition of labialization to a sound corresponds to the addition of a high value of the feature Round.

18 Wide

As we saw in Chapter 9, in a few languages vowels are distinguished by variations in the width of the pharynx. In most languages, however, the value of this feature is predictable from the values of other features, such as Height. Note that a low value of this feature occurs in pharyngealized sounds.

19 Rhotacized

This feature is also required mainly for the specification of vowels. In Chapter 9, it was noted that rhotacized vowels are clearly marked by an easily measurable acoustic property, the lowering of the frequency of the third formant. This feature differs from the value [retroflex] of the feature Place in that Rhotacized specifies an acoustic property, rather than a particular tongue position. Sounds that have the value [retroflex] usually have a high value of the feature Rhotacized. But it is possible and often happens that sounds having a high value of the feature Rhotacized are not [retroflex].

20 Syllabic

In the discussion of syllables it was pointed out that there is no agreed physical measurement corresponding to syllabicity. But there is no doubt that segments can be described phonetically as being syllabic (100 percent) or nonsyllabic (0 percent).

The Classification of English Phonemes

Table 12.3 shows how the prime features may be used to classify some of the phonemes of English. Many of the features are completely redundant from this point of view. No English phonemes are differentiated by one having the value [−glottalic] and another having the value [+glottalic]. Names of features that have no role in classifying the phonemes of English are parenthesized in this table.

Many features are relevant to the classification of English phonemes only in particular circumstances. For example, the value of the feature Nasal is relevant only in classifying stops. All other sounds are predictably [−nasal]. Similarly, the feature Voice is used to specify distinctions among stops and fricatives. With the exception of /h/, all other sounds are predictably [+voice]. The feature Lateral is used only in distinguishing between /r/ and /l/. All other sounds are predictably [−lateral].

Most of the redundant values of those features that are used only occasionally are enclosed in parentheses. It would, however, be possible to make more complex statements of the interdependencies that would show that some of the other values are redundant. For example, the only English phonemes that are [+sibilant] are those that are [fricative] and also [alveolar] or [palatal].

Some of the parenthesized values are somewhat arbitrarily assigned. When classifying phonemes, all that matters is that the contrasting sounds are classified differently. For example, when classifying /h/ it does not really matter what value we assign to the features Height and Back. It is only when making a phonetic specification that we have to state the precise values of each of these features for this sound. In English the phonetic specification of [h] is that all features except Voice have the same values as in the following vowel. Similarly, all the values for the feature Grave are largely arbitrary, except for those classifying voiceless stops and fricatives; and even these values are predictable in terms of values of other features.

Most of the classifications can be made using binary values of the features. But in the case of the feature Place the values are: [b(ilabial), d(ental), a(lveolar), p(alatal), v(elar)]. English does not have any need for the values [r(etroflex)], [u(vular)], [ph(aryngeal)], and [g(lottal)]. In addition, the values [l(abiodental)] and [pa(lato-alveolar)] need not be used in classifying English

Table 12.3

The classification of some English phonemes in terms of prime features. Redundant (predictable) feature specifications are enclosed in parentheses. When the values in a whole row are redundant, the name of the feature is also parenthesized.

	p	t	k	f	θ	s	ʃ	m	n	w	j	r	l	h	i	ɪ	æ	ɔ	ɒ
(Glottalic)	(−)	(−)	(−)	(−)	(−)	(−)	(−)	(−)	(−)	(−)	(−)	(−)	(−)	(−)	(−)	(−)	(−)	(−)	(−)
(Velaric)	(−)	(−)	(−)	(−)	(−)	(−)	(−)	(−)	(−)	(−)	(−)	(−)	(−)	(−)	(−)	(−)	(−)	(−)	(−)
Voice	−	−	(+)	−	−	−	−	(+)	(+)	(+)	(+)	(+)	(+)	(−)	(+)	(+)	(+)	(+)	(+)
(Aspiration)	(+)	(+)	(+)	(−)	(−)	(−)	(−)	(−)	(−)	(−)	(−)	(−)	(−)	(−)	(−)	(−)	(−)	(−)	(−)
Place	b	a	v	b	d	a	p	b	a	v	p	a	a	(v)	p	p	p	v	v
(Labial)	(+)	(−)	(−)	(−)	(−)	(−)	(−)	(+)	(−)	(+)	(−)	(−)	(−)	(−)	(−)	(−)	(−)	(+)	(+)
Stop	s	s	s	f	f	f	f	s	s	a	a	a	a	a	a	a	a	a	a
Nasal	(−)	(−)	(−)	(−)	(−)	(−)	(−)	+	+	(−)	(−)	(−)	(−)	(−)	(−)	(−)	(−)	(−)	(−)
Lateral	(−)	(−)	(−)	(−)	(−)	(−)	(−)	(−)	(−)	(−)	(−)	(−)	+	(−)	(−)	(−)	(−)	(−)	(−)
(Trill)	(−)	(−)	(−)	(−)	(−)	(−)	(−)	(−)	(−)	(−)	(−)	(−)	(−)	(−)	(−)	(−)	(−)	(−)	(−)
(Tap)	(−)	(−)	(−)	(−)	(−)	(−)	(−)	(−)	(−)	(−)	(−)	(−)	(−)	(−)	(−)	(−)	(−)	(−)	(−)
Sonorant	−	−	−	−	−	−	−	+	+	+	+	+	+	−	+	+	+	+	+
Sibilant	−	−	+			+	+												
Grave	+	−	+	+	−	−	+	+	−	+	−	−	+	−	−	−	−	+	+
Height	(4)	(4)	(4)	(4)	(4)	(4)	(4)	(4)	(4)	(4)	(4)	(4)	(4)	(4)	4	3	1	2	3
Back	(−)	(−)	(+)	(−)	(−)	(−)	(−)	(−)	(−)	(+)	(−)	(+)	(+)	(−)	−	−	−	+	+
(Round)	(−)	(−)	(−)	(−)	(−)	(−)	(−)	(−)	(−)	(+)	(−)	(−)	(−)	(−)	(−)	(−)	(−)	(+)	(+)
(Wide)	(−)	(−)	(−)	(−)	(−)	(−)	(−)	(−)	(−)	(+)	(+)	(+)	(−)	(−)	(+)	(−)	(−)	(−)	(−)
(Rhotacized)	(−)	(−)	(−)	(−)	(−)	(−)	(−)	(−)	(−)	(−)	(−)	+	(−)	(−)	(−)	(+)	(−)	(−)	(−)
(Syllabic)	(−)	(−)	(−)	(−)	(−)	(−)	(−)	(−)	(−)	(−)	(−)	(−)	(−)	(−)	(+)	(+)	(+)	(+)	(+)

sounds, for the fricatives that have these values at the phonetic level may be classified phonologically as acting with the [labial] and [palatal] sounds respectively.

The feature Stop has been used to classify these English phonemes in terms of the values: [s(top), f(ricative), a(pproximant)]. The feature Height has been used with the values: [4, 3, 2, 1]. This assumes that there are four values of vowel Height. Some linguists have suggested that there are really only three values of vowel Height in English. In their classifications of English phonemes they have used other features, for example, the equivalent of Wide, to distinguish between /i/ and /ɪ/, and other pairs of vowels that are represented here as being different in Height.

The Phonetic Specification of English

It is considerably more difficult to make a phonetic specification of some of the sounds of English in terms of percentage values of the prime features. The data are not available in many cases. The best estimates that I can make at the moment are shown in Table 12.4. The consonants specified are the allophones that occur initially in a stressed syllable before [aɪ], and the vowels are the allophones that occur in a stressed syllable. Many of the values shown in this table are simply educated guesses.

The value for the feature Glottalic is 50 percent for most sounds. This indicates that there is neither an upward nor downward movement of the glottis, and that these sounds are produced with a pulmonic airstream mechanism. But there is a tendency for the larynx to move upward in the production of English voiceless stops and downward in voiced stops. These sounds are therefore assigned estimated values of 60 percent and 40 percent respectively.

The value for the feature Velaric is obviously zero for all sounds in English. The values for Voice are zero for the voiceless sounds, and probably about 80 percent for voiced sounds. Remember that these values represent percentages of the possible range of positions of the arytenoid cartilages. 100 percent would represent maximum glottal closure (as in a glottal stop). Ordinary voicing has a value of about 80 percent. The small degree of narrowing of the glottis that occurs in [h] as in "high" is guessed to be 20 percent of the maximum closure.

The physical scale corresponding to the feature Aspiration is the length of time from the start of an articulatory closure until the start of vocal cord vibration. The degree of aspiration that occurs in English, and probably in all other languages, varies in accordance with the place of articulation of the stop. This is because of the pressure changes that occur in stops. As we saw earlier, the vocal cords will vibrate only when the airflow between them is sufficiently great. In order for there to be any airflow, the pressure of the air in the lungs below the vocal cords must be greater than the pressure in the vocal tract above the vocal cords. During the articulation of the voiceless

Table 12.4

A phonetic specification of some of the sounds of English in terms of percentage values of the prime features. The consonants are assumed to be the allophones that occur before the vowel [aɪ] in a stressed syllable. The vowels are assumed to be the allophones that occur at the beginning of a stressed syllable. There is a great deal of guesswork in this table.

	p	t	k	f	θ	s	ʃ	m	n	w	j	r	l	h	i	ɪ	æ	ɔ	oɔ
Glottalic	60	60	60	50	50	50	50	50	50	50	50	50	50	50	50	50	50	50	50
Velaric	0	0	0	0	0	0	0	0	0	0	0	0	0	0	0	0	0	0	0
Voice	0	0	0	0	0	0	0	80	80	80	80	80	80	20	80	80	80	80	80
Aspiration	90	95	100	70	70	70	70	0	0	0	0	0	0	60	0	0	0	0	0
Place	100	85	60	95	90	85	80	100	85	60	70	80	85	60	75	70	60	40	55
Labial	100	5	5	90	5	40	60	100	5	80	5	40	5	5	25	20	5	30	40–80
Stop	100	100	100	90	90	90	90	100	100	80	80	70	70	0	75	70	5	70	70
Nasal	0	0	0	0	0	0	0	100	100	0	0	0	0	0	0	0	0	0	0
Lateral	0	0	0	0	0	0	0	0	0	0	0	0	100	0	0	0	0	0	0
Trill	0	0	0	0	0	0	0	0	0	0	0	0	0	0	0	0	0	0	0
Tap	0	0	0	0	0	0	0	0	0	0	0	0	0	0	0	0	0	0	0
Sonorant	0	0	0	5	5	15	15	75	75	70	70	75	80	5	80	85	95	95	95
Sibilant	0	20	0	10	20	100	90	0	0	0	0	0	0	10	5	0	0	0	0
Grave	—	—	—	—	—	—	—	—	—	—	—	—	—	—	—	—	—	—	—
Height	100	100	100	100	100	100	100	95	95	90	90	90	90	5	85	60	5	20	30–50
Back	—	—	—	—	—	—	—	—	—	90	0	—	—	40	0	20	50	100	90–95
Round	0	0	0	0	0	40	60	0	0	90	0	60	0	0	0	0	0	40	40–90
Wide	50	50	50	50	50	50	50	50	50	50	95	30	50	50	95	60	50	20	60
Rhotacized	0	0	0	0	0	0	0	0	0	15	0	100	0	10	0	5	10	15	15
Syllabic	—	—	—	—	—	—	—	—	—	—	—	—	—	—	—	—	—	—	—

stops [p, t, k] the air pressure in the cavities above the vocal cords is the same as that below the vocal cords, and there is no airflow. In the case of the bilabial stop [p], the pressure decreases very quickly after the opening of the lips, since the outgoing air is released without impediment into the surrounding air. Consequently it is not very long before there is sufficient airflow between the vocal cords for them to be set in vibration. In the case of an alveolar stop [t], it takes slightly longer for the pressure to fall after the lowering of the tongue, as the outgoing air is slightly impeded by the narrowness of the vocal tract in front of the alveolar closure. Consequently the airflow between the vocal cords increases more slowly. In the case of the velar stop [k], the release of the outgoing air is considerably impeded by the plosion being in the back of the mouth cavity. After a velar stop it takes appreciably longer for the pressure above the vocal cords to fall so that the airflow between the vocal cords is sufficient for them to be set into vibration. Consequently [k] has a longer period of aspiration than [t], and both are more aspirated than [p]. English fricatives are also slightly aspirated when they occur before a vowel in a stressed syllable.

The percentage values for Place specify the distance from the glottis to the first narrowing (or closure) in the vocal tract. This figure is well determined for consonants, but less clear for vowels. The value assigned to [h] is that of the following vowel. Note that, with the exception of the feature Voice, the values for all features for [h] as in "high" are those appropriate for the beginning of the diphthong [aɪ].

The values for the feature Labial (the vertical distance between the centers of the lips) are 100 percent for bilabial and only slightly less for labiodental consonants. They are also significant for [s, ʃ, w, r], which involve supplementary actions of the lips. In the other consonants the lips take up the position of the vowel. In the case of [oω], two values are given as this vowel is a diphthong involving lip movement.

The feature Stop specifies the degree of articulatory closure. It has the same value as the feature Labial in the case of [p, f, m]. It is taken to be zero for [h] in "high," since the diphthong [aɪ] begins with the most open possible articulation. Estimates of intermediate values are given for all other sounds.

The specifications for the degree of lowering of the soft palate (the feature Nasal) are fairly straightforward. Most of the values are zero or 100 percent. A small degree of lowering of the soft palate is given for [æ], and for [h] as in "high." In low vowels the pulling down of the tongue tends to result in the soft palate also being pulled down.

The values for the features Lateral, Trill, and Tap need no comment. The values for Sonorant are in accord with the measurements of acoustic intensity shown in Figure 10.1. Those for Sibilant are estimated on the basis of very little acoustic data and should not be taken as more than illustrative of possible values. The values for the feature Grave have been omitted altogether because of insufficiency of data.

In the case of vowels, the values for Height and Back are well determined by measurements of the formant frequencies. The Height values for consonants may also be specified, since an articulatory closure always results in the first formant having a very low frequency. But except for [w] and [j], there is insufficient data for the specification of the values for Back for consonants. The values for Height, Back, and Round for [oω] reflect the fact that this vowel is a diphthong.

The values for Round are zero for most consonants before [aɪ]. But [s, ʃ, w, r] all have some degree of lip rounding. The values given for these consonants are all estimates and should be considered merely as indicative of appropriate values. The values for the vowels are based on actual measurements of a number of speakers (see Sources).

The values for the vowels for the feature Wide are based on measurements of x-rays of the vocal tract. In consonants in which the root of the tongue is not involved, the value is the same as that in the following vowel. But consonants such as [ʃ] and [j], which involve the body of the tongue being raised toward the hard palate, have a considerably widened pharynx. In the consonant [r] there is a quite consistent narrowing of the lower part of the pharynx.

Only the consonant [r] has a high value for the feature Rhotacized (the degree of lowering of the third formant). The small amount of lowering that occurs in some vowels and in [w] is also noted.

Finally, the values for the feature Syllabic have been left completely blank. As was noted, there is no agreed way of measuring the degree of syllabicity.

It should be emphasized that several of the values given in Table 12.4 are based on inadequate data. Nevertheless, since all the prime features are measurable in terms of physical scales, every sound at every moment in time should be specifiable in terms of percentage values. As I noted earlier, scientific description is, to a great extent, the statement of facts in terms of numbers that can be verified or rejected by other scientists. Statements about language that are not ultimately reducible to measurable observations cannot be proved. Phoneticians are concerned with providing descriptions of utterances that will form an adequate scientific basis for testing linguistic theories.

EXERCISES

Check that you understand the prime feature system by filling in the classification of the English phonemes shown in Table 12.5. Try to do this without looking at Table 12.3. The first seven columns should be identical with those in Table 12.3 except that the values for Voice (the third row) should all be [+] instead of [−]. Columns eight and nine (for /u/ and /ɷ/) should be identical with Table 12.3 columns 15 and 16 (for /i/ and /ɩ/) except that the values for both Back (row 16) and Round (row 17) should be [+] instead of [−].

Table 12.5

The classification of some English phonemes in terms of prime features.

	b	d	g	v	ð	z	ʒ	u	ɷ
(Glottalic)									
(Velaric)									
Voice									
(Aspiration)									
Place									
(Labial)									
Stop									
Nasal									
Lateral									
(Trill)									
(Tap)									
Sonorant									
Sibilant									
Grave									
Height									
Back									
(Round)									
(Wide)									

PERFORMANCE EXERCISES

The exercises at the end of the previous chapter were largely concerned with reviewing consonant articulations. The exercises below review vowels and semivowels. As noted in Chapter 9, the main features of vowel quality cannot be adequately described by means of written descriptions. Try to find a native speaker of at least one, and preferably all, the languages listed below, and imitate his pronunciation. Note that the symbols do not have the same values as they do in the transcription of English.

A French vowels. (Some speakers of French do not make all these distinctions.)

li	"lit"	(bed)
le	"les"	(the, *plural*)
lɛ	"laid"	(ugly)
la	"là"	(there)
lɑ	"las"	(tired)
lɔk	"loque"	(rag)
lo	"lot"	(prize)
lu	"loup"	(wolf)
ly	"lu"	(read, *past part.*)
lø	"le"	(the, *m. sing.*)
lœʁ	"leur"	(their)
lɛ̃	"lin"	(flax)
lã	"lent"	(show)
lõ	"long"	(long)
lœ̃di	"lundi"	(Monday)

B French semivowels.

mjɛt	"miette"	(crumb)
mɥɛt	"muette"	(mute)
mwɛt	"mouette"	(sea gull)
lje	"lié"	(tied)
lɥi	"lui"	(him)
lwi	"Louis"	(Louis)
ɥit	"huit"	(eight)
wi	"oui"	(yes)

C German vowels. (Note: German has so-called tense and lax vowels, which differ in both length and quality. The symbol [ʏ] denotes a slightly lowered high front vowel—a rounded version of [ɪ].)

tiːf	"tief"	(deep)
teː	"Tee"	(tea)
tɑːt	"Tat"	(deed)
toːt	"tot"	(dead)
ˈtuːtən	"tuten"	(toot)

ˈtyːtə	"Tüte"	(paper bag)
ˈtøːtən	"töten"	(kill)
tɪʃ	"Tisch"	(table)
tɛst	"Test"	(test)
ˈtatsə	"Tatze"	(paw)
tɔp	"Topp"	(top)
tʊʃ	"Tusch"	(flourish)
ˈtʏtəl	"Tüttel"	(dot)
ˈhœlə	"Hölle"	(hell)
ˈlaɪtən	"leiten"	(lead)
ˈlaʊtə	"Laute"	(lute)
ˈlɔʏtə	"Leute"	(people)

D Swedish vowels. (Note: Swedish has long and short vowels; the short vowels are followed by long consonants. The symbol [ʏ] denotes a slightly lowered high front vowel—a rounded version of [ɪ]. The symbol [ɵ] denotes a more centralized high rounded vowel—a slightly lowered [ʉ].)

ɹiːta	"rita"	(draw)
ɹeːta	"reta"	(tease)
ɹɛːta	"räta"	(straighten)
hæːɹ	"här"	(here)
ɹɑːta	"rata"	(refuse)
ɹoːta	"Rota"	(name of a valley)
ɹuːta	"rota"	(root)
ɹyːta	"ryta"	(roar)
ɹøːta	"röta"	(rot)
hœɹ	"hör"	(hear!)
ɹʉːta	"ruta"	(window pane)
ɹɪtː	"ritt"	(ride, *n.*)
ɹɛtː	"rätt"	(correct, *n.*)
hæːɹ	"herr"	(Mr.)
ɹatː	"ratt"	(steering wheel)
ɹɔtː	"rått"	(raw)
ɹʊtː	"rott"	(rowed)
nʏtːa	"nytta"	(use, *n.*)
ɹœtː	"rött"	(red)
ɹɵtː	"rutt"	(route)

E A fairly comprehensive review of general phonetic phenomena may be obtained from Table 12.2. Try to pronounce all the examples given in this table.

Glossary

Note: The explanations given in this glossary should be regarded not as formal definitions, but as general guides for use in review.

Allophone A variant of a phoneme. The allophones of a phoneme form a set of sounds that (1) do not change the meaning of a word, (2) are all very similar to one another, and (3) occur in phonetic contexts different from one another—for example, syllable initial as opposed to syllable final. The differences among allophones can be stated in terms of phonological rules.

Alternations Variations in words that can be described in terms of phonological rules, for example, the difference between [aɪ] and [ɪ] in "divine-divin(ity)."

Alveolar An articulation involving the tip or blade of the tongue and the alveolar ridge, as in English [d] in "die."

Alveolar ridge The part of the upper surface of the mouth immediately behind the front teeth.

Anticipatory coarticulation An action in which one of the speech organs that is not involved in making a particular sound moves toward its position for a subsequent sound. For example, the rounding of the lips during [s] in "swim" is due to the anticipation of the lip action required for [w].

Approximant The approach of one articulator toward another but without the tract being narrowed to such an extent that a turbulent airstream is produced. All vowels and (in many forms of English) /j, l, r, w/ are approximants.

Articulation The approach or contact of two speech organs, such as the tip of the tongue and the upper teeth.

Arytenoid cartilages A pair of structures at the posterior ends of the vocal cords. Their movements control different phonation types.

Aspiration A period of voicelessness after the release of an articulation, as in English "pie" [pʰaɪ].

Assimilation   The change of one sound into another sound because of the influence of neighboring sounds, as in the change of underlying [n] to [m] in "input" ['ɩmpɒt], or underlying [z] to [ʒ] in "does she" ['dʌʒ ʃi].

Bilabial   An articulation involving both lips, as in English [m] in "my."

Binary feature   A feature (for example, Lateral) that can be used to classify sounds in terms of two possibilities.

Breathy voice   See *Murmur*.

Broad transcription   A transcription that uses a simple set of symbols and does not show a great deal of phonetic detail.

Cardinal vowels   A set of reference vowels first defined by Daniel Jones. The vowels of any language can be described by stating their relations to the cardinal vowels.

Citation form   The form a word has when it is cited or pronounced in isolation.

Click   A stop made with an ingressive velaric airstream, such as Zulu [ʇ].

Closed syllable   A syllable with a consonant at the end, as the first syllables in English "magpie, pantry, completion."

Coarticulation   The overlapping of adjacent articulations.

Contour tone languages   Tone languages, such as Chinese, in which some of the tones have to be specified as gliding movements within the pitch range.

Creaky voice   See *Laryngealization*.

Diacritics   Small added marks that can be used to distinguish different values of a symbol. For example, the addition of [~] distinguishes a velarized from a nonvelarized sound, as in [ɫ] as opposed to [l].

Diphthong   A vowel in which there is a change in quality during a single syllable, as in English [aɩ] in "high."

Ejective   A stop made with an egressive glottalic airstream, such as Hausa [k'].

Features   For definitions of individual features as used by Chomsky and Halle, see Chapter 11. The prime features are described in Chapter 12.

Flap   An articulation in which one articulator, usually the tongue tip, is drawn back and then allowed to strike against another articulator in returning to its rest position. The /t/ in "dirty" is often a flap [ɾ] in American English.

Formant   A group of overtones corresponding to a resonating frequency of the air in the vocal tract. Vowels are characterized by three formants.

Frequency   The rate of variation in air pressure in a sound.

Fricative   Narrowing of the distance between two articulators so that the airstream is partially obstructed and a turbulent airflow is produced, as in English [z] in "zoo."

Geminate   Adjacent segments that are the same, such as the two consonants in the middle of Italian "folla" ['folla] (crowd).

Glottal   An articulation involving the glottis, as [ʔ] in many forms of English "button" ['bʌʔn].

Glottalic airstream mechanism   Movement of pharynx air by the action of the glottis. Ejectives and implosives are produced with a glottalic airstream mechanism.

Glottis   The space between the vocal cords.

Homorganic   Made with the same place of articulation. The sounds [d] and [n], as in English "hand," are homorganic.

Implosive   A stop made with an ingressive glottalic airstream, such as Sindhi [ɓ].

Impressionistic transcription   A transcription in which the symbols indicate only the general phonetic value of the sounds.

Initiator   A prime mover of an airstream. The closed glottis is the initiator in glottalic egressive stops.

Intensity   The amount of acoustic energy in a sound.

Intonation   The pattern of pitch changes that occur during a phrase, which may be a complete sentence.

Labialization   A secondary articulation in which lip rounding is added to a sound, as in English [ʃ].

Labiodental   An articulation involving the lower lip and the upper front teeth.

Laryngealization   Another name for creaky voice, a type of phonation in which the arytenoid cartilages hold the posterior end of the vocal cords together, so that they can vibrate only at the other end, such as Hausa [ʲ].

Lateral   An articulation in which the airstream flows over the sides of the tongue, as in English [l] in "leaf."

Lateral plosion   The release of a plosive by lowering the sides of the tongue, as at the end of the word "saddle."

Lax   A term with no specific phonetic correlates, used when dividing vowels into classes on phonological grounds. In English the lax vowels are those that can occur in monosyllables closed by [ŋ] such as "sing, length, hang, long, hung."

Liquid   A cover term for laterals and various forms of *r*-sounds.

Loudness   The auditory property of a sound that enables a listener to place it on a scale going from soft to loud without considering the acoustic properties, such as the intensity of the sound.

Monophthong   A vowel in which there is no appreciable change in quality during a syllable, as in English [ɑ] in "father." Compare *Diphthong*.

Multivalued feature   A feature such as Height that can be used to classify sounds in terms of more than two possibilities.

Murmur   Another name for breathy voice, a type of phonation in which the vocal cords are only slightly apart so that they vibrate while allowing a high rate of airflow through the glottis, as in Hindi [bʱ].

Narrow   Having the root of the tongue drawn back so that the pharynx is narrowed, as in one of the sets of vowels in Twi. Pharyngealized sounds can also be called narrow.

Narrow transcription A transcription that shows phonetic details (such as, in English, aspiration, length, etc.), by using a wide variety of symbols and, in many cases, diacritics.

Nasal A sound in which the soft palate is lowered so that there is no velic closure and air may go out through the nose, as in English [m] in "my."

Nasalization Lowering of the soft palate during a sound in which air is going out through the mouth, as in the vowel [æ̃] between nasals in English "man."

Nasal plosion The release of a plosive by lowering the soft palate so that air escapes through the nose, as at the end of the word "hidden."

Obstruent A fricative, stop, or affricate.

Open syllable A syllable without a consonant at the end, as the first syllables in English "beehive, bylaw, sawing."

Palatal An articulation involving the front of the tongue and the hard palate, as in English [j] in "you."

Palatalization A secondary articulation in which the front of the tongue is raised toward the hard palate, as in the so-called soft sounds in Russian.

Pharyngeal An articulation involving the root of the tongue and the back wall of the pharynx, as in the Arabic [ʕ].

Pharyngealization A secondary articulation in which the root of the tongue is drawn back so that the pharynx is narrowed, as in some so-called emphatic consonants in Arabic.

Phoneme One of a set of abstract units that can be used for writing a language down in a systematic and unambiguous way. See also *allophone*.

Phonology The description of the systems and patterns of sounds that occur in a language.

Pitch The auditory property of a sound that enables a listener to place it on a scale going from low to high, without considering the acoustic properties, such as the frequency of the sound.

Plosive A stop made with a pulmonic airstream mechanism, such as in English [p] or [b].

Prime feature A measurable property that can be used to classify the sounds of a language.

Prominence The extent to which a sound stands out from others because of its sonority, length, stress, and pitch.

Pulmonic airstream mechanism The movement of lung air by the respiratory muscles. Most sounds are produced with a pulmonic airstream mechanism.

Reduced vowel A vowel that is pronounced with a noncontrasting centralized quality, although in the underlying form of a word it is part of a full set of contrasts. The second vowel in "emphasis" is a reduced form of the vowel /æ/, as in "emphatic."

Register tone languages Tone languages, such as Yoruba, in which most of the tones are relatively steady state pitches that can be described as points, as opposed to movements, within a pitch range.

Retroflex   An articulation involving the tip of the tongue and the back part of the alveolar ridge. Some speakers of English have retroflex approximants in "rye" and "err." Retroflex stops occur in Hindi and other languages spoken in India.

Rhotacization   The auditory property known as *r*-coloring that results from the lowering of the third formant.

Rhotic   A form of English in which /r/ can occur after a vowel and within a syllable in words such as "car, bird, early." Most forms of Midwestern American English are rhotic, whereas most forms of English spoken in the southern part of England are nonrhotic.

Secondary articulation   An articulation made by two of the organs of speech that are not involved in the primary articulation. The English alveolar lateral at the end of a syllable, as in "eel," is often made with the back of the tongue raised, and thus has the secondary articulation of velarization.

Semivowel   A sound articulated in the same way as a vowel, and not forming a syllable on its own, as in [w] in "we."

Sibilant   A speech sound in which there is high-pitched, turbulent noise, as in English [s] and [ʃ] in "sip" and "ship."

Sonority   The loudness of a sound relative to that of other sounds with the same length, stress, and pitch.

Spectrogram   A machine-made graphic representation of sounds in terms of their component frequencies, in which time is shown on the horizontal axis, frequency on the vertical axis, and the intensity of each frequency at each moment in time by the darkness of the mark.

Stop   Complete closure of two articulators. This term usually implies an oral stop—that is, complete closure of two articulators and a velic closure, as in English [b] in "buy." But nasals, as in English [m] in "my," can also be considered stops.

Stress   The use of extra respiratory energy during a syllable.

Stress-timed   Having a rhythm in which stressed syllables tend to recur at regular intervals of time, as in English sentences.

Strong form   The form in which a word is pronounced when it is stressed. This term is usually applied only to words that normally occur unstressed and with a weak form, such as "to, a."

Syllable   A unit of speech for which there is no satisfactory definition. Syllables seem to be necessary units in the mental organization and production of utterances.

Syllable-timed   Having a rhythm in which each syllable tends to have the same duration, as in French sentences.

Systematic phonetic transcription   A transcription that shows all the phonetic details that are part of the language and can be stated in terms of phonological rules.

Tap   An articulation in which one articulator is thrown against another. In some forms of American English, /t/ in "pretty" is a tap [ɾ].

Target   An idealized articulatory position that can be used as a reference point in describing how a speaker produces utterances.

Tense   A term with no specific phonetic correlates, used when dividing vowels into classes on phonological grounds. In English, the tense vowels are those that can occur in stressed open syllables such as "bee, bay, bah, saw, low, boo, buy, bough, boy, cue."

Tone   A pitch that conveys part of the meaning of a word. In Chinese, for example, [ma] pronounced with a high level tone means "mother," and with a high falling tone means "scold."

Tone group   The part of a sentence over which a particular intonation pattern extends. There may be one or more tone groups in an English sentence.

Tonic syllable   The syllable within a tone group that stands out because it carries the major pitch change.

Trill   An articulation in which one articulator is held loosely near another so that the flow of air between them sets them in motion, alternately sucking them together and blowing them apart. In some forms of Scottish English, [r] in "rip" is trilled.

Uvular   An articulation involving the back of the tongue and the uvula, as in French [ʁ] in "rouge" [ʁuʒ].

Velar   An articulation involving the back of the tongue and the velum, or the soft palate, as in English [g] in "guy."

Velaric airstream mechanism   Movement of mouth air by action of the tongue. Clicks are produced with a velaric airstream mechanism.

Velarization   A secondary articulation in which the back of the tongue is raised towards the soft palate. In many forms of English syllable final [ɫ] as in "hill" is strongly velarized.

Velic   Involving the upper surface of the velum, or soft palate, and the pharynx. A velic closure prevents air from escaping through the nose.

Velum   The soft, movable part of the palate at the back of the mouth.

Vocal tract   The air passages above the larynx. The vocal tract consists of the oral tract and the nasal tract.

Voiced   Having vibrations of the vocal cords during an articulation, as in English [m] in "me." In a partially voiced sound, vocal cord vibrations occur during only part of the articulation, as often in English [d] in "die."

Voiceless   Pronounced without vibrations of the vocal cords, as in English [s] in "see."

Voice onset time   The moment at which the voicing starts relative to the release of a closure.

Vowel harmony   The sharing of a property or properties by all the vowels in a word. In Twi, for example, all the vowels in a word are either wide or narrow.

Weak form   The unstressed form of any word, such as "but" or "as," that does not maintain its full form when it occurs in conversational speech.

Wide   Having the root of the tongue drawn forward so that the width of the pharynx is enlarged, as in one of the sets of vowels in Twi.

Sources

Some of the data presented in this book are from published sources or from personal communications from colleagues.

The acoustic data on the formant frequencies of vowels (Figures 8.7 and 9.1) are from: Petersen, G. E., and Barney, H. L. "Control methods used in a study of the vowels." *Journal of the Acoustical Society of America* 24 (1956): 175–84. Holbrook, A., and Fairbanks, G. "Diphthong formants and their movements." *Journal of Speech and Hearing Research* 5 (1962): 38–58.

The x-rays of cardinal vowels used in Figure 9.3 were published in: Jones, S. "Radiography and pronunciation." *British Journal of Radiology*, New Series Vol. 3 (1929): 149–50.

The data on Spanish vowels in Chapter 9 is from Pierre Delattre, "Comparing the vocalic features of English, German, Spanish and French." *International Review of Applied Linguistics* 2, pp. 71–97 (1964). The data on Japanese vowels is from Mieko Han *Japanese Phonology* Tokyo (1962). The data on Danish vowels is from Eli Fischer-Jørgensen "Formant frequencies of long and short Danish vowels" in *Studies for Einar Haugen* (ed. E. S. Firchow and others) Mouton: The Hague (1972).

The x-rays of the Twi vowels (Figure 9.7) were provided by Mona Lindau.

The description of vowels mentioned in the first exercise at the end of Chapter 9 is published in: Stevens, Kenneth N., and House, Arthur. "Development of a quantitative description of vowel articulation." *Journal of the Acoustical Society of America* 27 (1955): 484–93.

The description mentioned in the second exercise at the end of Chapter 9 was suggested by Morris Halle and Kenneth Stevens. Historical descriptions of vowels mentioned in the third exercise may be found in: Helmholtz, H. *Sensations of Tone.* First published in German in 1863, the fourth edition was translated by A. J. Ellis and published in English in 1885. Reprint. New York: Dover Publications, Inc., 1954.

The lip positions in vowels in Table 12.4 are derived from data in: Fromkin, Victoria. "Lip positions in American English vowels." *Language and Speech* 7 (1964): 215–225.

Most of the data on particular languages are from my own investigations. Some of the language data have been published with appropriate acknowledgements in: Ladefoged, Peter. *Preliminaries to Linguistic Phonetics.* Chicago: University of Chicago Press, 1971. Ladefoged, Peter. "Features of the larynx." *Journal of Phonetics* 1 (1973): 73–84.

The data on Bariba tone in Chapter 10 were provided by William E. Welmers. Tonal data on other West African languages in that chapter were provided by Ian Maddieson.

The photographs of the glottis on page 122 were taken by John Ohala and Ralph Vanderslice.

Index

A

Acoustic correlates, of consonantal features, 180
Acoustic intensity, loudness and, 219
Acoustic phonetics, 159–91
  acoustic measurements in, 165–67
  articulatory descriptions and, 174
  formant charts in, 174–77, 188, 190, 201
  individual sounds and, 191
  loudness and intensity in, 163–65
  pitch and frequency in, 162–3
  sound waves and, 160–62
Affrication, of stops, 187
Affricates, 141
Air pressure, variations in, 160
Airstream
  initiators of, 113
  obstruction of, in vocal tract, 6
Airstream mechanisms, 113–21
  glottalic, 114
  pulmonic, 113
  velaric, 119
Air vibration, vowel formants and, 169
Akan
  labialization and palatalization in, 209
  palatal stops in, 141
Allophones
  defined, 36
  glottal stops as, 46
  rules for, 76–82
  of stop consonants, 43

Allophonic variation, in segment lengths, 223
Alternations, rule-governed, 35
Alveolar approximants, articulation of, 150
Alveolar lateral approximant, 33
Alveolar consonants, acoustic correlates of, 180
Alveolar nasal plosion, 48
Alveolar obstruction, 7
Alveolar ridge, 3
  in palato-alveolar sounds, 141
Alveolar stops, 139
  in American and British articulation, 55
  lateral plosion and, 48
American English
  articulation of [1] in, 55
  back vowels in, 237
  closed syllables in, 74
  diphthongs in, 70
  formant frequencies in, 189
  lax vowels in, 74
  Midwestern, 199–200
  rhotacization in, 71
  sonorant feature in, 264
  varieties of pronunciation in, 63
  vowel auditory qualities in, 67
  vowel formants and, 188–89
  vowels in, 63–76, 193–4
American Indian languages, voiced stops in, 260
Amharic, airstream mechanisms in, 115
Anterior-nonanterior feature, 240

Consonant Chart

	Bilabial	Labio-dental	Dental & Alveolar	Retroflex	Palato-alveolar	Palatal	Velar	Labial-velar	Uvular	Pharyngeal	Glottal
Nasal	m		n	ɳ		ɲ	ŋ	ŋ͡m	N		
Plosives	p b		t d	ʈ ɖ		c ɟ	k g	k͡p g͡b	q ɢ		ʔ
Implosives	ɓ		ɗ				ɠ				
Ejectives	p'		t'				k'				
(Central) Fricative	ɸ β	f v	θ ð s z	ʂ ʐ	ʃ ʒ	ç jˆ	x ɣ	ʍ wˆ	χ ʁ	ħ ʕ	
Lateral Fricative			ɬ ɮ								
(Central) Approximant			ɹ	ɻ		j		w	ʁ		h
Lateral (Approximant)			l	ɭ		ʎ					
Trill			r						ʀ		
Tap			ɾ								
Flap				ɽ							

Diacritics

Voiceless	̥	n̥	Dental	̪	t̪
Aspirated	ʰ	tʰ	Labialized	ʷ	tʷ
Murmured	̈	b̈	Palatalized	ʲ	tʲ
Laryngealized	̰	b̰	Nasalized	̃	w̃ ẽ
Velarized or pharyngealized	̴	ɫ	Long	ː	nː
			Syllabic	̩	n̩